# Power Dating Games

Safe Dating Through Personality-Based Research.

How would you like to be your own marriage broker and manage your personality-based relationships through power dating games? Match your personality to the character of your soul mate's. Soul mate foraging has evolved to personality farming in the power dating game.

What's really important to know about the person you will meet and marry? Here's how to avoid the pitfalls, gain insight, foresight, and hindsight, and avoid the pitfalls. Before you commit to a relationship, know what the warning signs are so that you can steer clear of Ms. or Mr. Wrong.

Here's how to play the power dating games. Avoid the personality stereotypes, receive marriage proposals from the right person for you, and investigate what makes the search for a safe and loving Ms. or Mr. Right a cottage industry aglow in a business-based marriage.

When you find your soul mate, that individual will be slow to anger. With credibility, responsibility, and visibility, your significant other will demonstrate why the mate can be trusted with your life under any circumstances. This book will show you how and where to find the one through personality-based power dating. Discard the character stereotypes, the pop psychology jargon, and investigate what will build you a safe home and a great match.

# Power Dating Games

## What's Important to Know About the Person You'll Marry

*Anne Hart*

Authors Choice Press
San Jose  New York  Lincoln  Shanghai

**Power Dating Games**
What's Important to Know About the Person You'll Marry

All Rights Reserved © 2001 by Anne Hart

No part of this book may be reproduced or transmitted in any form or by any means, graphic, electronic, or mechanical, including photocopying, recording, taping, or by any information storage or retrieval system, without the permission in writing from the publisher.

Authors Choice Press
an imprint of iUniverse.com, Inc.

For information address:
iUniverse.com, Inc.
5220 S 16th, Ste. 200
Lincoln, NE 68512
www.iuniverse.com

ISBN: 0-595-19186-X

Printed in the United States of America

To all of you who share a safe household with a partner with whom you can trust your life under all circumstances.

# *Epigraph*

Will familiarity breed abuse? Which Personality Type Is Right For You to Date or Marry? How do you avoid the personality stereotypes? Can you create a safe house with your partner? What are the personality games played in power dating? Marriage is a cottage industry. How do you know whether the right person for you will be a compatible partner or mate—even a soul mate, a Ms. or Mr. Right instead of a Ms. or Mrs. Always Right? In the business-based marriage, love means familiarity will not breed abuse, denial of hugs, withdrawal from burdens, anger pools, power struggles, or battles to be the centers of attention. How will you find rapport?

When you want a connection, will your partner shout, "Give me a break?" If God is love, what's marriage? Why will a generous woman who values money and beautiful homes but raised in poverty with parental abuse often marry a thrifty man because his style seems familiar?

How will your relationships end—or thrive? How do you choose a partner or mate based on personality and interests? Is choosing what's familiar always good for you, or only what you know? Will you marry at the level of your self-esteem of the moment? Are your standards realistic? Find out in Power Dating Games.

What do you really know about the person you're going to marry? What's important to find out? What would you look for if you investigate your soul mate before making a commitment to marriage or moving in together?

How do you forage for a soul mate? What do you need to know in order to be your own marriage broker? How do you get marriage proposals? What is personality-based power dating? How do you play the power dating games?

Did anyone ever tell you, "Welcome to the future battered women's society?" The men have their fight clubs, but soul mate farming and foraging is a healing art. Welcome to personality-based power dating. It's your turn to be an investigative reporter in future relationships.

# *Contents*

Chapter One
    Pitfalls to Avoid .................................................................1
Chapter Two
    Why Your Partner Calls You A Loser ............................................8
Chapter Three
    When Domestic Violence Spills Over Into The Workplace ........14
Chapter Four
    Perfectionists ....................................................................32
Chapter Five
    Is The Need To Control Driving You? ........................................38
Chapter Six
    Open Doors To Intimacy .............................................................44
Chapter Seven
    What Measures Your Personality? ...............................................56
Chapter Eight
    Don't Marry At The Level Of Yesteryear's Self-Esteem ..............61
Chapter Nine
    Love Is An Act of Behavior, Not An Emotion ...........................68
Chapter Ten
    The Marrying Table ....................................................................74
Chapter Eleven
    How Do You Find The Right Type For You? .............................80
Chapter Twelve
    How Do You Advertise For A Soul Mate? .................................87
Chapter Thirteen
    Log On The Information Superhighway ....................................91

Chapter Fourteen
    The Smoothest Marriages ....................................................... 109
Chapter Fifteen
    Road Maps. ................................................................................ 115
Chapter Sixteen
    How To Be Your Own Marriage Broker .............................. 123
Chapter Seventeen
    The Undeveloped Flip Side Of Your Soul Mate's Personality ..154
Chapter Eighteen
    Will You Marry A Bully? ........................................................ 306
Chapter Nineteen
    Check Out Your Partner's Compassion ............................... 314
Chapter Twenty
    Is Wife Battering Related To Violence
    In The Victim's Childhood? .................................................. 332
Chapter Twenty-One
    Do We Really Fall Apart According
    To Our Personality Preferences? ........................................... 336
Chapter Twenty-Two
    Once You Know Your Preferences
    And Type .................................................................................. 338
Appendices ..................................................................................... 397
Bibliography .................................................................................. 405

# List of Tables

1. Answer Sheet for Scoring
   Your Personality Choices Game  ....................387
2. Example of Filled-Out and
   Scored Personality Choices Game Answer Sheet  .........388

# *Foreword*

## Power Dating Games

Before you commit to a relationship, try some investigative personality-based power dating. What's important to know about the person you're going to marry before you meet your soul mate? Marriage is a cottage industry, and the business-based marriage is about finding a safe home for you and your partner. You want a soul mate. That's somebody so slow to anger that you can trust your life in your partner's presence regardless of the circumstance, stressors, or length of familiarity in your relationship.

To play the power dating game, you need to know how to be your own marriage broker and how to get marriage proposals, but first, you need to find your soul mate. What's important to know about the person you're going to date, mate, and marry? How do you forage for a soul mate? Do you hunt or gather? Personality-based power dating is about using facts and research studies to find out what personality in a significant other matches most closely with yours because similar personalities stay together.

### *The Dark Side of Dating by Personality Impressions*

The personality-based marriage can be a game. Studies can have flaws. The online marriage market is world-wide, and the world is growing smaller as far as instant communication. What personality in another is right for you do date or marry?

Will you have a business-based marriage, a personality-based marriage, or a fantasy-based marriage? Marriage is an emotional business relationship between two people. They may look for what they wish they could be in one another (attraction of opposite types). In marriage, you experience the upward gush of your own infancy.

There are many alternative classifiers of personality types, temperaments, styles, or neurological brain locations, and time and fun to try them all. Which one can help you find your soul mate? Which one can stand up to rigorous research and proof over many years? How many can be scientifically validated? This book discusses games soul mates play to survive and how it relates to good match/good fit/comfort and personality type.

What you will learn in this book are the following insight hindsight, and foresight. You'll learn how to avoid the pitfalls and how to tell before you commit to a relationship whether your partner might not be safe. It has been written that there's no way to tell beforehand whether your partner or spouse will abuse you in your relationship. Yet there are warning signals and red flags. You'll learn the following pitfalls to avoid as well as where and how to find your soul mate through personality-based power dating.

> How To Tell Before You Commit To A Relationship:
> 1. Whether Your Partner Might Use Anger To Get Power
> 2. Or Could Possibly Turn Into A Bully, Batterer, Controller,
> 3. Or A Perfectionist,
> 4. Or Rage-Filled Abuser,
> 5. Or Is Simply A Fearful Loner
> 6. Or Avoidant Person With A Sensitive System.
> What Can You Predict Beforehand, If You Can?
> 7. Your New Friend Rushes Too Fast Into Romance. Beware Of The Partner Who "Comes On Too Fast." If It's Love And First Sight, And A Proposal Follows Closely, Watch Out For Control And Dominance. Isolation Is What Might Be Ahead, Followed By Dominance And Control, Compounded By Future Abuse And Neglect Or Patrol.

What Are The Warning Signals Of Impending Intimate Violence Later On In The Relationship When You're At Your Most Vulnerable Time Of Your Life?

Strategies For Prevention: Foresight, Insight, And Hindsight—Before You Commit.
Are You A Candidate For The Future (Or Former) Battered Spouse's Club? Check Out Some Of The Strategies, Findings, And "Rules" On These Pages Before You Commit To That Relationship Or Decide To Steer Clear.

The Rules For Avoiding Domestic Violence According To Your Personality Preferences Before You Commit To A Relationship. One More Road Leading To Your Soul mate.

How Can You Find Out Whether Those Who Abuse Their Partners May Have Low Levels Of Serotonin In Their Brains?

What Science Tells Me About The Rules For Steering Clear Of Intimate Violence In Your Relationship:
Old-Fashioned Rules On How To Attract Really Great People And Steer Clear Of Those Who Would Put You Down To Build Themselves Up.

How Will Your Relationship End Based On Personality Preferences, Similarities, And Differences?
Will Your Relationship/Marriage End Up As Domestic/Intimate Violence Spillover Into The Workplace?
Can You Predict It Before You Commit To A Relationship?
Can You Tell Beforehand Whether Your Relationship
Will Spill Over Onto Your Jobsite As Domestic Violence?
Is Prevention Of Intimate Abuse Possible?
Can You Tell Beforehand?

Steering Clear Or Veering Near
When Domestic Violence Spills Over Into The Workplace
Perfectionism At Home And At Work:
Its Relationship To Intimate Abuse
Is Prevention Of Intimate Abuse Possible?
What Science Reports About Intimate Violence
When Domestic Violence Spills Over Into The Workplace
Ensuring Workplace Safety: A Reality?

# *Preface*

Have you ever investigated the soul mate hunt? Do you use personality-based power dating techniques to find out who might be most compatible with your preferences? Power dating games can be fun and safe if you can avoid the pitfalls. What's important to know about the person you're going to marry? Have you met Mr. or Ms. Right ? Have you looked in the hidden places? How can you investigate your partner or learn the warning signals and red flags that show you before you commit to a relationship, before you marry or move in together, whether you'll be in safe hands?

Marriage is like an insurance policy. It's also a cottage industry. You have to work together even if you're not together in the same work place. Would you choose your soul mate by personality? Do you want to investigate personality-based dating? How do you play the game? Relationships are show business, and you're on stage. By matching your personality to the character of your mate, you can find your comfort level, compare similarities, find out whether distances are too different to bridge, and use personality-based match making to find someone you can live with for the long haul.

Here's how to be your own marriage broker, online, in print, or in person. Find out whether the personality stereotypes have any validity. Is personality-driven dating worth your time? What if you don't want to date and would prefer to be matched with a compatible partner without having to play the power dating game? What insights can you glean from looking at personality preferences of two people who want to see whether they have anything lasting in common?

Your goal is to find a safe house of your own. Find out what you need to know about the person you're going to marry, even before you meet your soul mate, your Mr. or Ms. Right. Investigate personality-based power dating.

# *Introduction*

In this guidebook on personality-based power dating, playing the power dating game may help you learn how to avoid the pitfalls and gain insight, foresight, and hindsight. You'll learn how to watch out for the relationship that "comes on" too fast.

If you need answers to questions, you'll find out why your partner calls you a loser. Or if you haven't met your partner yet, you'll learn what steps you take when domestic violence spills over into the workplace. How can you ensure workplace safety: a reality?

If you want to learn more about love and it's flip side, you'll find answers to questions such as, "Is love a behavior rather than an emotion? Are you acting out of your weakest feelings?" You'll find out how the right partner affects your health. Would you like to be your own marriage broker? In times when marriage is a cottage industry, and most relationships are business-based marriages, finding the Right Mate takes investigation and caution. You'll learn how you know when you've found Mr. or Ms. Right—your soul mate. How do you know when the personalities match, when your personality is in a comfort zone with the character of your partner?

**Choose your soul mate by personality preferences and styles, by attitudes and choices, commitment and safety. Can you tell whether your partner will abuse you in the future before you commit to a relationship? Power Dating Games may be able to give you some answers and point you in the direction of further research and investigation so you can feel safe in a relationship once you know where to go to find it and how to get marriage proposals. The most important investigation of all, is to find what is important to know about the person you may marry, even if you two haven't yet met.**

# *Personality-Based Power Dating*

Power Dating Games can be fun if you put safety, compatibility, and harmony first. Investigate your soul mate before you even know where to find the personality to match with your character. You'll learn how to steer clear or veer near. When marriage became a cottage industry, the business-based marriage required a more efficient way of exploring the personality and even the genome of the one you want to marry, long before you two meet.

The Business-Based Marriage Is A Cottage Industry

Before You Commit To A Relationship: New Warning Signs For Future Intimate, Domestic, Or Dating Violence

Marriage is a cottage industry. Each marital relationship like each cottage industry is unconsciously chosen according to the personality preferences of each individual. Safe dating is based on knowing you can trust your mate with your life under any circumstances.

# *Chapter One*

## *Pitfalls to Avoid*

**B**eware of the relationship that "comes on" too fast. In marriage you experience the upward gush of your own infancy. Is your mate's attention love at first sight, or a warning signal of future violence, control, or emotional abuse? Are you and your mate perfectionists that have trouble getting close to anybody else? Will you have an angry marriage based on fear of abandonment, territory control, and loss? Are you a generous spender and your mate so tight, he'll put in uncomfortable lighting in *your* home-based office to save money even after you've agreed to pay your share?

Do you go shopping together and he (or she) puts back on the shelf the gourmet food you choose for your own self-indulgence and replaces your personal items with a large sack of beans? How great are the personality differences or similarities between you two?

Can you tell before you commit to a relationship, if you'll have a happy relationship or a fearful one in the future? Should you look for yourself in a soul mate? How will the differences and similarities between your personality and that of your mate's change your marriage?

There are many alternative classifiers of personality types, temperaments, styles, or neurological brain locations, and time and fun to try them all. Which one can help you find your soul mate? Which one can stand up to rigorous research and proof over many years? How many can be scientifically validated?

Will you be telling yourself, "Welcome to the future battered spouse's club?" Or will you be able to steer clear or veer near the relationship that's right for you. Beware of mar-rage (marital rage).

No one knows how the future will change you or your partner. However, here are some pointers and warning signs on how to tell before you commit to a relationship how your time together will be banked and spent. Before you commit to a relationship, here are the rules for steering clear of domestic violence possibilities related to personality differences.

## What Science Reports About Intimate Violence— Why Some Partners Beat, Shake, Chase, And Verbally Abuse Their Mates. Introduction: The Role Of Low Serotonin And Its Relation To Domestic And Intimate Violence

Science has a few good rules for those who fear judgment outside the home. Here's what science explores about taking some action and learning the warning signals for steering clear of intimate violence by looking at serotonin levels and narcisissm. Science offers diverse perspectives on domestic violence and shows a variety of facts on why some women without income of their own stay in such a marriage to avoid homelessness. Before you commit to a relationship, here are the rules for steering clear of domestic violence possibilities related to personality type differences.

(The pronoun "he" will be used throughout the book for brevity. However, a spouse or partner abuser may be male or female. Male abusers do outnumber female abusers. The abuser may be in a heterosexual or same-sex relationship with a partner. A spouse beater may be male or female. Please keep this in mind. At the present time, safe houses, battered spouse's shelters, and houses for persons of various religious or ethnic groups for women far outnumber safe houses or shelters for abused men.) Ironically, there are more homeless shelters for men.

**Those Who Abuse Their Partners Often Have Low Levels Of Serotonin In Their Brains.**

What is the most frequently-occurring trait in those who abuse or batter their mate, spouse, children, or domestic partner? It's low levels of serotonin. The more serotonin, the more affection your partner, and the closer he/she wants to be to you. The less serotonin, an amino acid, in the brain, the more impulsive, abusive, violent, depressive, aggressive, and suicidal the partner is.

Violence can be inner or outer directed, and violence is related to low serontonin. A group of Danish scientists measured 5-HIAA and other serotonin metabolites in a group and found that the lowest levels of serotonin were found in males who had killed a sexual partner or had attempted suicide. So, the best indicator of whether your soul mate will become a spouse batterer is to have the individual take a simple blood test at his or her doctor's office which measures the amount of serotonin levels in the blood.

Find out before you commit to a relationship by moving into that person's home or getting married or engaged whether you should steer clear or move toward a relationship. Low cholesterol diets are dangerous for spouse abusers. If the person with a low serotonin level is put on a low cholesterol diet, they usually become more aggressive, less affiliative, and show lower serotonin levels in their brain.

Beware of diet drugs that may sometimes permanently deplete the serotonin in your partner's brain, thereby setting up potential violence with the first sign of stress or frustration in the family or on the job. There are supplements, nutritional and health-related, and medicines available from your physician to regulate the hormones. Also, intimate violence may be sparked by a disorder known as "intermittent explosive disorder," whereby a person is normal and charming until a seemingly trivial phrase during normal conversation sets off an explosion of anger and violence, or the person may sleep walk and commit violent acts while asleep or in a semi-conscious state and not remember the acts. Check out these possibilities as well as brain allergies to certain foods.

An increase in depression, suicide, violent death, and spouse battering is rising for people on severely cholesterol-restricted diets or cholesterol-lowering drugs. Check out whether these are lowering the serotonin in yours or your partner's brain, thereby setting the stage for domestic violence. For further information, see the January issue of Life Enhancement magazine on serotonin and violence. (Life Enhancement, PO Box 751390, Petaluma, CA 94975-1390.

There's a relationship between alchohol, aggression, violence, and a craving for carbohydrates among people with low serotonin in their brains. In tests with animals, when they are given serotonin, tryptophan, 5-HTP, or an SSRI, their alchohol consumption drops.

Human studies have shown over the years that alcoholics have lower levels of serotonin function activity, showing low levels of 5-HIAA, an amino acid. In alcoholics who show science of becoming violent, as soon as drinking ceases, serotonin levels fall at the same time as the appearance of alcohol withdrawal symptoms appear. Abstinence must continue for a long period of time before serotonin levels slowly return to what they were formerly. If the person usually has a low serotonin level, the propensity for domestic violence is waiting to be set off by the slightest spark.

Research the field of reversing serotonin deficiecy before you commit to that relationship with someone who tests low at the doctor's for serotonin. In fact, when you get married, not only should the license show your partner is free from sexually-transmitted diseases, but also have normal levels of serotonin in the brain, or you could be setting yourself up for trouble. People with disabilities are vulnerable to domestic partners who can be aggressive and violent when the serotonin levels that are already low, move down lower to critical levels, thereby setting the stage for violence.

People with low serotonin levels are driven by appetites for food, water, sex, drugs of abuse, and are far more impulsive and unable to control extroverted feelings that explode outwardly like a volcano at you in the face of threat. They are less able to control their actions under stress.

Such partners are more likely to use aggression against you to get their way, obtain rewards, or keep you from blaming them. They will not be sensitive to your vulnerabilities, and they will not defer to any social control in the home. At work they may be charmers to keep their job and rise in the ranks, but watch out at home where you can't directly influence their future in the workplace where their security is focused. After all, you're looking for your soul mate in a partner.

What is the most frequently occurring trait in those who abuse or batter their mate, spouse, children, or domestic partner? It's low levels of serotonin. The more serotonin, the more affection your partner, and the closer he/she wants to be to you. The less serotonin, an amino acide, in the brain, the more impulsive, abusive, violent, depressive, aggressive, and suicidal the partner is.

Violence can be inner or outer directed, and violence is related to low serontonin. A group of Danish scientists measured 5-HIAA and other serotonin metabolites in a group and found that the lowest levels of serotonin were found in males who had killed a sexual partner or had attempted suicide. So, the best indicator of whether your soul mate will become a spouse batterer is to have the individual take a simple blood test at his or her doctor's office which measures the amount of serontonin levels in the blood.

Find out before you commit to a relationship by moving into that person's home or getting married or engaged whether you should steer clear or move toward a relationship. Low cholesterol diets are dangerous for spouse abusers. If the person with a low serotonin level is put on a low cholesterol diet, they usually become more aggressive, less affiliative, and show lower serotonin levels in their brain. Beware of diet drugs that may sometimes permanently deplete the serotonin in your partner's brain, thereby setting up potential violence with the first sign of stress or frustration in the family or on the job.

An increase in depression, suicide, violent death, and spouse battering is rising for people on severely cholesterol-restricted diets or cholesterol-lowering drugs. Check out whether these are lowering the serontonin in yours or your partner's brain, thereby setting the stage for domestic violence. For further information, see the January 2000 issue of Life Enhancement magazine on serotonin and violence. (Life Enhancement, PO Box 751390, Petaluma, CA 94975-1390.

There's a relationship between alchohol, aggression, violence, and a craving for carbohydrates among people with low serotonin in their brains. In tests with animals, when they are given erotonin, tryptophan, 5-HTP, or an SSRI, their alchohol consumption drops. Human studies have shown over the years that alcoholics have lower levels of serotonin function activity, showing low levels of 5-HIAA, an amino acid.

In alcoholics who show science of becoming violent, as soon as drinking ceases, serotonin levels fall at the same time as the appearance of alcohol withdrawal symptoms appear. Abstinence must continue for a long period of time before serotonin levels slowly return to what they were formerly. If the person usually has a low serotonin level, the propensity for domestic violence is waiting to be set off by the slightest spark.

Research the field of reversing serotonin deficiency before you commit to that relationship with someone who tests low at the doctor's for serotonin. In fact, when you get married, not only should the license show your partner is free from sexually-transmitted diseases, but also have normal levels of serotonin in the brain, or you could be setting yourself up for trouble. People with disabilities or some women who become financially dependent on others are vulnerable to domestic partners who can be aggressive and violent when the serontonin levels that are already low, move down lower to critical levels, thereby setting the stage for violence.

People with low serotonin levels are driven by appetites for food, water, sex, drugs of abuse, and are far more impulsive and unable to control extroverted feelings that explode outwardly like a volcano at you in the face of threat. They are less able to control their actions under stress. Such soul mates are more likely to use aggression against you to get their way, obtain rewards, or keep you from blaming them.

They will not be sensitive to your vulnerabilities, and they will not defer to any social control in the home. At work they may be charmers to keep their job and rise in the ranks, but watch out at home where you can't directly influence their future in the workplace where their security is focused.

\* \* \*

# Chapter Two

## Why Your Partner Calls You A Loser

Does he put you down? If he doesn't make you feel good about yourself, drop him now. The verbal abuse will escalate after marriage. At first he'll complain how bad your room smells, or that he can't stand you slobbering over the table when eating in front of him.

The average person wouldn't mind the crunchy sound of eating crispy foods. The wife beater will be angered by the slightest noise you make eating. He'll order you to clean off the tops of the kitchen counters, but he'll never put items away himself. If you refuse, that will be enough to warrant a beating or a chase where he'll corner you and push you around.

Some wife batterers complain that their own wife is the only woman who can provoke them to violence. Others will beat any woman in any location if she doesn't defer to his commands.

**Does He Cuss Out The Car In Front Of Him For Cutting In Front Of Him On The Road? Does The Car In Front Become An Extension Of Your Partner's Personality?**

A potential spouse beater sees the car in front of him (or her) on the highway as an extension of his own personality. If any quick moves are made that cause him to react fast, a rush of adrenaline in his body sets off his temper. He'll cuss, yell, explode in anger, or express bad feelings to you. The wife beater is the kind of man who expresses angry feelings freely to his wife or girlfriend, but holds in his feelings at work or around other men.

After you know him awhile, the angry feelings will increase and the affection will decrease. By the time you're married awhile, your foremost complaint will be that the only emotion he shows you is anger, never love. Yet on the phone with his fellow employees, both male and female, he's a scared rabbit who can never say no, a people pleaser who will readily hit you before he'll say no to a neighbor or co-worker.

He'll use terms like "can't you keep the house clean?" or "I'm so embarrassed at your housekeeping," each time there's a visitor to the home, such as a repairman or guest. No matter how well you clean the house, he'll find something wrong with your housekeeping just at a time when you're working on solving a work-related problem at home.

## Does He Control And Patrol You In The Name Of Being Protective Or Jealous?

The leading female character from the opera 'Carmen' is stabbed to death just after stating that she's a free spirit whom no man can own. This archetype of the battered woman resounds throughout time and geographic location. In our society today as yesterday, a woman doesn't break off a relationship without getting physically beaten or killed-unless the man wants to break off the relationship first.

To not defer to a man, elicits an angry and violent response. One quarter of the policemen killed in the line of duty die responding to a report of domestic violence. It's up to the woman to change this pattern that goes back to stone-age times. One of the most common reasons women are fired from jobs is for "not deferring to men." Several years ago, TV anchorwoman Christine Craft was said to have been fired from one of her TV jobs for being (as one newspaper reported her then employers as saying she was) "too old, too ugly, and she doesn't defer to men."

Is your partner confusing sex and aggression? A young child's exposure to his parent's sexual relations can cause inhibitions later in life or sadism. Children often interpret sex between parents as physical combat. If the child buries his awareness in a fantasy which is later associated with sexual arousal in a violent style, he's masking his terror to close out memory of the "sex fight" between his parents. How many theatrical films depict sex occurring right after extreme violence? Does your boyfriend use extreme violence on the screen to arouse him sexually? Watch out.

Where psychologist C.G. Jung was on target with his theories, S. Freud ignored actual patterns of family interaction such as the high frequency of incest in families. How does your boyfriend use fantasy? Does he think 'fantasy' is a dirty word? Or does he think fantasy means using your imagination to create a better world? Is he so down-to-earth practical and realistic as to respond with violence to your softly intuitive imagination to escape to a better world or create serenity?

If the way fantasy is used is very different between the two of you, look out for trouble. What's wrong here is a type difference. You may be intuitive and open-minded. He may be using his senses to observe the world around him in visual details. He may not trust his imagination or intuition, thinking it 'flaky.' You may trust your intuition because it keeps open the possibilities for bettering your self or your surroundings.

The type difference, itself could lead to violence, if he has a low tolerance for ambiguity or other people's differences in type and temperament. To find out, both of you could take a Myers-Briggs Type Indicator given by most adult education counseling centers, schools, and colleges.

## What Kind Of Woman Becomes A Battered Wife? What Type Of Man Becomes The Batterer?

To get a closer look at what kind of woman makes a battered wife, in contrast to what kind of man becomes a batter, see Terry Davidson's book, Conjugal Crime: Understanding and Changing the Wife-Beating

Pattern. In Davidson's book, therapist Carol Victor surveyed eighty clients, all victims of wife beating, all socio-economic classes.

In Victor's survey of 80 clients, four of the battered wives completed graduate school, six completed college, and seventeen had attended college. Nine of the wife beaters completed graduate school. Several were PhDs and MDs, and nine had completed college.

The stereotypical myth that wife beaters come from lower socioeconomic classes is false. Domestic violence from child abuse to wife abuse to elderly abuse cuts across all economic classes from dropouts to those with many graduate degrees, from the most poverty-stricken to the rich and famous celebrities.

In therapist Carol Victor's study, the type of women who were beaten listed their occupations as one or more of the following: "social worker, psychologist, librarian, teacher, artist, nurse, designer, manager, medical technician, computer programmer, law enforcement officer, banker, secretary, and accountant. One woman was a waitress."

The wife-battering men listed their occupations as: "physician, self-employed businessman, draftsman, engineer, teacher, pharmacist, medical technician, librarian, police, career military, and computer programmer. There was one sanitation worker."

The abusers of battered spouses and partners are found in all walks of life, from members of high IQ societies, physicians, lawyers, to repair technicians, the unemployed, and everything in-between. The battered spouse or partner may also come from any type of occupation or no occupation—from highly educated to little formal education. Anger management is a problem for the abuser, regardless of whether the person is mopping floors for a living or practicing medicine.

Often it's the case of a man who can't take care of his wife marrying a woman who can't take care of herself. Taking care refers to an emotional state, regardless of the education and skill of either party.

Occasionally, it's the woman who married young or who took a general liberal arts education or the woman who dropped out of high school who is most dependent. However, dependency in women upon a batterer's income is seen in women who are members of high IQ societies who had some college, in women with a variety of types of panic disorders, agoraphobia, and in women with high dependency needs to be taken care of by a father figure.

Sometimes it's the woman who fears not being able to support herself and her children who stays in an abusive relationship to have a place to live. And just as often, it's a working woman emotionally dependent upon the abuser who can earn a living but really doesn't trust her body to hold up under the strain and stress of earning a living. In some cases, the man is abused by a woman and is too embarrassed to admit the abuse to his work buddies.

It's a myth and stereotype that women who hold independent jobs or who own and run businesses can't possibly come home and change like Jekyll and Hyde into a battered wife. Battered wives aren't only the stereotypical submissive, shy personalities.

They're also the outspoken, independent thinking women who refuse to defer to their husbands controlling, patrolling, manipulative behavior. By refusing to defer and standing their own grounds, asking assertively for respect, the hostile/dependent man is provoked. When he loses the control over a woman who seeks control over her own life, he batters her.

The other type of battered wife is truly the shy, demure woman who suffers from the "battered woman syndrome." She has seen so much domestic violence in her parent's home as a child, or escaping violence in childhood, feels unable to take responsibility for her own financial and emotional independence.

She can be overwhelmed by the stress of caring for children, a body that breaks down physically, the wrong job skills or none, or an overwhelming desire to be taken care of and a deep fear of seeking employment. She feels incompetent and incomplete and fears rejection by employers. She's the type of woman who would rather stay at home at any cost rather than have to go out and work again for so little compensation-financial, emotional, and physical.

The sociophobic battered wife feels she could never earn enough to support her own children alone, so she stays long in a marriage where verbal and emotional abuse is high, but physical violence is low or only a once-a-year occurrence.

*     *     *

# Chapter Three

## When Domestic Violence Spills Over Into The Workplace
## Ensuring Workplace Safety: A Reality?

Another person under a restraining order because of threats against his estranged spouse went to her place of work at a national City Bank office recently, shot her to death and then killed himself in Carmel, Indiana. In addition to those in private employment, 30 percent of state, federal, and local government employees, including supervisors and managers, are assaulted at work each year, according to the National Crime Victimization Survey, (NCVS) which conducts interviews with more than 100,000 individuals over the age of twelve annually. Respondents who reported a violent victimization also said they were on duty or working when asked what they were doing when the assault occurred.

Forty percent of Americans view workplace violence as a growing problem, according to a recent Time/CNN poll. According to the CDC, each week 15 people are murdered at work. By 1992, homicide became the leading cause of death at work. Nearly 13 percent of deaths occurred in an office or factory, as a result of disputes between workers and customers, and 4 percent of the time due to a female worker's ex-boyfriend breaking into the office and killing her for trying to leave the relationship, especially when there is disputed child custody.

At the state government level, harassment and fighting or threats used to be less of a problem than violence from the public directed at state employees and supervisors. Today, the primary threat to state supervisors and employees is from domestic violence spilling into the jobsite. Northwestern National Life Insurance Company found in 1993 that 2.2 million workers are physically battered at work, 6.3 million are threatened on the job, and 16.1 million workers are harassed annually in the office or plant.

Stress (frequent, unexpected change) is the major cause of workplace violence, and the most frequent cause of stress leading to battering, vandalism, or intimate violence spilling over into the office is the "swing shift blues"-placing employees one workday on the night shift followed quickly by switching the employee to the day shift-so that the body rhythms and brain chemicals are disturbed. It takes the body two weeks to adjust to a work shift change.

Men assaulted at work in a state government office were more likely to be attacked by a stranger, but, according to NCVS, five percent of the women assaulted, victimized, or killed at work were more likely to be attacked by someone known to them, usually as a spillover of domestic violence that had followed them into their workplace.

Usually, the attacker of women was not another disgruntled employee, but an ex-boyfriend or estranged spouse reacting to the woman's desire to leave the relationship. Women who were in the process of leaving a relationship were more likely to be murdered by the person they had recently left rather than attacked by a total stranger, such as a caseworker's client frustrated by the system suddenly exploding in anger when claims are rejected.

Remarkably, more than half of all state government office victimizations sustained at work were not reported to police. When individuals were asked why, forty percent replied that they thought the incident was a private matter. Twenty seven percent reported the assault to a security guard or their supervisor and not to the police.

Among state government employees, when some is victimized at work, men are more likely to experience a violent crime, and women most often are victims of theft and purse snatchings while at work. Working victims were as likely to face armed offenders as those victimized while not working. More than 30 percent of victims working during an assault faced armed offenders, and a third of the offenders carried hand guns.

Nationally, workplace violence cost 876,800 lost workdays each year, costing employees more than $16 million in wages, not including days covered by leave. Interestingly, thirty percent of victims of workplace violence are state employees, since government workers make up only 18 percent of the total United States workforce. Six out of ten incidents of workplace violence occurred in private companies. That leaves four out of ten episodes of workplace violence happening at government worksites.

What may be responsible for the overrepresentation of government employees involved as victims of violent workplace crime, include a high risk of victimizations for certain government jobs such as state public safety personnel and the state police or highway patrol.

As domestic violence spills over into government offices, nineteen percent of female state employees assaulted at work were battered or killed by their estranged husbands or boyfriends, compared to only 10 percent of males were assaulted or killed being victims of domestic violence carried into the workplace. Of those attacked at work, 84 percent had sustained injuries. In most cases the offender wasn't armed (62 percent unarmed compared to 32 percent armed). Yet only 43 percent of those incidents were reported to the police, and 56 percent of the assaults were not reported to anyone outside the office.

Of all workers assaulted 61 percent, by far the majority, worked in private corporations, 8 percent were self-employed, one percent were working without pay, and 30 percent worked in state, local, or federal government jobs.

The violence occurred 23 percent of the time at another commercial establishment and only 14 percent of the time in the office.

Frequently, workplace violence in government offices occurs in the parking lot or garage (11 percent of the time) because of tight government building security. Yet 22 percent of the time the violence takes place on the streets or other public property.

Other places where violence against state employees occurs include campuses or school property, or at a restaurant, bar, or club, where state government workers frequently go for lunch. Volunteers, such as retirees, aren't as likely to be assaulted at work as paid workers of any age, although older supervisors in state government are more likely to be assaulted by younger employees than younger supervisors. Hatred against the older person seems to build into a resentment that easily explodes out of impatience.

## What Are The Warning Signals?

State government employees who exhibit "red flag" warning signals of impending workplace violence or spillover of intimate violence to supervisors and managers often go unnoticed because there are few behaviors that attract attention. The profile of the perpetrator of intimate violence brought into the office can be an employed "Mr. or Ms. Reliable" who goes far beyond duties to help people on the job, yet be a spouse batterer at home. That person usually is a loner who has trouble coming up with alternatives and possibilities to use when under sudden stress.

The individual appears normal on the job, but when under physical, work-related, personal, or financial stress, lacks the outgoing intuition to make less angry or more patient decisions concerning domestic matters. That person is most likely to follow an ex-spouse to work and explode in violence, physical, or even verbal abuse.

Warning signals include a long history, as much as 20 or 30 years of putting the spouse down verbally to raise one self up, and putting all efforts into doing a good job at work. The person can be a charmer at work or a loner, but chances are the partner at home is isolated and verbally abused, with increasing physical violence ending up in workplace-focused assaults. The workplace violence usually takes place in the spouse's place of employment, not the office where the perpetrator works.

Supervisors should be alerted that the highest indicators of impending employee violence toward managers, supervisors, peers, or ex-spouses on the job-for state employees and managers include the following, as outlined by the National Crisis Prevention Institute (1-800-558-8976) or email: cpi@execpc.com (Nonviolent Crisis Intervention is a registered Service Mark of the National Crisis Prevention Institute.)

## Indicators For Supervisors

There are alternative ways of interpreting key warning signs associated with the potential for violence in the workplace and/or at home (later spilling over into the worksite).

1. Excessive tardiness or absences from work.

2. Reducing the workday by leaving early or without authorization, or using excuses for shortening the workday. The National Crisis Prevention Institute considers this a very significant indicator if the employee previously has been prompt and committed.

3. Increased need for supervision. The 'normal' employee over times requires less supervision as the individual becomes more proficient. Employees who insist supervisors spend an inordinate amount of time with them could be signaling a need for help.

4. Reduction in productivity. A sudden drop in performance from an employee previously very productive. This is a classic warning signal of

dissatisfaction that needs an immediate meeting of supervisor and employee.

5. Inconsistency. State employees habitually are consistent in their work. When they become inconsistent, determine why immediately and find out whether resentment is brewing.

6. Strained workplace relationships. State government supervisors most frequently fire women "for not fitting into the group" and fire men "for incompetence," according to crisis intervention consultant Sally Tucker.

Complaints brought against female employees to the personnel department include such accusations as "urinating blood on the toilet seat in the women's room," whereas complaints against male workers to supervisors are almost always work-related or accusations of bullying.

Workers display disruptive behavior most frequently in reaction to strained work relationships, differences of personality type and different ways of handling conflict or communications. To diffuse a potentially violent situation, the supervisor in a state government office, according to the Crisis Prevention Institute (CPI), needs to intervene right away and offer professional employee assistance.

7. Inability to concentrate. Distracted workers could be in trouble and need help before frustration and impatience turn into violent anger or suicide.

8. Violation of safety procedures. Stress can make some employees careless, or they may need a lot more training on the job. An employee who always has been careful suddenly may become involved in accidents on the job or safety violations. This is a clear warning signal of deep stress, and possibly impending violence or self-destructive behavior. Find out why it's happening fast.

9. Changes in personal health or hygiene. When your employee suddenly stops bathing, using deodorant, or starts dressing in filthy clothes, neglect of personal health or grooming signals trouble, such as depression, which could easily erupt outwardly as violence or inwardly as

suicidal or other self-destructive behavior. Even anorexia or eating problems such as bulimia, may signal work-related depression, fears, desire to control the inner world, work-related financial insecurities.

The extension of the worker's personality applied to any passerby, even a vehicle that cuts in front of the person could signal impending violence or great difficulty in handling stress. When hygiene or health changes, it's time to talk first, then send the employee to a physician for evaluation as to why the change happened.

10. Any sustained change in behavior is often an indication of difficulties that are not expressed orally or in writing-where they should be-in a current file or database and presented to supervisors.

11. Substance abuse. Street drug, alcohol and prescription pill addicts, are prone to workplace violence. Also, certain food allergies or allergies to medicines and medical pill interactions are susceptible to violence due to brain allergies to the particular food or substance causing personality changes. Drug test results can be falsified.

Pay particular attention to following up any substance abuse problems or results of workplace counseling results. Sometimes substance abusers are bullies or secret drinkers and overly quiet or loners, while other loners may merely be normal, healthy introverts who prefer to concentrate on their work with the door closed for maximum production results.

12. Stress due to changes in time schedules. Identify and intervene promptly.

Encourage personal wellness and preventative discussions, programs or stress relief training.

14. Blaming or blame-throwing excuses. This kind of 'flaming' signals inability to find alternative ways of inquiring into the situation that caused the employee or supervisor to blame first and ask questions later. Solution is to stop and think first, cool down, and ask for explanations or 'why' the situation occurred, then analyze results listing pros and cons, checks and balances, etc. with employee.

Blamers are most likely introverted, practical, "Mr. or Ms. Reliables" with undeveloped intuition who have trouble listing enough alternatives to blaming the person closest to them at the time or at home. Blaming can escalate into physical violence when no witnesses are around or be used only at home directed toward the spouse, while at work the person stops at verbal blaming.

Some nonverbal types may be spouse-only blamers who like to help people at work, but are absent emotionally from intimate relations or neglectful and abusive or merely silent and withdrawn or demanding and commanding in relationships. These people are often 'mouses' at work and can't say no to volunteering to help people at work with projects no one else wants.

15. Depression. Not all depressed employees are prone to violence. Some are self-destructive for long periods of time. Since violence can come after a long period of depression, help should be offered immediately, before the inward turning employee turns the anger and hurt outward toward the people closest.

It's one step from depression to blame and then onto violence.

Supervisors at the state government level are most concerned with the State Police whose job it is to protect the security of state government buildings, and the Highway Patrol. (The State Police are under the umbrella of the Highway Patrol). State Police officials emphasize that there are almost always warning signs of an employee who needs help fast. As a supervisor, you need to be aware of these indicators through experience and judgment.

Warning signs or indicators can be used as tools of experience. The signs are pleas for help that are impossible to communicate at work, only because the employee is unable to find alternatives, intuition, ideas, or the right words to ask for intervention. There also may be fear of intervention, or fear of being singled out for help. A timely, positive response helps to create a more secure workplace by empowering workers who feel a need to control and manipulate the team at work.

## How Can Supervisors Curb Workplace Violence (Often Spilling Over From Domestic Or Dating Violence)?

Whereas most state employees who are assaulted by a supervisor file a civil lawsuit against the government (and collect damage fees), most government supervisors assaulted by an employee end up physically injured or dead with the employee arrested by the State Police. The solution is to always look for alternative ways of interpreting behavior.

The supervisor who attacks an employee most often is still on the job long after the employee files a civil suit. Sometimes, despite complaints to higher management, no action is taken when an employee is injured by a supervisor, especially in the private sector. Sometimes the company will merely say the supervisor in question is "not a people person," and let it go at that.

According to news reports, when an AT&T supervisor pleaded no contest to a criminal charge of battery against an employee, in the mid-nineties, AT&T refused to take action against the supervisor, but the State Court of Rockdale County, Georgia, sentenced him to 24 hours of community service and 180 days probation for literally kicking ass. According to news reports, he allegedly kicked a female technician in the seat of her slacks while she was bending over a box at the AT&T facility in Conyers, Georgia.

"I couldn't believe he had actually kicked me when he said, 'and that wasn't my hand," the employee said, according to news reports. This workplace violence incident and similar information appeared in the mid-nineties on the Internet at the Website http://www.portal.com/~dblan, entitled "A Leader in Workplace Violence!" There are dozens of Internet Weblinks and sites under the search term, "Workplace Violence" to explore, a cornocopia of workplace incidents and reports on violence, and surveys as well as articles on "Ticking Bombs: Defusing Violence in the Workplace." at http://galaxy.einet.net/gala.

Each year nearly a million victims of violent crime are injured while working or on duty. Workplace violence accounts for 15 percent of the more than 6 million acts of violence experienced by United States residents over the age of 12. More than 2 million personal thefts and 200,000 car thefts occur each year while persons are at work.

Crime victimizations in the workplace cost half a million employees 1,751,000 days of work lost each year, an average of 3.5 days per crime. According to the National Crime Victimization Survey, the missed work results in more than $55 million in lost wages annually not covered by sick leave or vacations. Workplace violence results in nearly 160,000 physical injuries annually.

State Police and the Highway Patrol whose job it is to guard state buildings and roads from bombers and violent freeway shooters, can't go inside the minds of employees or supervisors to prevent theft or violence at work before it actually occurs. The National Institutes for Occupational Safety and Health has declared workplace homicide a public health problem, not a State Police dilemma. Homicide is the leading cause of workplace death for women and the third leading cause for men. Violence on the job includes rape, robbery, assault, and 'trailing' domestic violence.

State employees who deal with the public, especially social service workers and retail clerks in the private sector are the most affected. Only 20 percent of workplace violence is perpetrated by co-workers. Employees are twice as likely to be attacked by clients or customers as by co-workers or randomly-met strangers.

Maintenance supervisors are the most likely government workers to be murdered at work by their own employees as are postal supervisors, and video store owners, cab drivers, restaurant managers, pawn-shop owners, convenience store clerks, psychologists, sanitation managers, tavern owners, cooks, fishermen, and furniture store owners are more likely to be killed by customers.

Every state supervisor should have de-escalation, assault prevention, and crisis training to learn how to diffuse a potential problem long before it escalates into impulsive, unpremeditated violence or murder based on a random remark that became "the last straw." Agitated, disruptive people may be the most likely to commit violence at work, but workers who travel on business, work night shifts or are paid to handle disruptive people want their supervisor's commitment to their own safety.

According to Judith Weiss of the Assault Prevention Information Network, (Personal Power Assault Prevention Training) found on the Internet at Website: http://galaxy.einet.net/gala, assault prevention focusing on de-escalation and wellness programs show supervisors and employees how to work together to strategize about personal safety, self esteem, and personal power.

It's the powerless employee who strikes out at the supervisor, the powerless client who stabs the social worker, and the powerless supervisor who lashes out physically at an employee who cannot be controlled. What affects your employees positively in all areas of their lives? What makes them confident in new environments, able to assess risks, negotiate contracts, and set visible boundaries?

Supervisors aren't counselors, but they can empower employees for teamwork by letting them know they are on their side and partners in personal growth, because it's profitable and productive to the workplace and the government. Does the supervisor have a duty to provide a safe workplace for employees and clients? Can OSHA make rules to prevent occupational homicide? What can the Occupational Safety and Health Act do to help employers provide a safe workplace? OSHA has started to give citations under its general duty clause, which requires a workplace free from hazards, to employers who aren't protecting workers from being physically battered or injured by others on the job due to violent tempers.

The threat of citations imposes financial penalties and government-ordered abatement requirements. Worker's Compensation places liability on workplace violence injuries. Worker's compensation liability defines the extent of an employer's liability for employee victims of violence from clients or other employees. Some states bar employees from suing for negligence co-workers who assault them on the job. The question for supervisors, is, did they use reasonable care in selecting and retaining employees?

An informative Website on a variety of state's rulings on compensation for workplace assault is at http://venable.com/wlu/rocke on the Internet. Unions must address workplace safety issues, because employees seek union protection. If the fundamental need for safety at work isn't met by an employer, an employee will turn to outside sources, especially unions, for help. In fact, the Service Employees International Union (SEIU) developed sample contract language to protect employees from on-the-job violence. At the state government level, the need is high right now for negotiation of specific contract language to help bring into reality a safer workplace.

## Who Is Most Likely To Bring Domestic Violence Into The Workplace To Assault An Employee Or Supervisor?

The profile of the person most likely to bring domestic violence into the workplace in a state government office building is a male in his forties living primarily in California, Texas, or Florida (but could be anywhere), who exhibits the following characteristics: He is rigid, controlling, manipulative, and pathologically jealous either an employee who works at the given site or, if he, also, is a government employee, the jealousy is directed to his supervisor, or he covets his supervisor's job and feels he has earned the rights to it and is being denied what's his.

At work he is distant from others, aloof, and "not a people person." He's unable to understand and appreciate another's feelings and has difficulty in expressing emotions other than anger. The individual may or may not be a state government employee himself, but if he's not, he will follow his estranged partner into her office. The profile of the stranger most likely to bring domestic violence into the workplace where the object of his assault works is as follows:

The guy most likely to walk into a state office building and evade security measures is there to target an ex-partner. He has poor impulse control, an explosive temper, and very limited frustration tolerance. If he also works in the same office or both parties work for state government, he may deny his behavior or try to justify it. At work he's anxious about his feelings and views himself in a negative light.

On the job he's self-centered, but lacks self-esteem, feeling he's out of control. He reacts by trying to control his estranged spouse who most often is the one with the government job, although sometimes both partners work together for the same supervisor. The man with out-of-control feelings seeks to control both his supervisor and his spouse.

Employees who follow their wives or partners to work in order batter them in front of co-workers are often traditionalists who hold to hierarchical and stereotypical patriarchial roles in the family as well as on the job. Promotion is up through the ranks, not by merit, originality, or creativity. This ranking order of command is followed rigidly at home, too. Substance abuse is a problem for many persons who commit violence in the workplace, particulary, domestic violence at work. Frequently, but not always, the workplace domestic batterers have witnessed abusive childhood backgrounds.

Individuals who bring domestic violence into the workplace are not all alike. Studies of state government employees reveal that there are developmental stages in this behavior and different clusterings of personality characteristics. Some researchers include Gondolf, 1985, and Hamberger & Hastings, 1986.

The picture painted of someone who brings domestic violence into the workplace is one of an immature person who fails to accept responsibility for his actions. There are far fewer females who assault their boyfriends or husbands at work than there are males who assault their female partners or estranged spouses.

Immaturity is the key description of the typical batterer who follows his/her partner to work to express anger violently in front of strange employees. Persons with short tempers have problems that need anger management behavioral modification counseling and workshops, or in severe cases, other treatment. People with intermittent explosive disorder have a problem with an explosive temper that may have an organic, biological, or medical basis and may need to be under treatment by a medical professional. The first step is to get a physical and find out whether the problem is biologically-based, chemical imbalances, hormonal, or related to anger management behavior.

According to studies reported in the mid-nineties in various journals and bulletins of personality type studies, on the Myers-Briggs Type Indicator, (MBTI) ™, the most frequent types encountered for male batterers was ISTJ and ISFJ, and ISFP slightly less frequent. Women with high dependency needs such as INFP and ISFP need to be cautious whom they marry. INFP females may too easily marry ISFJ or ESTP men with repressed anger coupled with low self-esteem. With a lack of confidence, too many INFP women may harbor morbid fears of being fired repeatedly. The dominant introverted feeling may encourage such dependent women to conclude they always will remain unable to support oneself financially apart from the batterer.

Why does workplace domestic violence happen so frequently, especially in government offices? The batterer knows how much the employee or supervisor values the financial independence offered by a stable, secure government job that builds seniority. The batter focuses on the fact that the victim will only leave a job as a last resort and targets the deep fear of financial dependence in both the victim and the batterer.

The most frequently found wife "battering" personality types on the MBTI, the ISTJ, is followed closely by the ISFJ, but it's only hypothesized by studies showing statistically significant numbers of ISTJ and ISFJ males in counseling groups for male workplace batterers. That leaves out all the workplace violence perpetrators who refuse to come to counseling or support groups for batterers. ISTJ stands for introverted sensing thinking judging and ISFJ stans for Introverted Sensing Feeling Judging. ISFP stands for introverted sensing feeling perceiving and INFP for introverted intuitive feeling perceiving.

The most frequently found type, the ISTJ male is logistics-oriented on the job and seeks stability. When he batters, it's because he has passed judgment on co-workers or a domestic partner, or overrided a more meek individual. His reactions usually are unpredictable when his attempts to be rigid and controlling or patriarchal is thwarted. (Keirsey and Bates, 1978).

At work, the ISTJ is socially isolated and unable to verbally express emotions, except anger (Myers & McCaulley, 1985). On the job, when anger is expressed by frustration over production speed, for example, some ISTJs use action statements, including threats of violence that may escalate into physical force.

Sensing-thinking personalities are least able to use intuition to find alternative ways of getting out of the situation or leaving the site for a break. This individual, whether a supervisor reprimanding an employee or a spouse jealously following an estranged partner into the office, is least able to foresee the consequences of violent actions before they occur.

There are normal ISFJs like normal people of any personality. The ISFJ only when a perpetrator, goes to extremes of the normal ISFJ desire for order. In the extreme or under heavy stress, such a person *might* hold order at utmost importance, both in the home and on the job. Everything must be in its place-job, supervision of employees, wife, kids, the 'right' medical plan, retirement pension arrangements, etc. Over-structuring and over-organizing the smallest details of life can be frustrating to the INFP wife who's literally a free spirit, who will not be measured or controlled or made to "walk on egg shells" or postpone labeling files, cleaning the house, or doing any other organizing-related task.

His introverted sensing clashes with her extroverted intuition and, bang-zoom, to the moon. She's beaten into orderliness, and most frequently at home. When she decides to leave, he may follow her into her office and either assault her or worse, break her equipment, and without hesitation, turn the weapon on himself when the acts of violence toward others is over.

Harmony for the ISFJ and the INFP is the priority. The feeling of being undervalued at work and in the home is what drives the ISFJ to violence in the workplace, or more frequently, at home when he can isolate his spouse. ISFJ feels angry when a partner doesn't live up to his standards or when a supervisor or co-worker doesn't meet his inner ideals.

Normally under assertive at work, at home any feelings of being undervalued will be transferred to verbal and physical abuse and emotional neglect. As nonverbal as the ISFJ and ISTJ are, anger is released in a steady stream of put-down words directed at the spouse, and when in a depression, the anger also is directed to co-workers or the supervisor, even though the job is highly valued.

The work-oriented ISFJ sometimes cannot say 'no' to work-related requests from supervisors and co-workers. They internalize anger which leads to depression, dependency on the job and the spouse, and very low self esteem. Note that all this information applies only to the ISTJ and ISFJ types who do commit workplace violence, not the thousands of those who do not, for 38 percent of the population are ISFJ or ISTJ types, and most are stable, logical, harmony-seeking workers whose only wish is to keep their jobs until retirement.

Men most likely to commit workplace domestic violence suppress their emotions (other than anger) in order to act more stereotypically forceful on the job while still trying to present a picture of being dutiful and loyal to their supervisors. Male batterers who spill over into the workplace to 'get their spouse' on the job use aggression to compensate for their feelings of inadequacy, for which the ISFJ male is most prone of all the types studied.

The workplace domestic violence batterer presents a profile of being obsessed with inner sense reactions that are not filtered through a mature judging process. These inner sense reactions are full of fear of being hurt unjustly and without cause. Instead of asking, "is it worth it?" or "Is it logically the best for me in the long run?" the workplace batterer shows obsessive jealousy toward the supervisor and at the same time severe controlling behavior toward the domestic partner at the worksite and at home.

The workplace domestic batterer distrusts intuition or the act of seeking alternatives to the angry attitude. His partner's complaints are exactly what he states as being his own needs.

The workplace batterer who brings intimate violence into his domestic partner's office is distressed when every detail doesn't go his way all the time. He is stuck in the rut of looking at domestic and work situations only in ways that he has actually experienced before many times (Hirsh & Kummerow, 1989). The batter finds it impossible to create other strategies to deal with workplace stress.

Studies have not looked at females who bring domestic violence to the workplace because there have been so few. In the mid-nineties, a newspaper story told of the first 'female, black employee in her forties to shoot up the workplace,' as if it were a landmark of women's achievement crossing a threshold into a formerly all-male domain, it has been stated. With the ISFP workplace batterers, they stop adapting and won't give an inch, when a cherished inner value is frustrated. They stop being flexible. The ISFJ workplace batterer suffers from inferiority feelings and a loss of self-confidence at work together with a distrust of the spouse and family or life in general.

The self-critical workplace assaulter neglects to share his feelings with others and becomes negative towards all supervisors and destructive in attitudes. A most common reaction to reprimands from supervisors is to urinate on the carpet in the office without the supervisor noticing. Workplace vandalism may be frequent. The constant internalizing of feelings of anger and rejection toward the supervisor escalates and increases the individual's anxiety, leading to mental and physical stress reactions directed at management and co-workers who are perceived to put them down verbally.

The workplace batterer who brings domestic violence into the office of his partner often neglects his own needs in favor of trying to please the supervisor and co-workers at the same time. Feelings often are immature and not expressed in outer behavior in a positive way. Battering at the office is an expression outwardly of stored-up resentments against a critical supervisor (trying to improve work production) and the rejecting domestic partner at the same time. Above all, jealousy of someone else's job perceived as better, sometimes is involved in violence or vandalism.

Acting reasonable at work is difficult when immaturity is an issue. It's the underdeveloped "frustration function," the way an individual handles frustration under stress, that needs to be tested by supervisors before hiring someone, and that's hard to do. No job applicant wants to experience how he or she will react under stress during an interview or early on the job. That's called 'hazing' and can provoke a law suit. When violence erupts, it usually is directed to the person closest to the batterer.

Few studies or literature are available on women who batter in the workplace at the present time. Suggestions for supervisors in state government would be to discuss with employees how they will react under work stress or how they see bringing domestic violence issues into the workplace. Training in dealing with repressed anger in the workplace is necessary. Self-esteem is a frequently discussed issue in government employment, but the self-esteem of the unemployed spouse who follows the employee or supervisor to work rarely has been discussed, let alone training classes opened to handle such problems. Workplace violence is on the increase. The question of repressed anger and low-self esteem also in the domestic partner is an issue, including a legal issue, for employers to look at. Who's responsible for damages when a woman is beaten by her ex-spouse or disgruntled ex-boyfriend at her job in a state government building and her ex-partner is not employed there?

\*     \*     \*

## Chapter Four

## *Are Perfectionists Are More Inclined To Be Involved In Domestic Violence Spillover In The Workplace?*

Perfectionists dominate workplace trauma scenes in cases where domestic violence at home sometimes spills over into the office or worksite. "I know because I'm one myself, migraines and all," said a retired consultant who asks anonymity. "I beat my former wife and verbally abused her early in the marriage by calling her a loser and someone who can't hold a job or make any friends," he confessed.

"I followed her to work and confronted her until she was fired 'for not fitting into the group,'" he added. "That was thirty years ago. "Today, I'm no longer a perfectionist, but that came long after retirement and becoming a recluse by choice to stop the criticism from hurting my sensitive feelings. I was all touchy-feely inside and all tough manager outside, until my health broke in midlife."

A 10-year study of perfectionism involving more than 9,000 supervisors and managers in the mid-nineties noted that "the single most important finding is that perfectionism makes you sick," according to the late Clayton Lafferty, former director of Human Synergistics, a Plymouth, Michigan research and consulting company that in the mid-nineties studied the perfectionist behavior of supervisors. The article was well publicized in newspapers nationally in 1996.

"The illness rate is much higher for perfectionist supervisors and managers as well as perfectionist employees," according to news articles in which the late Clayton Lafferty was interviewed by reporters. Most frequently, they are victims of "hypertension, cardiovascular diseases, migraines, and tension headaches."

Such supervisors are competent, hard-working, intelligent workers who may fear their ability to compete in the workplace. However, perfectionist could be deadly in the workplace, especially in government jobs that value long-term security and stability in employment.

Who's A Perfectionist?

According to a stress research firm, Essi Systems, Inc., San Francisco, Esther Orioli, chief executive, reported in news interviews in the mid-nineties "perfectionists score lower on the compassion scale." In mid-nineties news interviews with the late Clayton Lafferty, he described the traits of perfectionists. The traits of perfectionist supervisors also include the following:

1. Feeling that doing the best job you could is not enough to please your own supervisor.
2. Feeling that you should instead of you could.
3. Feeling that you must control and be on guard against what could happen in the future.
4. After doing a good job, you feel you could have done better, or you feel slightly sad, hostile, or sorry that you worked so hard and did such a bad job, after all that trying. 5. Everyone tells you that you drive yourself and your employees too hard and you're not satisfied with yours and everyone else's work.
6. You feel guilty at the thought of playing or relaxing instead of working.
7. Weekends, you're sick with migraine, headaches, or hypertension-related problems from working too hard. Or weekends you're working and feeling sick while working without enough breaks to meditate or

"waste time" playing or socializing, or a feeling that socializing and making small talk wastes your time. You think about work when you try to relax.

8. You dominate conversations and finish other people's sentences, or talk fast to get it all in before time interrupts you.

9. You feel angry, hostile, or slightly impatient standing in lines, waiting, getting inferior service, or even if anything is out of order or line, even a little bit.

10. Nobody meets your standards of doing a good job, correctness, perfection, or just doing anything at home or work "the right way."

## Does Anyone, Including You, Measure Up To Your Standards?

Take the case of (Mr. Anonymous), for example, a typical perfectionist, by his own definition, on the job for 25 years. "All I wanted to do was to make complex things simpler for my computer industry employees," the former supervisor admitted. "I was always afraid of downsizing, afraid my job was hanging by a thread because our jobs depend upon seniority."

He admits he's a true perfectionist. "My compulsion was to do more and be better. I drove my employees nuts by holding off decisions, waiting for more information to come in. I feared quick decision making, feared losing money if I didn't hold off for endless details to come in. I was always waiting, afraid to make a decision, fearing it wouldn't be perfect."

Mr. Anonymous was never satisfied with his own efforts or with the efforts of others. "I was too locked into my own need to be exactly right," he said. I didn't even look up to notice the distress it caused my employees."

Regarding still another personality indicator, (Mr. Anonymous) explained, "I even took the TDI, a type of personality classifier based on the Myers-Briggs Type Indicator, which showed I had a very low score on compassion and a very high score on worrying.

"I scored high on being methodical. About compassion, I strived to be far more rational than compassionate. It's true that I didn't take the time to think about how others were feeling, only whether they saw my job details were performed perfectly correct. When I got out of the military I took military accuracy and perfection to my new job."

Mr. Anonymous admits he couldn't take a step back or show empathy. "I could never forgive myself for not being perfect, and I drove others who worked under me harder until I thought I could make them perform perfectly, a trait that I could never find in myself."

Perfectionists are hard on everyone around them, but hardest on themselves. Frequently perfectionists contribute to their employees' divorces by the hard-driving manner they use to maintain total control over employees in all aspects of their work lives.

Often, the supervisors also go through divorces due to their need to control everything in their lives over the long-term.

Perfectionists are among the brightest people in the world, but their curiosity and high intelligence drives them to search for better ways of doing their work or making decisions. Non-rational people are perceived as wanting to be deceived in exchange for comfort. When perfectionists under stress can't find the patience to wait for a better way of doing their job or running their home life, they want very much to get rid of any obstacles in their way by letting employees go or divorcing a spouse. Most of all, perfectionists need to learn patience and stepping back calmly from the problem or task.

Many are "hot reactors," meaning they react emotionally with raised blood pressure and pulse to the hundreds of stressors each day that come with their jobs. Most often, they react hotly to the unpredictability of people. Contrast this physiology reaction to those spouse abusers whose pulses slow and blood pressure goes down as they beat their partner.

Those abusers have under stimulated nervous systems that seek the excitement of spouse or partner abuse in order to normalize their pulse rates and blood pressure, stimulate their nervous systems, and awaken their senses. These types are different from perfectionists whose pulses and pressure rise when angry at their spouse and have over stimulated nervous systems on the edge of volcanically erupting in anger.

Almost all perfectionist supervisors will never see their perfectionism as a problem to be solved, not even if it's pointed out to them. It takes much more, like a disease or health problem hitting them from their hard-driving work style and lifestyle.

"Vigilance took over my lifestyle," Mr. Anonymous said, "I had to be on guard all the time, and it raised by blood pressure permanently. My motto always was 'be prepared.' I was always looking for a threat to my job or my company. My life was based on looking for fine details that would eventually create problems. I loved to find problems and solve them, especially people problems in supervision."

Recently, it was found that people who show photographs or portraits with one eye pulled inwards that reflects the light in an inwardly manner when seen from a portrait and one withered side of the face may have a variety of abnormalities of the autonomic nervous system. A short article appeared in *Egypt Revealed* magazine in May 2001, noting reference to a medical journal that reported physicians were looking at painted portraits of Egyptian mummies in order to check out findings about the way one of the portrait's eyes appear to be pulled inward and the tendency of one side of the face to be withered (on the portrait).

Medical findings are showing that the tendency in living people of having the eye and one side of the face appear that way is related to certain abnormalities of the autonomic nervous system. It's worth checking out if you or your partner fit the description.

This has nothing to do with spouse abuse, but if you have certain abnormalities of your autonomic nervous system, you surely don't want to get into a relationship where you have to walk on eggshells to keep your spouse from losing his or her temper, or where more stress is put upon your already sensitive nervous system. In fact, you would be more likely to be the partner who requires more calm and serenity in a marriage and to steer clear of people who harbor a pool of anger or who might have the tendency to blame you first and take responsibility or think clearly later.

*   *   *

# Chapter Five

## Is The Need To Control Driving You?

This type-A behavior is based on perfectionism and the need to control anyone under one's supervision. "I constantly pushed myself to higher levels of achievement by pushing everyone under my supervision to the same goals," Mr. Anonymous said. "I'm a questor, a champion of high quality. In fact I championed quality so much until there was high turnover among my employees."

Low morale is the trademark of the perfectionist supervisor. "All I saw was that I set high standards," Mr. Anonymous explained. The demanding, perfectionist supervisor or manager creates a problem in all the employees because standards are so high, the average working person cannot reach them.

The perfectionist demands that employees under supervision meet personal requirements that only one tenth of one percent of employees in any capacity will ever achieve. And even if the high standards are met, as soon as that's accomplished, the perfectionist boss will raise standards higher, as if playing the limbo bar game.

### What If You Work For A Perfectionist Supervisor?

Internet-related and multimedia company employees working under a perfectionist supervisor or manager usually retaliate by telling a supervisor in writing to back off or else legal action will be the next step. What a perfectionist supervisor needs most is to give employees latitude, more responsibility, and more author. The supervisor must delegate and reign in on the need to control people.

Any change must be one hundred percent supportive. The goal is growth for everyone. The perfectionist's first goal should be to develop patience.

Unfortunately, if the perfectionist is going to come down with a disease, it usually hits just as the supervisor is trying to become mellow. Patience, less hostility expressed, more support for people, these are the changes necessary in a perfectionist who's in charge.

The whole view of life needs to go from vigilant to patient. Control over details and people needs to be delegated to others along with responsibility and authority. Someone has to take away the perfectionist's need to control, and that something usually is health problems following divorce. Stress problems can come to either the perfectionist supervisor and/or employees working for a perfectionist.

If health problems don't get them first, problems may continue until job loss or divorce-and frequently all three occur in a short space of time-together. The first sign of a perfectionist at work is his or her inability to get close to anybody.

Home-based telecommuting computer industry perfectionists are loners. At home, there is lack of intimacy with a spouse. Getting close means losing control, and the perfectionist won't give up the being on guard.

Some perfectionists are neatness controlled at home, or constantly criticize a spouse for not being neat enough, or "a good housekeeper." This leads quickly to divorce, the desire of having to have things in a certain order of arrangement. At home, concern for the spouse's feelings are unrecognized.

Attention to detail drives perfectionists and makes them tough to work with at all times. They're still at work when at home. The problem is called micro-management by researchers. Perfectionist supervisors and employees are so detail-oriented, that their entire focus is on correcting or avoiding mistakes in themselves and others. Perfectionist supervisors are hired because they offer any organization benefits such as efficiency.

Perfectionists seek out positions of authority where they can have the chance to watch quality, but who's watching the watchers? Perfectionists Are Attracted By Quality Control. Quality-control areas of Web page supervision attracts the perfectionist above all other kinds of work. In private sectors, perfectionists tend to be proofreaders and editors looking to improve the quality of other people's work. Frequently, the first symptom is headaches from trying to find flaws.

Supervisors who must manage perfectionist employees, the best way to keep perfectionism under control is to give deadline markers all along the way, not just an ending date to a project. Web and multimedia supervisors need great patience working with perfectionist employees. The corporate animation design profession attracts the quintessence of the perfectionist personality trying to express creativity without detectable flaws.

The perfectionist employee needs a specific job description to follow. No ambiguity. Tell them what must be done and what must be avoided to do the work.

## When You Need More Responsibility and Authority

If you're an employee with a perfectionist supervisor, you need more responsibility and authority so you won't be sandwiched between two perfectionist supervisors with no power of your own to make decisions. If you feel tormented, prepare questions in advance so it is absolutely clear what is expected of you. Put your job details in writing and have them approved by the perfectionist so there is no excuse for leaving out important points. The perfectionist supervisor wants to clarify things for you before you start. Problems arise when such a supervisor doesn't have enough patience to explain everything due to time urgency demands.

Perfectionism is hard to change because it's based on the need to control, but attitudes can be modified with training in how to set reasonable goals. The perfectionist supervisor sets a goal called 'more,' but 'more' isn't a goal at all. It's an open-ended space, much like Mr. Anonymous's goal of "waiting endlessly for more information to come in before deciding with difficulty."

Waiting for more means being afraid to make the wrong decision because all the facts may not be in yet. Another mistake is for the perfectionist supervisor to make getting better" a goal. That's not a goal either. The perfectionist keeps telling himself/herself that something should be done better or more often rather than saying it could be done differently. By substituting 'could' for 'should', there is less pressure and control to meet a certain unrealistically high standard of competence that just is not attainable.

Perfectionist supervisors keep raising that bar just beyond their reach, then fret and assert more control when their reach exceeds their grasp. Patience lessens the self-demands. What helps most to change behavior is to constantly take up hobbies and tasks that the perfectionist is no good in, to experience that you don't have to be good at something to engage in that activity.

"I took organ lessons, knowing I was no good at playing music," Mr. Anonymous said. "I gave myself permission to fail at a few hobbies, to fall on my face. What resulted was that I soon gave my employees permission to make human errors. I let them fail without trying to control the way they worked.

What opened my eyes was finding my therapist, like a third of all therapists, was as perfectionist as I. After that experience, I took up illustration, knowing I have no talent. Is that putting myself down again or merely being realistic?"

When you tell perfectionists they are loners, they will deny it. Extroverts with many acquaintances will perceive themselves as having many friends and being very outgoing. However, ask their friends how many deep and meaningful relationships they sustained over long periods of time, and you'll find a history of unhappy marriages, domestic violence or psychological abuse and neglect, superficial friendships, and the like.

Even in a crowd and among friends, they are internally and deeply loners, however superficially surrounded by people with whom they work or live. It's the perfectionist extrovert most likely to deny being a loner, and the perfectionist introvert who relishes in the thought of enjoying being a recluse because the danger of being criticized or appearing flawed to those in authority or power is lessened.

Workplace perfectionism in the computer industry loner is harmful to your health and to the health of your employees and family. Why spend time trying to measure up, to please the authority figure inside yourself as if 'it' was a controlling parent and you were still a child (searching for a better way to make decisions)?

The perfectionist is in this state of 'wiredness' because of fear of authority figures, possibly as a result of having a stern, dominating parent who constantly criticized minor flaws in early childhood. To compensate, the perfectionist is internally driven to improve upon everything and to correct hard. Improvement means as much to the perfectionist and the perfectionist perceives that it means to the individual he or she is driving.

In short, the perfectionist is all about knowing more than others, having better skills, because the perfectionist's skill level is that person's main source of security, not the job. Like the hacker, the perfectionist wants to point out everybody else's weak points.

Perfectionists are interested in practical, marketable, useful, or technical knowledge currently in demand and worth some type of security-money or family cohesiveness and control. Perfectionism comes from an intellectual desire to figure out how people or gadgets work and the desire to showoff just how much the perfectionist knows and how important that knowledge is and is valued by society. Do you know when to stop and say "I did my best?"

Are you driven by finding flaws in everybody else's work or relationship? Whereas the hacker turns outward, the perfectionist, being similar in makeup, turns inward to drive the self and anyone else supervised without knowing when to stop, think, and say, "I did my best ."

# Chapter Six

## *Open Doors To Intimacy*

For what did you settle? Do you frequently say, "If I were looking for a relationship, I'd be satisfied with a guy who would settle for putting the toilet seat down, if only he were slow to anger, and I knew him long enough to see how he'd react toward me and others under stress. I'd be happy if both of us would act from our stronger not our weaker feelings, out of thinking as opposed to acting on impulse without pausing to consider the consequences…and out of a need to keep serenity in our lives." What did you settle for?

Let's take a look at a few of the popular personality indicators and classifiers to see how they view people with different preferences. How many ways does the Enneagram (compared to other character and preference classifiers) predict that a man can love a woman? Falling in love again? Stop right there. Let's discuss how much in control you feel, and how much you feel on automatic pilot. How much would you risk for the perfect soul mate?

Pick your mate by personality preferences-such as type, temperament, behavior, and style. Personality preference matching type mates is a fascinating way to open doors with people. If you were shown 37 ways to pick your mate, how many ways would you explore? How would you like to know the partner who'd be the perfect mate-your soul mate? Together, you'd make a type matched couple.

If you're tired of being lonely and ready to meet your special partner, try type mating.

If you knew you could match your personality type to the character of someone with similar preferences, style, and temperament, how far would you go for the perfect match? If you could see patterns in people, in nature, in everything, how would you match those patterns, like in a jigsaw puzzle, to find two people enough alike to call each other soul mate? Does repackaging your personality for a marital or personal comparison-shopping mate search seem unreal or humiliating? Would you like to learn how to position yourself first in the eyes of your mate or future long-term companion?

Do you wonder why everyone you form a relationship with is afraid to commit to you? Do you want to bond with one other person for many years without being miserable most of the time? If you could see maps of your mind, locations in the brain, the neurology of personality preference, would you be interested in choosing your perfect match? Would you like to begin a personal search for a Mr. or Ms. Right Personality?

Are you seeking someone with similar enough preferences to yours, having like interests in the home, in hobbies, and in the workplace? What if you were alerted to the warning signals of possible future dating, gender, or domestic violence in your relationship-before you commit?

## How Do You Know When You've Found Mr. Or Ms. Right Personality Match?

Do you want to beat the odds in love? When you decide to pick a mate, listen to what your partner cares about. How do your partner's values fit in with your own? You know you've found your soul mate when your significant other brings out the best in you and you bring out the best in your soul mate.

Do you reflect a sensitivity to your soul mate and does your soul mate reflect a sensitivity to you? Are you being treated fairly? Do you know you are appreciated?

Does your soul mate have a positive, centered, and balanced impact on all your actions and decisions? You know you've found the right mate when there is no uneasy feeling being around your partner.

Most of all, does your soul mate encourage everything that really matters to you?

If finding the right mate could produce some type of healing from within, how much would you risk to find the best possible person (and people) with whom it would be easiest to live and love? (If you have to say I love him or her, but I don't like him or her, that person is not your soul mate.)

## Falling In Love, The Emotion, Versus Maturing-In-Love As An Action-Oriented Behavior

Would you rather "fall" in love or rise in love? Would you prefer to grow in love? Would you prefer to grow wiser together as a mutually supportive couple? It has been said by mental health professionals that love is a behavior, not a feeling. Your soul mate is the person with whom you choose to grow wiser together.

It's the person you're with for the final curtain and the renewal after. How do you find that perfect match of personality preferences?

## Thirty Seven Ways To Pick Your Traditional 1900 Soul Mate Versus Futuristic 21$^{st}$ Century Soul Bait: Are There Rules And Laws In Tradition Or New Paradigms In Relationships?

There are many more ways to love your soul mate than is imaginable. In order to make finding and loving your soul mate more concrete and realistic, there are more than 37 personality questionnaires, classifiers, indicators, and preference measures available ranging from the general to the neurological.

There are measures of locations and positions in the right or left hemisphere of your brain, categorizing the preferences of people as limbic or cerebral, left dominant, or right dominant based on the research of neurologists and scientists such as Giambattista Vico.

There are studies of cognitive neuroscience predicting personality type. That's the study of the different left brain hemisphere-right brain hemisphere locations and positions that help determine how we make choices.

Slightly to the right, you'll find the sensing function. Sensors are people who prefer the practical to the imaginary. Scientists have located areas of the brain slightly to the left, where you'll find the seat of intuition. Futurists (using intuition) who see patterns, possibilities, and alternatives in everything use the left hemisphere of the brain more when using their intuition to take in information.

Pragmatic realists (using sensing) who prefer to focus on the details and specifics of the moment, use the right hemisphere of the brain more frequently. Sensing or intuition are means by which people take in information.

You either use one more naturally or the other, and usually prefer a mate who processes information the same way you do. It makes it easier to communicate (and understand each other).

Where the personality traits are located in the brain upsets the notion that imagination is seated in the right hemisphere of the brain with imagery-and that sensing facts in a linear order is always located in the left hemisphere of the brain.

Studies have found that the sensors are a little more right-brained and intuitives are a little more left-brained so to speak. Your personality preferences determine how you pull your soul mate into the whirlwind of your activity-or why your mate needs so much space and time away from you to feel balanced and centered.

## What Your Personality Says

Take the Myers-Briggs Type Indicator at your local continuing education school's counseling office or career center, or your local community college counseling center to find out the four letters of your personality type. And take the Keirsey test as in Dr. David Keirsey's best-selling book *Please Understand Me*, to find out your temperament. There are four temperaments: NF, SP, NT, and SJ. And these four temperaments combine to make up the sixteen personality types of the Myers-Briggs Type Indicator (MBTI™ ), one of the world's most popular personality classifiers. It also has been translated into several languages.

If you're in college, go to your career counselor and ask for the MBTI™. Write down your four letters of your personality type. If you need to find another way of taking this personality indicator, get in touch with Consulting Psychologist's Press in Palo Alto, CA, and ask them to refer you to someone in your area who can let you take the MBTI ™. Once you know your four letters you can look up research in the Journal of Personality Research or Bulletins to find out what studies are going on with the various types.

You also can join Association for Psychological Type (APT) or the Center for the Applications of Type (CAPT) if you have at least an undergraduate degree. If you're a member of APT, you can attend local chapter meetings for type enthusiasts and professionals in your area. Read books about type and temperament that use one of the world's most popular personality indicators. Online, look at the newsletters and Web sites on personality type and temperament. There are other personality classifiers based on personality styles. So do as much comparative research on who you are before you begin looking at what you'd like in a soul mate, a partner, a mind mate or play mate, or in Mr. or Ms. Right.

Your type determines how you'll handle crisis situations in your marriage. It lets you know how resourceful and ingenious you'll be in getting things done around the house. Your type helps you know how you come across to your mate and how your mate with a different type perceives you as similar or different.

Some people may read differences in personality as being honest and straightforward when that has no relationship to personality type. People are intuitive (abstract) and sensing (concrete) in various degrees. Also they are introverted or extroverted in degrees. People have different time schedules and may wait longer or less for new information to come in, or may want to make quick decisions to come to conclusions faster, depending upon their personality difference. Some people express themselves volcanically and others oceanically. Whether you keep your emotions to yourself or express them loudly depends upon your personality preferences.

A sensing mate wants you to tell it like it is. Your intuitive partner may be adaptable, but not want to take risks. Therefore, your mate may exaggerate or hold back the truth to escape reality. This may cause you to get impatient with the abstract way your mate lectures on and on about theories or wants to talk about the relationship when you want to talk about the budget that won't make the ends meet.

Your mate may be impulsive and unpredictable when you need stability, dependability and commitment to feel secure. Your mate may create a crisis to have something exciting to do. So you feel the fear of abandonment and clamp down on the controls. Your mate feels manipulated by your tight reign, rules, and need for obedience. Your mate may not want to take a stand or become indecisive the more you try to control.

## Beware Of Trying To Change Your Mate

By picking a mate using personality preferences, you tend to be aware of your need to rebuild your mate in the image of your own personality type. You know what you're picking.

Although the different scores on a variety of personality questionnaires make for different degrees of any one type, all individuals of every type are unique and different. There are enough similarities to speak of types, temperaments, or styles of personality.

One introverted intuitive feeling perceiving (INFP) or Extroverted sensing thinking judging (ESTJ) type can be totally different than another INFP or ESTJ. In addition, any one type can use the traits of another type to solve a problem requiring that type function. We naturally prefer to use sensing or intuition, thinking or feeling, introversion or extroversion, or judging or perceiving more frequently because it feels more comfortable. There are too many people playing the "*My Fair Lady*" or "*House of Wax*" game of trying to change the personalities of a partner. It's much easier to find someone similar to yourself in interests, hobbies, philosophy of life, staying at home or socializing, ideas about family size, pets, foods, faiths, or occupations.

## Your Mate's Preferences And Attitudes Influence Your Health

With the right mate, you communicate more easily. Your heart rate and blood pressure go down, not up, when your mate walks into the room unexpectedly. (When you pet a household animal, your heart rate and pressure go down.)

We can use our personality preferences to pick compatible mates who extend our life spans by making us feel good about ourselves. When we feel good at home, our immune systems tone up.

In contrast, the wrong mate lifts himself/herself up by putting you down. With the wrong mate, your heart rate rises above 95 beats a minute during an argument and you're blood pressure stays up longer.

## The Right Mate Leads To Commitment

With the right mate, one whose preferences are compatible with our preferences, you focus on the commitment. You can see through the pain to bring up the positive and the optimistic-the joy the two of you have together-even when going through extreme loss and grief-instead of the blame, contempt, ridicule, criticism, and disrespect.

Unfortunately, more than half the adult population of the United States has gone through a divorce. What methods are we not using to pick our mates?

The answer is that in all the ways we have of meeting people-the personal ad, professional association, convention social, video interview, the dating games, parties, religious organizations, travel, same-age-group clubs, ethnic groups, senior centers, apartment complex parties, introductions, friends, marriage brokers, singles networking, occupations, hobbies and hobby groups, sports, dances, courses, personal growth seminars, television talk shows, singles bars, and recreational interests, few have tried matching people by their personality preferences, types, styles, temperaments, and neurocognitive brain area similarities-until now.

## Personality Classification In Other Cultures

In India, Ayurvedic medicine emphasis three personality types not so much by locations in areas of the brain, but by body types: the thin, nervous Vatta type who suffers from anxiety under stress; the well-built, bigger-boned, muscular, square-jawed athletic type with its hostile heart, explosive temper, pot belly when sedentary, and propensity toward heart disease; and the round, apple-shaped, shorter-lived, obese, relaxed and jolly type who takes life easier, lazier, and moves slowly without anxiety, never making waves.

The various body types in the medical literature of other cultures around the world, especially in Indian and Chinese medicine, are classified as prone to different illnesses. In the West, types are classified according to personality preferences, temperaments, and styles.

In Japan, different personality types are classified by their blood groups. Mate hunting Japanese style may call for a man whose blood type is of the A or O group. The man with B type blood is sometimes shunned by employers or by the parents of prospective mates, based solely on the personality characteristics attributed to men who belong to the B type blood group.

Say, you are on a blood type O "hunter's" diet. This diet emphasizes high protein and low carbohydrates. You marry someone with blood type A.

Your blood type A partner is a "settled farmer type" on a largely vegetarian diet. You worry because you've read that blood type A might clot sooner than blood type O if on blood type O's high animal protein and diet.

You don't want your blood type A partner to eat blood type O's high animal protein diet rich in eggs, fish, lean meats, but high in fat. You've also read that if anyone is a fast metabolizer, a fast burner of carbohydrates, they need some protein in the morning to keep insulin from pouring out when they eat a high glycemic index breakfast of foods that turn to sugar too quickly such as oat meal, rice, or cold cereal. Or maybe your partner with AB type blood has hyperinsulinism, where insulin pours out whenever high carbohydrate foods are eaten, and shows up as a big belly. What do you do now? Would you be able to cook compatible meals for both types to stay healthy if you're living together? Let them cook their own meals. (Check out the book **Eat Right for Your Type**, by Dr. D'Adamo.)

## The Biology Of Type Matching

In Western medicine, medical students study the life expectancy and chances of getting ulcers or stomach cancer of men and women who belong to the various A, O, B, and AB blood groups, predicting everything from chances of getting a thrombosis to life expectancy. Science is discovering new ways to observe why people behave as they do when they look for a mate.

The most important type differences are not personality type differences, but the blood type incompatibility of babies born of Rh Negative women and Rh Positive men. If Rh positive men were only to mate with Rh positive women, there wouldn't be any Rh negative babies born with blood incompatibility medical problems from antibodies. Matching marriage partners by Rh negative or Rh positive blood types never has been part of a standard courtship.

Few people inquire about incompatible blood type or inheritable genetic disorders before they match and mate to breed. This book is about matching soul mates not by a postive or negative allele or the right gene, but by similar preferences for lifestyle.

During courtship, people compare personality types, tastes, backgrounds, ages, ethnicities, religions, and similar interests. Matchmakers bring people together based on astrological signs and similar educational or vocational backgrounds. People join clubs of single book lovers and art lovers.

We marry and we hire our peers who are most like ourselves in age and background. Or we marry the self we wish we could be if only we were smarter, luckier, or richer. We marry the person who makes us feel good about ourselves. How many people look at a partner's brain waves on an EEG or other biofeedback machine printout, or ask to see a polygraph test before they commit to a long-term relationship? Who asks whether one's soul mate chooses a marriage partner who makes decisions with the cerebral or limbic mode of the brain, the right or left hemisphere, or whether he or she uses more metaphor or irony in everyday conversation?

Does anyone wonder whether a marriage partner's thinking style is all about contraction, expansion, solidification, or dissolution? Maybe you should if contraction is related to being a cold, withdrawn penny-pinching miser, a Mr. Takeaway man, contracting everything from minced words to thrifty eating.

Would you prefer a mate whose thinking style is all about expansion, when expansion is related to being a generous romantic? The mate whose thinking style is about expansion talks and writes in metaphor. He or she believes marriage is a stage to present your life and everything else is a stage, even your toilet must show off it's contents on a platform (as in Erica Jong's, Fear of Flying).

What about irony, a mate whose thinking style is born to the cerebral mode, a thinking partner whose forever logical focus is on dissolution? He or she believes in what's ironic about marriage, that change only makes everything even more the same. (See Brain, Symbol, and Experience, by Charles D. Laughlin, Jr., Shambala, Boston, 1990 and The New Science of Giambattista Vico, Cornell University Press, 1991.)

Brain research reports that people have different personality types or preferences that are with us from birth to death. Our personality traits evolve as type is developed during a lifetime. If our type is biological, genetic, neurocognitive, and only slightly modified by environmental influences from birth, why bother to try to change our mate's type any more than we would try to force a left-handed child to use his right hand because we do?

Instead, before marriage, we could search for the type that's right for us. What we'll find is that within one type, there is a variety of people, all unique, and all very different from one another. All people of one type have varying scores on type and various other personality classifiers.

We use what we can to match and mix until we find our soul mates. People too often are thought of as being interchangeable as computer peripherals. We are diverse and unique, but all of us fall into a finite number of personality types, styles, temperaments, and preferences.

This book is on how to pick your mate. It is written in clear, easy-to-understand and followup language, for average readers trying to decide which person to marry.

It's about how to begin searching for your soul mate, Mr. or Ms. Right Personality. This book will clarify your preferences, values about marriage or relationships, and interests-so that you can do what you really want to do and still feel your values, health, interests, and life goals are supported and enhanced by another with similar goals, according to that mate's personality preferences.

Whichever way you choose to pick your mate, that unique person is going to have different preferences from you. You may be similar in outlook, but your internal clocks (biorhythms) aren't synchronized. The closer you can get in agreement and the more you can accept your mate's right to disagree without suffering a loss of self, the better selection of a mate you will have made.

\* \* \*

# Chapter Seven

## *What Measures Your Personality?*

Your personality preferences are measured by indicators such as the Myers-Briggs Type Indicator (MBTI) (Registered Trademark), which lists sixteen universal types, the Enneagram, which lists nine types, psychoanalyst, C.G. Jung's eight types, all for relatively mentally normal people.

Personality preferences also have been classified by the four temperaments of Dr. David Keirsey. There are the thirteen normal personality styles found in the excellent and highly recommended book, *Personality Self Portrait*, (Why You Think, Work, Love, and Act the way You Do) John M. Oldham, M.D. and Lois B. Morris.

Dr. Oldham's 13 personality styles for normal people have been revised for the average person. They are based on personality inventories for abnormal people, such as questionnaires based on the DSM-III-R (Diagnostic and Statistical Manual of Mental Disorders), the Minnesota Multiphasic Personality Inventory (MMPI), and many more measures of preferences.

In addition by reading Dr. Oldham's *Personality Self Portrait*, you'll find available personality inventories, including the corporate and marital issues personality assessment questionnaires, the measures of creativity, intuition, and original thinking, and measures of anger, harmony, and similar tastes. It's a "must" along with books on the MBTI ™ personality indicator and the Keirsey Temperament Sorter such as *Please Understand Me*. You want to read these books to get a well-rounded view of the search for self-identity. Only when you know yourself can you start looking for a mate or partner with qualities not so different form your own that the future will bring much irritation and dissonance.

What if you took all the questionnaires, and found you came out similar on all them? What if your endless search for self-identity reached the same conclusions with each preference questionnaire you answered? Would you then be able to put yourself in a box, even though you hate stereotyping people in boxes and putting labels on them, and leave the roof of the box open so that your soul mate could join you?

## Be What You Are And Look For Yourself In Your Soul Mate

Whether you're single and looking for your significant other, a future spouse, a Mr. or Ms. Right Personality, it's equally important to be what you are than to do what you are. When you marry or live with another person, above all you want to get along in harmony on a long-term basis.

You want to work out conflict smoothly. You want to avoid violence, intimidation, humiliation, resentment, contempt and constant criticism. You want to avoid matching up with a person who puts you down to lift himself/herself up.

## Match Your Type To The Character Of Your Mate

How do you pick the person with whom you're most likely to get along? The answer lies, partially, in matching your personality type to the character of your soul mate. You're encouraged to take the MBTI ™, and then go on to take the other questionnaires and indicators of preference type, temperament, style, and character available. Discover the perfect mate through the strategies of personality preferences.

## Type match People For Marriage

If you want to be your own marriage broker, learn how to type match people, and watch out for your type mate. First, to understand what personality preferences and type really is, let's begin with the Myers-Briggs Type Indicator. Each of the sixteen MBTI ™ personality types are the following:
ISTJ, ISFJ, INFJ, INTJ, ISTIP, ISFP, INFP, INTP, ESTP, ESFP, ENFP, ENTP, ESTJ, ESFJ, ENJF, ENTJ.

The definition of the letters are listed below:

E is extrovert
N is intuitive
F is feeler
J is judger
S is sensor
T is thinking
I is introvert
P is perceiver

There are sixteen personality type combinations, according to psychologist C.G. Jung. The MBTI ™ was developed by Katherine Briggs and Isabel Myers in the sixties based on Jung's research in the twenties.

If you're good at seeing "what is" and you meet your soul mate who likes looking at "what could be," your mate and you could have some pretty rough times pulling each other into different realities. You grasp the details. Your mate wants to see only the big picture. You begin to fight over money or over who tells who what to do and how they can do it or how to spend money.

One of you is practical, the other is imaginative. One of you has to keep their feet on the ground while the other tries to expand. One sells reality, the other sells fantasy as escape entertainment. One is abstract and puts you to sleep with long talks about theory and "what ifs." The other is specific and bores a mate with dull and dry facts. One watches the ball game on television while the other wants to watch a documentary on ancient Egyptian archaeology or UFO research.

One describes facts first, the other makes a general point and leaves out all the facts. Can the two ever understand each other? Or are the soul mates like two ships passing in the night, each feeling empty, neglected, and desperately alone with nothing to say that would ever interest the mate?

## Position Yourself First In Your Soul Mate's Mind

We are different because we have different preferences that come naturally to us. It feels difficult to walk a mile in our mate's shoes, to think and feel like our mate does, to like the same things. When it comes to finding our soul mate, our significant other with whom we expect to spend the best years of our lives, it's better to position yourself first in your soul mate's mind. It's better to pick someone with the same preferences as ourselves-or just a tiny bit different-enough of a difference to see our blind spots and point them out without criticism, contempt, or lack of respect.

## How to Marry A Mate for His/Her Genes

If personality is mainly genetic, do we marry a man or woman for his or her genes? From symmetrical face to concordant brain chemicals, we marry at the molecular genetic level of fitness for the healthiest progeny. We want mates that are alert, bright, able to tolerate stress, and healthy. We tend to move toward people of our own personality preferences as in "personalities of a feather flock together." When we marry, however, we fly toward the excitement generated by the opposite personality type.

Then as the excitement wears off and the difference in personality types becomes real, as the courtship mask comes off, we may realize but not be so surprised that "what our mate likes is not our first choice."

So why marry someone who will eventually abuse you? Learn to see the warning signals before you commit to a relationship. Find your soul mate, the best possible person for you.

If your self-esteem is low, you'll tend to want someone of a different personality type because we secretly hate our own preferences. We judge them to be weak or deficient in some way. That's called low self-esteem, low self worth, and a distorted self-image.

\* \* \*

# Chapter Eight

## *Don't Marry At The Level Of Yesteryear's Self-Esteem*

We all marry at the level of our self-esteem of the moment. It takes time to raise self-esteem. While we are growing, we can still look at personality preference matching. Align your mate with his own expectations.

There's a strong tendency for self-concept to determine destiny- especially who we choose to marry or live with as our lifelong companion. When our internal thinking doesn't match our external experience of our soul mate, we try to manipulate our mate (and everything else external) until our mate aligns with our expectations.

If our mate is not a compatible type, living with the person no longer feels natural, comfortable, and easy. Do you want to achieve consistency at the cost of self-esteem? No! You only want to pick your soul mate.

When it comes to picking a mate, do you really think you're on your own? Or do you believe you bring all the baggage of your own family life and childhood with you, including your personality preferences?

## You Bring Old Baggage To A New Marriage

You bring the lifetime experience of your personality preferences which did or did not match smoothly with your parents, siblings, close relatives, and best friends. You use your personality type, temperament, style, and preferences to create self-fulfilling prophecies about exactly who your Mr. or Ms. Right Personality should be.

Self-fulfilling prophecies can be constructive. We use personality preferences such as type, style, and temperament to show that the future conforms to the past. People with good self-esteem define their soul mate as a person who has the same likes and dislikes as themselves.

## Different Preferences Make, Break, Or Contrast The Moods Of A Marriage

Those with the same likes as ourselves use the same methods of taking in information, of making choices and decisions, and of choosing to stay open minded or seek quick closure. Either we choose subjectively by our inner values, such as our likes and dislikes. Or we choose objectively by logic and making a list of pros and cons and weighing the yes against the no answers.

Some like to plan, others want to be surprised. Some can change horses in midstream and be spontaneous, others get greatly disturbed by having their plans changed by events beyond their control.

Some talk off the top of their heads without stopping to think through how what they say will affect the feelings of their partner. Others pause to think before speaking, wonder how accurate and precise their words are and what long-lasting impact it will have on their image in the eyes of their mate.

Some mates use intimidation to control their lover. Others tape notes of appreciation on the refrigerator door. Some manipulate through hugs. Others withdraw when their mate wants affection, because demanding attention makes them angry.

## Do You Confuse Being Loveable With Being Competent?

When you search for your mate, you may confuse being loveable and being competent. Would you rather be right or be loved? Your personality preferences give you that feeling that it is best for you to be either loved or right. Your personality type, when matched with the same or similar types where there is no conflict in the "wrong places" can help you arrange your life to align with the belief that you are loveable. If you are competing with your mate, does your mate feel he or she has suffered a loss each time you win in any competition with your mate in any situation or subject?

For example, say you have introverted intuition. You are a man whose personality type is INFJ (introverted, intuitive, feeling, judger). You marry a woman who is an INFP (introverted, intuitive, feeling, perceiver).

You think that because everything else is alike in your personality type: (you're both introverts, both intuitive (imaginative), both feeling types, making decisions based on personal likes and dislikes and values of worth), you should hit it off.

Wait a minute! The INFP woman has extraverted intuition. That's going to rub you the wrong way because you have introverted intuition. You're being driven crazy by what you call your mate's selfishness.

Your introverted intuition sees patterns coming from inside yourself about how people behave, and you write them down. You're full of insight, like a psychic, oracle, and overseer.

Your INFP mate with her extraverted intuition is a resource person, looking to take in global impressions of everything out there that see can bring together as a catalyst. She uses her extraverted intuition to write romance novels. Also she's spontaneous and open-ended.

Her open mind is constantly waiting for more information before seeking closure. She has a high tolerance for ambiguity. She will wait and wait and finally decide at the last moment, thriving on that rush of adrenaline at the end as she works faster in an environment of time urgency.

As a "J" or judger, you seek quick closure. You're more comfortable making a decision. As a "P" (perceiver), she's more comfortable waiting until the last possible minute before making a decision, often missing the opportunity.

Her lack of punctuality drives you up the wall. She is disorganized, and her desk is a mess-a sure sign of high creativity. She doesn't want to hold down a "real" job because it stifles her need for creative expression and going from project to project.

You need the security of a paycheck, a regular job, and a chance to work with people in a human resources type company. You're not as spontaneous, but you're regular. You publish newsletters or work as a reporter or an English or psychology teacher, or manage the personnel department.

Secretly, you wish you could afford to be a poet. She writes the fiction in the family or illustrates the magazines or is the poet and cares little for holding down a regular job.

She likes working at home, but not doing housework. You express feelings. She expresses imagination.

How do you end up? Calling another woman, an ENTP, to tell a perfect stranger how selfish your wife is-instead of asking your wife why she feels the need not to answer your correspondence.

Your INFP wife would say, because your "J" is a controlling trait, and the free-spirit INFP woman does not want to be controlled-or told what to do by her husband. The INFP woman has different interests, a different career, and wants you to answer your own correspondence.

She may secretly hate secretarial work, especially answering her husband's letters. She wants to work on her own projects using any of the forms of creative expression by understanding what makes people act as they do. So you stop using your "J" to control her "P". Or else, she'll get passive aggressive on you. She knows you talk behind her back to strangers and call her selfish.

INFP is not selfish. With dominant introverted feeling (feeling turned inside herself instead of outgoing to others), she has a tendency to nurture herself first, not please you. Although the NF temperament is described as "desiring to please in order to preserve harmony." If there's a choice between your project and hers, she'll tell you to do your own homework.

She'd never expect you to answer her correspondence. Asking her to do your work steps on her inner personal values, morals, and ethics. It's not ethical for an INFP to be asked to do your work for you.

The INFP feels horribly exploited without pay when asked to do something you could do for yourself. She'd probably shout, "I'm not your slave, secretary, maid, or housewife. I'm a career woman, even if I don't earn a dime and do my projects for love. So don't treat me like your father treated your martyred mother."

Ask an ISFJ mate, and he or she will do it for you to be of service, if not overburdened at work at that time. The INFP would rather express her values in print or illustration than mend your socks or answer your correspondence if you are physically capable of doing your own work.

The INFJ man needs to control his wife. The INFP woman feels man and woman are equal but different, and as equals everybody does his own homework. She wouldn't think of asking you to wash her laundry either or do her creative work. This artistic type of woman will never take orders from her mate. She'd rather live in the world of art and imagination.

What you do have in common is the need to inspire and motivate others through the written word. So work together on separate projects where each of you can truly "do it by yourself" and then join each other to appreciate each other's freedom, optimism, and joy. Those two NFs need to put on an audio tape of laughter for twenty minutes, then take a personal growth experience or attend an uplifting convention together.

Therefore, no matter how close in type you are, the difference of one aspect of personality type could make, shake, or break the relationship. If you marry your exact type, the only bad that could come of it is that both of you have the same blind spots and could make the same mistakes about the same details, future plan, decision, or big picture.

## Should You Marry Your Own Type?

With the same type, you have less chance of contempt, criticism, lack of respect, and intimidation in the relationship. Your soul mate is the one person for whom you will never lose respect. However, respect depends upon how your mate behaves.

How should your mate behave? What interests, hobbies, work, health practices, and vacations should your mate have? Do you prefer romance, travel, and excitement in the last decade of your lives together or solitude with each of you working in your separate rooms on your own personal computers trying to create immortality through a creative project?

Will it be desperately and dependently lonely vacationing together as a couple in your later years? Will familiarity breed contempt? Or will you still walk down the beach holding hands at eighty as you did at fifty or at thirty?

## Secrets Of A Type Matcher

Will you become another divorce statistic by having chosen a mate with preferences too different from your own to be reconcilable? In California, nearly 58% of marriages end in divorce, leaving children to suffer the life-long separation anxiety. Can personality preference matching help to bring people together with compatible preferences?

Could you and your significant other be busy developing your type together instead of looking for differences about which to bicker? Type is all about the way you do what you do.

Type tells you how you face the universe. If there are finite ways of facing the world, you have the chance to choose someone who faces the world like you do. Then as a couple both of you may work together to develop your type and your mate's to each individual's maximum potential of type development.

If your mate's type is different than your own, you can encourage each other to develop individual type diversity to the best it can be. The world is full of diversity. Type diversity is only one kind of variation on a natural theme. Your type doesn't limit you. You don't have to pick a mate of the same type in order to get along or stay married.

Be aware of which types find it easier to agree with which other types. Your goal is to match your type to the character of your mate's or date's. Different types may disagree with one another on a variety of important issues.

Are you constantly using your senses to experience your environment? How would you get along with a mate who constantly uses his or her intuition or imagination to escape from reality in order to feel healthy? How would this natural preference affect your socio-economic level? Your surroundings? Your interests, livelihood, and recreation?

You share some strengths and use other strengths privately. Either you show your feelings to your mate or you keep them to yourself. Either you tell your mate what to do or you give information and let your mate make up his or her mind independently.

You either show your thoughts to your mate or use your thinking only in your inner world. You share the way you take in information with your mate, or you keep your imagination inside. You are better expressing yourself orally and spontaneously, or with a plan in front of you, or only in writing when you're by yourself.

\*        \*        \*

# Chapter Nine

## *Love Is An Act of Behavior, Not An Emotion*

Love is the behavior you use to take action and express what is best for the other person, not yourself. Narcissism is closer to the emotion of wanting to possess a person to fill up a vacuum in yourself. Love is the action you take to make life better for the person you love. Love is not a feeling or emotion.

It is the act of improving the quality of life of another human being by connection and having rapport with you or people you provide. Love is not possession, jealousy, ownership, or protection of territory. Love is not limited to sex because love exists when sex leaves the body and where sex never existed, as in love between family members or between a person and a pet. Love is bonding as between an infant and a parent.

Love can be a behavior we have toward a person, a place, an object, or a spiritual connection. Love is not the act of marrying out of fear of loneliness or having children so they can support your long- term care insurance in old age. Love can inspire hormones in the brain to heal or make changes in behavior, but it is more than chemicals at the molecular level of neurons and synapses, electricity and amino acids. It is the act of making the quality of life for another being better by being near or cherishing another person or animal.

When you search for your soul mate, you're really looking for someone most like yourself and most like your ideal impression of what a playful mother figure would be like if he or she was most compatible with you.

You'd look at a father figure differently than a mother figure, and if your own parents didn't measure up, you want a mind mate, play mate, soul mate who will have faith in you and show support in helping you be all that you can be when you need help and fostering your independence when you want to be independent or interdependent.

It's important to act from your strongest thoughts and feelings after pausing to consider the consequences on your harmony, serenity, and happiness in the longest run. Don't act on your weakest or impulsive feelings. Consider acting from your strongest intuition plus what your judgment and experience tell you about the facts. Then verify everything to make sure your conclusion is based on a reality check. In the end, you'll have toughed it out and will be proud of yourself.

By now you're wondering what is love? It's a behavior. It's what we do. It's the action we take. It's not a feeling we have. It has been said by mental health professionals that love is a behavior whereby the significant other (your soul mate) promotes enough serenity in the environment so that it's possible to experience the following thoughts or feelings about yourself in your lover's presence. Frequently radio talk show hosts expound on the fact that love is a behavior, not a feeling. What is meant by a behavior? It's an act performed—something we do to show love in the concrete rather than in the abstract form.

Love is tangible as a washing machine. What the word "love" means in the abstract is different and is closer to fear of loss through competition and protection of territory. So don't marry out of fear of abandonment. Marry in order to show your mate a behavior. Love in the intangible sense means each time the one closest to you wins a competition, it's your loss because you didn't win. Love in the concrete sense is shown to your mate or family by how you behavior and measured through your actions. These actions promote the quality of life for those you love as well as for yourself. Mr. or Ms. Right becomes "right" for you when you can promote the quality of life for others as well as yourself at the same time. If you don't have to give up being you to love your mate and be loved back equally, that's the measure of love.

**You Know You're In Love When:**
1. Your soul mate makes you feel important.
2. Your soul mate makes you feel good about yourself.
3. Your soul mate supports your maximum educational and career growth, even if it means separating for years while you get your training or work location settled.
4. Your soul mate sets you free so you can return of your own choice and never tries to control or manipulate you out of fear of abandonment.
5. Your soul mate never shows resentment, contempt, or holds onto grudges used to blame you or rub your nose
in the mess.
6. Your soul mate always respects you so that you find
dignity in your mate's presence.
7. Your soul mate never humiliates or criticizes you to put you down so he/she can be uplifted, or intimidates you instead of taking responsibility for his/her role in the problem.
8. Your soul mate never blames you without looking first at his own responsibility and role in the situation.
9. Your soul mate always focuses on the problem and asks how
both of you could do better to solve it in the present.
10. Your soul mate never brings up the past wrong decisions either of you made to put you down.
11. Your soul mate walks a mile in your shoes and feels empathy for your different preferences.
12. Your soul mate would never hit you, no matter how angry
you feel or how great your partner's sense of loss is.

13. Your soul mate would never hit you if you disagreed with his viewpoints.

14. Your soul mate, even under stress, would be slow to anger.

15. Your soul mate would never try to control you or make you over in your mate's image or change your
preferences to be more like your mate's.

16. Your soul mate would never take your money.

17. Your soul mate tells you love is a behavior, not a feeling, and acts like he loves you, not only says the word. Your mate's body language is receptive.

18. Your soul mate places your children's happiness first.

19. Your soul mate cares for you when you're sick or frail.

20. Your soul mate can be trusted to be truthful.

21. Your soul mate makes you feel centered and balanced
when you two are together alone or in public.

22. Your soul mate does everything to extend your lifespan,
and empower you, including being in rapport.

23. Your soul mate emotionally supports your lifetime dream or passion, be it a career, destination, diploma, work of art, achievement, or hobby.

24. Your soul mate commits to you, inspires and motivates you.

25. Your soul mate's presence affects your mood, body and emotions in measurable and positive ways for at least two years after you start going together.

## Choosing Your Mate

You want to steer clear of someone with intermittent explosive disorder. This type of tightly-wound person is so obsessive about keeping everything in order that when stress upsets the way the "bowling pins are lined up" so to speak, the usually charming, quiet, private person will explode like a volcano and become extremely violent and abusive.

Before you make a final decision about your personality preferences or your partner's, understand that there's a huge difference in the way mates get along with one person has introverted feeling that he or she keep in and seeks serenity, and the other person expresses emotions outwardly in a volcanic blast.

Intermittent explosive disorder is not related to having extroverted feeling or expressing emotions outwardly. Normal people who express feelings freely don't have volcanic tempers that explode in your face. What they have is feelings directed at you, facial expressions that show emotions, and warmth or anger that they are not afraid of expressing in public or in your face.

Intermittent explosive disorder is not a normal personality type at all. Don't confuse it in any way with extroverted feeling. The basically normal person may have introverted feeling or extroverted feeling and still be either an introvert or extrovert in that person's preference to be around people more or less.

Extroverts are energized by people engaged in activities. The introvert is drained by having to "perform" and be judged before many people or lots of activity. Basically, an extrovert has more of an under aroused nervous system that needs the stimulation and excitement of meeting many people or working with people, going to parties or other activities, and talking to people. The introvert's nervous system is over aroused.

Sometimes an introvert will be so over aroused as far as sensitivity to information coming in from people, sounds, lighting effects, or other stimulation of the senses, the individual needs solitude to relax and recharge. It's the introvert who is more likely to come out of a movie shaking from over stimulation of the senses, feeling drained by the intrusion and invasion of noise and disturbing scenes. It's the extrovert who prefers to be stimulated by special effects and noise, people, and action. Extroverts don't like to be alone most of the time. Introverts look at solitude as a way to unwind from being overwhelmed by stimulation of the senses from people, noise, sound, action, or stress. Introverts may prefer jobs that allow them to work alone, such as teaching online, writing, illustration of books and magazine articles, counseling on a one-to-one basis, or working in libraries or with computers. Extroverts enjoy jobs that allow them to be with people, such as teaching and training face to face, public speaking, traveling, or driving.

When you know enough about your own personality preferences, you can match the character of your soul mate to your own personality preferences. Pick your mate by what feels comfortable. Will you marry out of fear, loss, abandonment, or love, connection, and similar interests? Stand back and make an objective, logical analysis of the warning signals and signs of possible future domestic abuse before you commit to a relationship. Make a decision based on the pros weighed against the cons before you make a decision based on values. Ask yourself whether marriage to your partner is worth risking your health for or shortening or lengthening your life span?

Pick your mate by the impact that the individual makes on you. Are you still choosing your mate by how secure the person's real estate or stock holdings and career appear? Pick your mate by how dependent you intend to be on that person's financial support. Choose your mate according to your preferences matched to your partner's character. When you have done that, your concern will be whether your mate has also chosen you on similar bases.

\*      \*      \*

# Chapter Ten

## The Marrying Table

Personality Preference Matching Choose Your Mate From Among Any Of These Groups Of Two. Match Your Personality Type To The Character Of The Type mate Next To Yours. Or Pick Your Soul Mate From Among Your Own Type

### Marrying Group One: These Two Possible Soul Mates Are Compatible
### Dominant Extroverted Sensing

ESTP sensing: extroverted and dominant
thinking: introverted and auxiliary
feeling: extroverted and third
intuition: introverted and inferior

ESFP sensing: extroverted and dominant
feeling: introverted and auxiliary
thinking: extroverted and third
intuition: introverted and inferior

### Marrying Group Two: These Two Possible Soul Mates Are Compatible

### Dominant Introverted Sensing

ISTJ sensing: introverted and dominant
thinking: extroverted and auxiliary

feeling: introverted and third
intuition: extroverted and inferior (fourth)

ISFJ sensing: introverted and dominant
feeling: extroverted and auxiliary
thinking: introverted and third
intuition: extroverted and inferior (fourth)

## Marrying Group Three: These Two Possible Soul Mates Are Compatible

## Dominant Extroverted Intuition

ENTP intuition: extroverted and dominant
thinking: introverted and auxiliary
feeling: extroverted and third
sensing: introverted and inferior (fourth)

ENFP intuition: extroverted and dominant
feeling: introverted and auxiliary
thinking: extroverted and third
sensing: introverted and inferior (fourth)

## Marrying Group Four: These Two Possible Soul Mates Are Compatible

## Dominant Introverted Intuition

INTJ intuition: introverted and dominant
thinking: extroverted and auxiliary

feeling: introverted and third
sensing: extroverted and inferior (fourth)

INFJ intuition: introverted and dominant
feeling: extroverted and auxiliary
thinking: introverted and third
sensing: extroverted and inferior (fourth)

## Marrying Group Five: These Two Possible Soul Mates Are Compatible

### Dominant Extroverted Thinking

ESTJ thinking : extroverted and dominant
sensing: introverted and auxiliary
intuition: extroverted and third
feeling: introverted and inferior (fourth)

ENTJ thinking: extroverted and dominant
intuition: introverted and auxiliary
sensing: extroverted and third
feeling: introverted and inferior (fourth)

## Marrying Group Six: These Two Possible Soul Mates Are Compatible

### Dominant Introverted Thinking

ISTP thinking: introverted and dominant
sensing: extroverted and auxiliary
intuition: introverted and third

feeling: extroverted and inferior (fourth)

INTP thinking: introverted and dominant
intuition: extroverted and auxiliary
sensing: introverted and third
feeling: extroverted and inferior (fourth)

## Marrying Group Seven: These Two Possible Soul Mates Are Compatible

### Dominant Extroverted Feeling

ESFJ feeling: extroverted and dominant
sensing: introverted and auxiliary
intuition: extroverted and third
thinking: introverted and inferior (fourth)

ENFJ feeling: extroverted and dominant
intuition: introverted and auxiliary
sensing: extroverted and third
thinking: introverted and inferior (fourth)

## Marrying Group Eight: These Two Possible Soul Mates Are Compatible

### Dominant Introverted Feeling

ISFP feeling: introverted and dominant
sensing: extroverted and auxiliary
intuition introverted and third
thinking: extraverted and inferior (fourth)

> INFP feeling: introverted and dominant
> intuition: extraverted and auxiliary
> sensing: introverted and third
> thinking: extraverted and inferior (fourth)

## Who Gets on Whose Nerves?

- All types have to work together, and all types have to get along well with one another in any kind of relationship. Yet, what if you really had a choice with whom to live for the rest of your life? Would you choose someone the same type as yourself or someone close, say with introverted feeling if you have introverted feeling or extroverted feeling if you have extroverted feeling? Or the same for thinking, perceiving, judging, sensing, or intuition? In all of these groups, the partner with extroverted sensing or intuition may get on the nerves of the mate with introverted sensing or intuition. This means that on a trip, the introverted sensor or intuitive could tire more easily of the many sights, travel, or new events long before the extroverted sensor or intuitive.

Intuitives may only want to notice, observe and enjoy an unlimited whirlwind of people, ideas, surroundings, colors, sounds, smells, textures, restaurants, tours, nightclubs, art, and tastes. The partner with the extroverted thinking or extroverted feeling may get on the nerves of the partner with introverted thinking or introverted feeling.

The mate with extroverted intuition will sometimes irritate the mate with the introverted intuition (third or less developed function). However, if these two soul mates allow for their different energy levels while taking in information or having fun, they can have a wonderful marriage.

To find your soul mate, pick your partner from among those who have the same dominant function in personality preference. That means dominant feelers together, dominant intuitives together, dominant thinkers together, and dominant sensors together.

If one mate has sensing as a second function and the other mate has intuition as a second function as in the marriage of INFP to ISFJ, the partner with extroverted intuition as a second function (not dominant intuition as in the ENFP or ENTP, may find happiness married to the partner with introverted sensing-as with an isfj, but only if the introverted sensing partner has feeling as a second function.

The INFP married to the ISTJ will feel bullied and controlled by the STJ combination of the controlling partner. The INFP partner will feel patrolled, controlled, and squeezed or crushed under the ISTJ partner, unless it's a marriage of convenience for one partner's financial support of the other partner's artistic pursuits.

Good combinations include ISFJ and ESFJ married to INFP and ENFP or ENFJ. Sensing married to intuition will communicate about different subjects and have different interests, hobbies, and career interests, even in the same company. For example ESFJ may sell concrete objects like appliances or medical records software, whereas ENFJ may sell counseling, psychology services, advertising and public relations services, communication services, or other intangibles...and still work for the same firm.

The sensing and the intuitive types with the same dominant functions of personality could very well have a good marriage because at the same stage of life they are getting in touch with their third functions (after age 25) and fourth or inferior functions (after age 50).

## Chapter Eleven

## *How Do You Find The Right Type For You?*

You can go to the Internet and find available mates. Pick the interest group of your choice according to your faith. There are Buddhist Singles at http://buddhist.forsingles.com/, Moslem Singles at http://moslem.forsingles.com/, Jewish singles at http://jewish-single.12match.com/find-personals.htm, Hindu Singles at http://hindu.forsingles.com/, and Christian Singles at ChristianCafe.com at http://www.christiancafe.com/index.php3?id=1000 and other Christian singles groups such as those at Lutherans Online at http://www.aal.org/LutheransOnline/mboards.html or Catholic Singles.Com at http://www.catholicsingles.com/. The Internet is teeming with online singles groups by religion, ethnic group, age group, and more. Pick your category or interest and look online. You can still use friends, people at work, classes, hobbies, social centers, tours, and dating services.

Where do you go to find your soul mate? Where would you go if in the best possible of all environments, you had the chance to go somewhere to find Mr. or Ms. Right Personality Type? I'm a marriage broker's daughter, descended from at least nine generations of old world matchmakers.

Each special interest group may have a singles group attached to it in many types of categories. For example, singles writers associations often advertise in the personals and classified ad sections of writers magazines. As an example, international associations such as the European Union of Science Journalists' Associations at

<http://www.esf.org/eusja/Resources.htm> have a special focus on not only journalists in Europe, but science journalists' associations. So if you're going to Europe for a vacation and wish to attend any functions where science journalists would be present, you can narrow your focus.

What would you say once you met a science journalist in Europe? You might ask how you can be introduced to single scientists or journalists or just meet more people to interview yourself while you're overseas. If journalists or scientists aren't of interest to you, find an association you like and see how you can meet single people who make contact with others in that association or other groups you want to explore or join, or if you're not able to join, interview for information or to write about them, promote them, or research their work, favorite recipes, friends, or favorite vacation places. You choose the subject matter that you can use to make life a little gentler and kinder for all the people you meet.

Some people become wedding planners to meet eligible singles invited to weddings. At almost every wedding there are single friends and relatives of the couple, classmates, and neighbors or other people of the same ethnic or religious group and sometimes of the same interest or work group. Meeting singles is best when you're doing something you like to do, such as a hobby or study in a field of interest.

I took a course in wedding planning a few years ago to learn more about a variety of ethnic weddings and to re-create ancient wedding themes. As an investigative reporter/anthropology researcher writing about wedding and life transition planning, ancient historical event planning, costume dramas as life transitions events, I wanted to find out a lot more about matchmaking customs around the world.

Each year, I'd write a novel that had to be researched for authentic wedding customs from food to fanfare, dress, adornment, and related customs. By the early seventies, before Internet pen pals, I sought out snail-mail pen pals, but the real people behind them were different from the letters then. It hasn't changed much on the Internet now more than thirty years later. Back then, in 1972, I was 32 years old and wanted to find my own soul mate. In those days some people snickered at the daydreams of a woman in her thirties finding the same quality of soul mate as she could at twenty-one. In your dreams was the common response.

As a book author, creative expression half-scientist-half artist type, an introverted intuitive feeling perceiver (INFP), #4 on the Enneagram, (with a #5 wing) and unable to go to most parties after dark because I'm a non-driver by choice, too cautious a monastic questor to singles bar hop, I placed a husband-wanted ad in selected trade magazines that held my life-long scientific interest, and newspapers going to people of similar interests.

(I bought the most appropriate mailing lists and studied the demography from mailing list brokers) to see where Mr. Right would most likely go for further training, intellectual stimulation, entertainment, work, fun, travel, recreation, vacation, continuing education, job hunting, recreational reading, career networking, counseling, and self-improvement.

The mailing lists told me Mr. Right Personality's demography: his religion, ethnic origins, languages spoken, hobbies, income, occupation, educational level, even the publications to which he subscribed as well as the subject interest of the books he read. By contacting a variety of type organizations, attending their conventions, training seminars, and meetings and subscribing to their publications, I could narrow down my search to his personality type.

## What Type Are You Going To Choose?

I chose someone introverted like myself. I wanted him to be a sensor, someone using practical skills to earn a living in a routine job, someone who didn't like too many changes. I wanted what in Ayurvedic medicine is called a "Vatta" body type-thin and small boned, like myself-someone who'd never protest when I set up my art studio, my writing den, or my scientific research databases and library space in certain areas of psycho-anthropology or when I'd write a book of poems about taking on Wall Street in a chastity belt.

I preferred him to be a judger, someone who would need closure and make decisions quickly, someone who was going to be using his extroverted feeling to loyally be of service. Someone responsible. Steady in his work. In short, I needed to find an ISFJ-an introverted sensing feeling judger, whose dominant function (way of taking in information) was through introverted sensing. Six out of every one hundred persons in the United States are ISFJs.

As an INFP, my ideal INTP type was a bit too scarce to find quickly. I had to choose between ISFJ and INTP. As far as interests in common, the INTP would have been an exact match of interests. My hobby was molecular genetics and archaeology—ancient DNA. So INTP would have been perfect. I couldn't find INTPs who were single and marriage minded in the time between my early and middle thirties. Before the bags under my eyes drooped any further, I chose the available ISFJs who make up about 38 percent of the world's population, and focused on an ISFJ with the values I held in high esteem. These values were: nonsmoker, spiritual, held a job for a long period of time in a large firm, kind to animals, and enjoyed staying at home to going to bars drinking on weekends. My values were similar, but my interests were different: writing novels, fine art, paleo-anthropology, journalism, reading about personality type research, history and geography of human migration genetics, ancient history, reading mystery novels, the stock market, and orange cats.

The next choice was ISFJ with a steady job. My own INFP type was found in about one to one and a quarter percentage of the same population. There are about two and a half million INFPs in the United States. My job now was to narrow that ISFJ search down to males of my own age decade who were single, employed, stable, non-smoking, non-drinking, nonviolent, slow-to-anger, and marriage-minded.

A dominant introverted sensing man with feeling, an orderly judger, would have a lot in common with me, a computer nerd lady who spends all day alone at home at her computer writing practical, useful, how-to, career development, popular anthropology, and self-help books about how people feel in their relationships, about marriage and finding soul mates, and about how we take in information and deal with technology as learning and entertainment.

As a futurist, I needed to visit everyplace sensors (who are rooted firmly in the present) go. As an intuitive, any place I went had few sensing judgers or ISFJ men. In my creative writing circles, I kept running into ENFP and INFP women with the same interests in writing both novels and self-growth books or popular anthropology books, just like I write.

## Narrowing Down Your List To A Few Compatible Types

Sensing Judgers represent about thirty-eight percent of the U.S. population. Now I had to narrow that down to not only sensing judgers, but ISFJs, introverted sensing feeling judgers, leaving out the extroverted sensing judgers and the introverted and extroverted thinking sensing judgers.

The differences between extroverted and introverted attitudes are profound when it comes to living together. How do introverts search for a soul mate?

As an idealist INFP, I needed to motivate and inspire a responsible, ISFJ man in order to coax him out of hiding behind his need to serve those underdogs and bosses who required his dutiful services.

If he felt I didn't need his "Guy Friday" helpful services any longer, he would become disinterested. So I emphasized the word, "responsible." I invited telephone company communications technicians (most likely to be ISFJ males) to a fundraiser I put on for their unions. That was the only way I could get anyone to come to my $32^{nd}$ birthday party.

Where do ISFJs hang out? I placed ads in all the newspapers and magazines they would most like read....such as Popular Science,

Handyman, PC computing, and a variety of news and TV review magazines as well as the Sunday Newspaper classified section. I even inquired about placing ads in the various union's newspapers (trade journals) in the industries most likely to employ single ISFJ males age 30-39.

I wanted a man with a steady job, and back in 1974 when I was husband hunting, the utility companies hired a man for life, and he was usually following in his grandfather's footsteps. I found the publications of the Unions for a variety of utility unions and wrote the them, advertising when it was permitted, in the classified ads.

At the time I was 32 years old. The man I met turned out to be the ISFJ I wanted, age 35, and we celebrated our $28^{th}$ wedding anniversary last week. He's been with a particular utility company for more than 30 years. So I targeted my search on someone who expected to stay with the same company until retirement. In those days before the huge wave of downsizing, it still was possible.

## Where Do You Begin Your Search?

To find Mr. or Ms. Right Personality type, I started my search for Mr. Right Personality at the broad base of an inverted pyramid of using my extraverted intuition to seek and find all of the possible publications, organizations, hobby groups, unions, recreational places, classes, vacations, interest areas, and work areas a man of the "right type" would be in a given season.

It's important to know that I did not want an ISTJ-an introverted sensing thinking judger. I wanted a feeling man who loved to nurture his job as a nurse would a sick patient, because I'm an "introverted feeling" woman who deals with the outside world through extroverted intuition. In the case of an ISTJ man married to an ENFP woman, there was the danger that his introverted sensing pitted against her dominant extraverted intuition could provoke his frustration to wife beating.

I had to do a lot more research. As an avid reader of anthropology, I had to make sure I wasn't creating type stereotypes in my head or putting people in boxes without scientific validation of my findings. What I wanted was an emotional, feeling type man to complement my cool-headed introverted feeling expressed mostly in my writing. The ISFJ was most likely not to crush my personal values of serenity and harmony in the home. I wanted a man with a sense of history.

It didn't matter what he looked like, as long as he was clean, a similar body type to mine, and most of all, compatible. My idea of a soul mate was strictly a mind-mate, someone who would not argue with me about philosophy, faith, or theory. An INTP would want a mind mate to argue various points of philosophy or abstract theory. The ISFJ emphasized not wanting to argue a point on an abstract idea. He was more interested as a concrete-detail person rather than an abstract idea person to focus on working in the garden or fixing the house. That left me time to write my novels or research my nonfiction books and visit museums and galleries. For an INFP, there is much joy in aesthetics.

I wanted someone who would be down-to-earth and make common sense. What I found twenty eight years after marriage, is that he was there one winter, at age 55, to mop up my stomach flu vomit from the floor at three o'clock in the morning and tell me not to worry about cleaning it up myself. That's an ISFJ male whose "primary desire," according to Dr. Keirsey's book, **Please Understand Me**, is to "be of service and to minister to individual needs."

\*        \*        \*

# Chapter Twelve

## *How Do You Advertise For A Soul Mate?*

The best place to advertise in print for a soul mate is to select a publication of special interest that closely matches your most important life-long interest. Use both print and electronic media. If you are interested in a special division of science or business, advertise in a scientific journal or business trade journal. Choose wisely to focus on what you want. For example, an advertisement in a medical journal will be read by scientists or physicians. A law journal is read by attorneys. If you place your ad in a magazine read by anyone, such as a general sports or general consumer magazine, you have ruled out the selected audience you want. If I wanted to meet and marry an architect, I'd place an advertisement in the personals of architectural magazines most often read by architects. Do your demographic research as to who reads the publication.

If the magazine is read by more women than men, be aware of that fact. If you want a travel agent, place an advertisement in professional trade magazines in the personals classification, of trade journals read by travel agents, or dentists, or doctors. Be aware of who your intended audience really is. If you want a literary person, choose the literary magazines, and focus on those who have a larger male audience.

People who don't read the singles magazines but do read publications in their occupations, will see your ad where you place it. My favorite publications would be the trade journals read by stockbrokers and fund managers if I were looking for a mate who liked to talk stocks and hopefully own them. Go to the public library and go through most of the trade journals and professional magazines, medical journals, and other special publications. If you like to discuss personality type, there are many journals on type. On the Internet, take a look at NF Journal Press at http://members.aol.com/NFJournal/. Here you see a magazine devoted to publishing articles that are about the NF temperament, that includes the personality type INFP, INFJ, ENFP, and ENFJ. Regardless of what publication you meet people through, find out whether you can place a personal advertisement, or advertise what you are interested in most and ask for pen pals. There are magazines for many kinds of personality categories as well as special interests online of anything from studies of medieval Khazaria to writing children's books. So if you don't see print publications in the field you enjoy most, look for publications online, or start your own Web site or discussion group.

If you're over 60 and want to get married, your chances of finding someone on a tour or cruise with other singles over 60 is great, but don't overlook the publications for people in your age demographic with specialized interests in a specific subject. You're looking for something in common, something beyond going out dancing, traveling on archaeology tours, or taking ethnic cooking classes. Keep adding to your list of interesting subjects you have enjoyed for years.

All kinds of personalities will read these specialty magazines. Target your intended audience. Place the ad in the personals section and advertise for what you really want. You may get your wish. Your advertisement might end up anywhere as it's passed along from friend to friend and co-worker to peer. I was groping against statistics, because there are so many more thinking men (about 66 percent) in the United States than feeling men (about 33 percent). And feeling women (about 66 percent) outnumber thinking women (about 33 percent) in the United States.

To find your soul mate, you can visit various ethnic and religious groups, do volunteer work, and study the buying habits of people from direct mailing lists. You can look at a person's demographics and consumer interests, even put personal advertisements in the special interest magazines to which he most likely would subscribe. I found my mate through my husband-wanted ad in a daily newspaper personals column in the end.

If you wanted to find Mr. Right Personality Type, you could subscribe to and advertise in any of the type-related newsletters, bulletins, journals, and related publications. For example, if you're of NF (intuitive feeling) temperament, like me, you could now subscribe to the NF Journal. (The addresses of all type-related publications and associations mentioned are listed in the appendix at the back of this book.)

The Association for Psychological Type (APT) is open to any person interested in the Myers-Briggs Type Indicator (MBTI). They publish a quarterly journal and a bulletin. People who publish other publications on type frequently advertise in their bulletin.

You could join APT and attend conventions, regional meetings, four day training seminars, parties, and read the occasional ads for pen pal groups, newsletters for singles on type, etc. In fact, I do attend some of their conventions. At the 1993 Newport Beach convention, I met some very interesting people. If you sell something, you can rent a vendor's table and really work the room networking, for research, business, or social purposes.

As an NF, the reader most likely to pick up this book first, note that APT currently has more than 3,200 members nationwide, of which about 50 percent are NFs. Intuitive Feelers make up only about 12 percent of the entire U.S. population. My own INFP type, (NF temperament), which emphasizes the search for self-identity as a perpetual life pursuit, represents only one percent to one and a quarter percent of the United States population.

If I wanted an INFP mate, more like myself with the same blind spots as myself, I could have focused on places where INFPs usually hang out to please themselves-at one of the national associations for career counselors, in psychology courses and art galleries, or teaching courses in novel writing, type research, cartooning, magazine illustration, or in pastoral counseling in the ministry.

Instead, I focused on finding gal pals, or best girl friends to remain in rapport with for a lifetime (if possible) who were INFPs, like myself, and I knew exactly where they were most likely to be found. However, in searching for a husband, I wanted an anchor in a homestead.

I wanted a soul mate as interested in computers at work as I was interested in the future of computers in telecommuting from the home. As a home-based homebody who loved freeing as well as channeling imagination as a career, I wanted a husband loyally devoted to his routine work in some large, traditional, hierarchical company.

There was no way I could get along with someone of a dissonant type in the same occupation. Mr. Right Personality had to be more than interested in computers, not a "thinking type" programmer, designer, engineer, analyst, or repair technician.

He had to be an emotional, sensitive, feeling man servicing and nurturing the needs of others along the future information superhighway, a gentle, quiet man who obeyed rules.

Most working people have so little time to spend on searching for a soul mate, they need shortcuts-strategies that work best with lasting positive results. What do you want in a soul mate, and where are you likely to find that person today?

\* \* \*

# Chapter Thirteen

## *Log On The Information Superhighway*

If your soul mate hunt takes place in the decade of home computers, you can use your home computer and modem to tap into the Internet network of publications, bulletin boards, e-mail lists, and discussion groups. According to news reports, back in the mid-nineties, conservative radio personality, Rush Limbaugh, married a woman he met through a computer electronic bulletin board while networking nationally on CompuServe.

Soul mate hunting through electronic mailing lists has become as popular as sending electronic resumes around the globe when job hunting. On your home computer, you can receive electronic mail on whatever subject is assigned to the particular mailing list. One such source is tapping the Internet mailing lists and discussion groups.

There are mailing lists for all NF types on Internet, a computer network anyone can access for a small fee. For example-INFPs, INFJs, ENFJs, and INFPs have their own Internet mailing lists. Back in the mid-nineties, the newsgroup on Internet called alt.pscyhology.personality, (that's what you typed when you log in) collected type-related articles. Today, group discussions online, chat rooms, electronic magazines, and message boards, lists of singles online, and other Internet-based communication methods, including the matchmakers offer people with similar interests or personality styles a chance to connect.

More people today are using a personal computer in the home to track down a database of potential mates. According to a 1994 survey conducted by the Times Mirror Center for the People and the Press, one in three homes has a computer. Today, many more homes are connected to the Internet, and anyone can walk into a public library and ask for time on the Internet in most cities of the USA.

Access to electronic bulletin boards, electronic mail, and information services provide people around the world or locally a chance to chat by typing on their computers at home any messages to singles bulletin boards or computer networking boards for almost any area of interest or occupation.

A proliferation of telephone and computer services has made it easier for introverted people to meet on a one-on-one basis without extroverting, without leaving their homes to push against the crowd or to compete.

The Internet, it's World Wide Web, discussion groups and mailing lists, and your personal computer, resemble the way that the military services take care of all your extroverted needs. The military issues you uniforms. You don't have to go out and look over the clothing. The Internet issues you companions, perhaps future spouses—online. You can sit in your room and cruise the Internet for people with similar interests, careers, or hobbies.

You can meet, chat, and exchange interests, preferences, attitudes, and lifestyles without ever showing how we look or how old or asymmetrical you are, unless we want to incorporate video on our multimedia CD-ROM laser disks. If you want a wife or husband, there's software available or an electronic mailing list to help us locate Mr. or Ms. Right Type. There are fax clubs for singles, where people can fax one another love letters. And the Internet offers sites where you can look over "mail-order" brides from nearly every nation. There are even Web sites where you can look at international adoptions should you want to adopt a child from another country, viewing pictures of people available as children for adoption or as adults for relationships and marriage.

- Do you want to adopt a child from Kazakhstan in Central Asia? Look at the Web site at http://www.adoptingmoms.com/kazkids.html. How about the Ukraine or China? Look at http://www.adoptingmoms.com/iap.html. Or if you're not a single parent or married couple and you don't want a child yet, but want a mate at this time, well pick the nation. Web sites such as Arab Girls International at http://arabgirls.freeyellow.com/. Or type in the key words "mail-order brides" in your search engine, such as www.google.com and the search engine will bring up a list of Web sites to click on, such as the sites with the following headings:

- RUSSIAN MAIL ORDER BRIDES, EASTERN EUROPEAN SINGLES, DATING ONLINE

- ARAB MAIL ORDER BRIDES - Arab Mail Order Brides

- Beautiful Ukrainian Women Arab Mail Order Brides

- AUSTRALIAN MAIL ORDER BRIDES, JAPANESE PERSONALS, EUROPEAN SINGLES

- COLOMBIAN MAIL ORDER BRIDES

- All Best Phillipino Mail Order Brides And European Marriages Are Here!

- Young Russian Mail Order Brides Swedish Bride

- Russian Girls Gallery Korean Mail Order Brides

- South American Mail Order Brides Australia Pen pals

- CANADA PERSONAL ADS, MAIL ORDER BRIDES SINGLE WOMEN, RUSSAINMAILORDERBRIDES

There may be more women searching for men, but as far as Web sites for persons in other nations wanting to marry someone in America, the sites for available women far outnumber the men. So the point is the Internet may be used for searching for someone from a particular country, or if you aren't looking for a mate but a son or daughter, the Internet has children available for adoption with some of their photos, from a variety of countries, particularly Asia and Eastern Europe.

The reason why less foreign men are looking for American wives blatantly online is that there is a double standard. American women usually want a man who has a job and will contribute to the household, supporting them when they take time off at least for childbirth. Many women want to have the option to take time off from work or work at home part time when children are small.

If a man is in another country with no job in the United States, can't speak English well, or doesn't have the type of job skills where he can easily find steady work, he may not look as attractive to a women in the United States looking for personality first, but success and confidence in a man about his skills, career, and where he's going.

There's also a fear on the part of women that the man will marry her only to get a card to work in the United States or in any large urban area of any major city in Europe, Canada, Latin America, or the Pacific Rim, and leave her as soon as he's a permanent resident or a naturalized citizen.

When a young bride from a remote area of anyplace marries a man with a steady job, business, or skilled career who is earning income, it's not necessary for the bride to speak English well at first. It's not important that she find work immediately as long as he will marry and support her. So the double standard still exists.

Note how many ads there are for Asian, Ukrainian, and Russian brides available compared to almost no grooms available for the same areas, mainly Eastern Europe, Central Asia, and the Pacific Rim. It all has to do with where the groom will work, his English skills, and career ambitions. For a bride, the common attitude is that all she has to do is marry.

## Narrowing Your Search By Occupation-And Personality Preference

What would you be looking for, if you wanted to narrow down your soul mate search by type to a certain personality style within a certain profession? You now have the option to become a temporary marriage broker-librarian and specialize in database searching or, for computer-avoiders, soul mate location strategies.

Now you're mate searching in the competitive intelligence industry. For example, if you specifically want a lawyer of your own personality type, and you happen to be an INTJ (introverted intuitive thinking judger) personality type, you could log onto a library's database and come up with the entry that in the July 1993 issue of the ABA Journal (American Bar Association), there appeared an article by Larry Richard about attorneys' personality types.

The article would inform me that Richard surveyed approximately 3,000 practicing lawyers. His findings revealed that 57 percent of the lawyers he surveyed reported themselves as introverts. Fifty seven percent of the same lawyers also reported themselves as intuitives. Seventy-eight percent of these same attorneys said they were thinkers. And sixty-three percent of these lawyers reported themselves as being judgers. (INTJ).

Now all you have to do was to find a common way to reach those lawyers who reported themselves in the research as INTJs, and you would find a way to track an audience of INTJ lawyers. If you were also an INTJ lawyer, would you have found a way to advertise for a soul mate by reaching the same publications they read, or somehow logging onto the same electronic networking systems they use, or getting into their E-mail? Or maybe even going as far as obtaining the researcher's mailing list, if it wasn't confidential.

It's possible to find out which lawyers were single and the age group you want to consider. You could write a letter to the ABA Journal or take out an advertisement stating you were searching for an INTJ lawyer as a soul mate. In this age of classifying people by all types of demographics, you certainly can advertise for a specific personality type and a particular career interest as well as age, income level, faith, ethnicity, or any other category, even by the rising sign on one's astrological horoscope.

Today, you can use your own computer or your social networking skills. Or advertise in the print or electronic media, or connect with personality type-watching organizations and associations. The next generation will have interactive multimedia sources from your telephone, television, VCR, computer, and other imagination machines interwoven to make electronic mate (and job) recruiting easier online.

Most frequently used by busy professional people seeking serious relationships are the computer bulletin boards, E-mail, and computer networking information services. Some are even arranged according to personality type, available on information services through Internet. For further information on the Internet, call toll-free 1-800-695-4005.

## Personal Ads Take A New Twist

If you're not into computers, there are always the publications, trade journals, newsletters, social and professional associations for personality type watchers. You can write away for catalogues of books and services from the Center for Applications of Psychological Type, http://www.capt.org/, The Association of Psychological Type, http://www.aptcentral.org/aptsite.htm, and the dozens of small presses, trainers, and publishers, who bring out videos, books, training materials, or maintain speaker's bureaus on the subject of type and relationships.

When I searched for a spouse and soul mate in April 1974, they didn't have computerized spouse hunting from your own home through your computer modem. I used the daily newspaper in my local area. Open to me also were the many trade journals, special interest magazines, and one of the best sources of all, the newsletters and journals published by professional and business associations.

If the newsletters of these national associations and their local chapters can be used to exchange information and offer classified, display or personal advertising, it's all right to put a personal advertisement there asking for what you really want. My husband-wanted advertisement emphasized what I was looking for in a relationship with another person. I stated my interests, education, and appearance: ( 5'4" 112 lbs, red hair, hazel eyes, 32 years old, graduate degree, published book author, hobbies: molecular genetics and archaeology, anthropology, writing novels, two orange cats.).

When I first began to look for a mate in 1962, I went to a computer matching service. I was in college and shy. I paid a fee and was matched with several computer dates. The first date was with a physicist in his mid-thirties who took me to dinner and played classical music on his car radio. He never called me back a second time, and I can't remember the subject of our dinner conversation.

The second date was with an accountant in his early thirties. He never called back after the first date either, but he did have the courage to tell me that at age 20, I was too young for him. I'm not sure why the computer matched me with a physicist and with an accountant. All I said was that I was able to do algebra in the third grade.

What was completely ignored was the fact that I was a university student majoring in creative writing and minoring in visual anthropology and that my hobbies included pre-history, art, and the social sciences.

I would have matched me with a professor of biological anthropology and genetics or an architect, since another of my hobbies was interior design. The computer emphasized only that I had taken to learn algebra on my own at age eight and nine.

It matched me thereafter, with men in math careers such as physicists and accountants, none of whom ever called me for a second date. The 1962 early computer matches in Manhattan were with men over age thirty. For a university student, I would have preferred being matched with someone about age 25-26, someone probably just finishing graduate school.

I really wanted to get married at ages 20-21. As a full-time student, suddenly homeless and without any money, I quickly found a job in the public library and switched to working my way through college at night. The moral of the story is to find one subject you like more than anything else and emphasize that in your search for a mate. For me, that one subject is writing books, fiction and nonfiction about what makes people do as they do with a subtitle interest in archaeology. It hasn't changed since 1962, when those room-size monstrous computers matched people for the first time—sometimes by childhood hobbies.

## Face-To-Face Networking At Type Meetings

Today, if you want face-to-face contact with a person who likes computer software as much as you do, you can find a future significant other browsing on a Saturday night in a computer store or at nine o'clock on a Saturday morning at the local IBM or MAC computer user's group, or at almost any international computer convention in Las Vegas. My favorites are the Comdex (international computer and electronics) convention each November in Las Vegas, the film festivals, and the annual American Booksellers Convention, usually in Los Angeles or Miami.

Find your mate at trade shows. Offer to sit in a booth at a convention or conference, seminar or meeting. Set up speakers to give presentations on panels at conferences. You can volunteer to professional associations to help them set up the speakers panels or the special interest groups. Help arrange internships. Volunteer to edit the professional or business association newsletter.

If you are an older woman looking for a large group of older men, join your local computer society and participate where you'll be visible, such as on the newsletter or vendor booths at meetings. There usually are more men over age 60 at computer clubs than there are at folk dancing classes. The same situation repeats at clubs for persons interested in wood turning or wood carving or model railroad.

If you're not interested in any of these subjects that older men show up in larger numbers, try the book clubs in your local community center or house of worship. If mostly women show up at the book clubs and you're a woman looking for a man, go to meetings of professional and business associations or work on political campaigns. Also visit travel clubs of persons who exchange houses in other nations for people vacationing abroad. These travel friendship clubs often have larger groups of older men. Arranging conventions, meetings, events, club sales of computer parts, or going to meetings of archaeology and anthropology clubs also interest older men. Volunteer to work on the newsletters of scientific organizations and associations.

What if you hate tekkies and computers? Where do you find your soul mate if what you like most attracts only women to women's interest circles? What if you're mainly interested in going to personal growth conferences instead of professional association conventions?

You can still find Mr. or Ms. Right Personality today by handing your business card to vendors at a trade show or exhibit in any large city or resort convention town. Attend some trade show, expo, exhibit, convention, conference, or event you like that attracts men and women or more men than women if you're looking for a man.

Visit your local convention and visitor's bureau. Ask for a list of conventions in your city or the city you'd like to visit. Go to that city's convention and visitors bureau and chamber of commerce. Ask for the convention schedule. You can attend the conventions. To get into conventions free of charge, obtain a press pass in advance and ask most professional associations whether it's all right to submit an article to their newsletter or other publication on the highlights of a particular convention or conference. You can attend the convention without charge on a press pass if you write an article by assignment or as a freelance writer for any type of publication that would interest the readers about that convention. The quickest way to get such a writing assignment is to ask to write an article for the newsletter of an association, professional or business.

Then ask some of the free newspapers, particularly the computer newspapers if you can submit a short article interviewing any of the speakers at the conference or convention or highlighting the meeting. Pick large, national conventions of particular interests such as technology, business, science and medicine, or whatever interests you. Once you're in a convention, socialize and interview people for information. Leave your business card as a freelance writer.

You can even make a part time business out of highlighting the events at a convention and writing it up into a 15-page newsletter with your personal computer. The material you write can go into a template and up on the Web, giving free publicity to the convention or conference or writing for the convention's own newsletter. Most conventions are sponsored by national associations such as professional, business, or technological associations.

Ask to write for their newsletters as well as other free publications that need someone to write articles as a volunteer. If you want a mate with a high IQ, volunteer to attend a meeting of a high IQ society and write about them for some publication. However, you get a more specialized reach when you target a particular scientific or business association to attend meetings, conventions, and highlight what happened there in a newsletter. You can create a newsletter for the duration of the meeting only and put it on the Web or have it printed.

Almost everyone's passionate subject interest, hobby, or recreational past time has a trade show, exhibit, conference or convention. Find something you're enthusiastic about and join a chapter of people with the same interest. There's a national group or convention for everything from UFO investigations to skeptics, from doll designers to marriage counselors.

## Some People Classify Personality Types By Their Hobbies

Every personality type has its own interests and wishful dreams in some special subject-quilting, woodcarving, history, writing, speaking, comics, Biblical archaeology, computers, photography, health and fitness, pen pals. Look in the Encyclopedia of Associations in your main or university library.

Find several national or international associations that interest you. It's a good way to meet people sharing interests similar to yours by attending national conventions and perhaps, volunteering to be on a panel or to register attendees.

There are telephone numbers to call and for a fee meet single strangers. People are still placing personal ads in professional, scholarly, and trade journals trying to match up with someone with similar interests in everything from the arts to genealogy, from screenwriting to UFO experimental genetic research, from children's books to interactive multimedia, or from global trade to vegetarianism.

## Other Personality Style And Preference Classifiers

More recently, people started to pick their mates by personality type. There are several different personality preference classifiers on the market. Many of them have personality assessment specialists who enjoy grouping people in similar categories. Some groups have national conventions for persons interested in meeting people of different or similar personality types.

Some individuals have started publishing newsletters on type. (See the appendix for addresses.) Others have opened singles matchmaking services using type as one of their guides. Type-related dating or singles matching services sometimes advertise in the type-related bulletins, club chapter newsletters, national newsletters, and in other publications on personality types, temperaments, preferences, or styles. Several publishing companies are devoted to books and other writings on type.

If you weren't limited to only one personality type classifier, you could attend the International Enneagram conferences. Contact the International Enneagram Association. The association's Web site is at http://www.intl-enneagram-assn.org/. The Enneagram is another popular personality classifier, more psycho-spiritual in content and original sources. The Enneagram system was first brought to the West by Gurdjieff, as a model for the flow of energy within processes.

Each number of the nine personality types in the Enneagram system refers to one of the primary strengths or weaknesses in the personality. According to the International Enneagram Association, the Enneagram symbol is a nine-pointed, star-like figure. The nine lines comprise a perfect triangle and a twisted hexagon contained within a circle. Sufis used the Enneagram system as part of their mystical training practice.

There are many alternative classifiers of personality types, temperaments, styles, or neurological brain locations, and time and fun to try them all. Which one can help you find your soul mate? Which one can stand up to rigorous research and proof over many years? How many can be scientifically validated?

Are there many good measures of personality style, type, temperament, behavior functions, and neurological brain locations and positions that tell us why we act as we do in marriage? How many out there can't be dusted off as "pop psychology" by the skeptics? Which can we successfully use to find our soul mates?

## Advertising For Your Soul Mate By Personality Style And Type

This is how I found my soul mate twenty-eight years ago. I didn't want to marry a man with exactly the same interests as myself, which would be another writer or video producer/writer. That's fine for a business relationship or platonic friend. I wanted someone with a steady job, an SJ, who would offer practical common sense and constant exposure to the reality and finer details of married and working life.

My career as a writer includes writing novels, plays, scripts, and nonfiction books on behavior and on the teaching of professional writing skills. I sell escape and entertainment as learning for those whose living rooms have become a center of both entertainment and learning, including vocational training. I write books to train other fulltime writers as well as self-help books about marriage and relationships.

My Mr. Right Personality for me had to be someone grounded in the here and now, because I'm always reaching into the clouds for ideas. My work depends on selling my imagination. The ISFJ is a conservator, a guardian of the family finances and homestead. Since change and working on new projects continually is my career, I needed a man who wished more than anything else that there would be no changes in his job, marriage, or address. I found Mr. Right Personality by advertising in print.

My April, 1974 personal advertisement read: "Futuristic hazel-eyed intellectual female book author, 5'4", 112, age 32, with a graduate degree and an interest in creativity enhancement studies seeks down-to-earth steadily employed marriage-minded mate interested in science or computer software. Hobbies: visual paleoanthropology, archaeology, genetics, ancient DNA, painting Mandalas, illustration, reading, walking."

My advertisement brought 172 letters during the several weeks I ran it in the Sunday personal classified ads of my local daily newspaper. The same ad in a variety of trade journals brought fewer letters, but from persons of backgrounds ranging from career military types to several biology professors, a gynecologist, a lawyer, and a medical instruments salesman.

The daily newspaper brought a flood of letters from blue collar workers with a year or two of college, utility workers, and others who worked at temporary menial jobs while attending school making career switches after the age of thirty-five.

I picked the ISFJ steadily-employed utility worker with two years of college who had the same hobby interests as myself. By December 21, 1974 we were wed and are currently married. Twenty-eight years later, I'm now over age 60 and in the stage of life where I want to live my dream job in these golden years of doing anything I want—from sculpture to writing mystery and suspense novels with a psychotherapist sleuth as my leading character. How INFP can you get?

## Analyzing A Soul Mate's Dominant Personality Characteristics

Today, we have our own computers and avidly use them in our own private computer dens. When you're an introvert married to another introvert, evenings of solitude are blessed when you rely on creative expression as your only fulltime occupation. Both of us use introverted sensation in very different ways.

As an introverted intuitive feeling perceiver or INFP, My dominant personality type is introverted feeling, but I used my auxiliary function or second best, extroverted intuition with introverted sensing as my third best function in my work as a creative writer. My husband, as an ISFJ, uses his dominant introverted sensing to work with computer code, taking in tremendous amounts of facts and routine data.

His auxiliary or second best is extroverted feeling which he uses to fix equipment people use every day, thereby being of service to help people. His third best function is introverted thinking, which he uses to think his work through in sequential order using facts and data for routine, unchanging software service technician work in the field of telecommunications.

There's a specific reason why I chose to advertise for this particular personality type to locate my soul mate. Introverted sensing judgers (SJ) (especially ISFJs and ISTJs) normally do not go out to participate in self-growth groups like my own intuitive feeling (NF) temperaments do.

A group is supposed to make the SJ temperament feel more nurtured. However, according to Dr. Eve Delunas in her book, ***Survival Games Personalities Play***, (Sunflower Ink, Carmel, CA, 1992), SJs won't join a group solely for personal growth nurturance because they interpret joining such groups to be self-centered, fostering self-absorption.

I was concerned that the essence of my INFP personality was the tendency toward total self-absorption because introverted feeling was my dominant personality characteristic.) So I had to watch myself and needed a down-to-earth, service-with-a-smile ISFJ to remind me how to be of better service to others through my personality's drive to motivate, inspire, teach, and empower others with enthusiasm through written communication.

INFP is a catalyst who excels in bringing people together for a worthy cause to better the world in some way. Six out of every one hundred people are ISFJs. This guardian and conservator's personality is about, according to Dr. David Keirsey, in his book, ***Please Understand***

*Me*, ministering to individual needs and being of service in traditional ways. ISFJs want to be around people who really need them. ISFJs love helping those less fortunate.

Sensing-Judgers (SJs) thrive on servility and really appreciate servility in others. ISFJs always show respect to strangers. The trick is to get them to show the same respect to their spouse. They don't mind routines, are dependable, responsible, and loyal to their supervisors at work.

This idea of self-absorption horrifies the SJ who emphasizes being humble as the ideal behavior. I wanted to reach a man who feels accountable to service the needs of others. I had to communicate to him through the correct media, to reach him in print through the publications he read which informed him of the welfare of others.

## Tracking An Audience Of Soul Mate Possibilities

In 1974, nearly 18 years before Dr. Delunas's 1992 book, I was tracking my audience of soul mate possibilities, using the direct mail advertising approach by using the personal ads in the generation before "Fatal Attraction," "Single White Female," and similar films scared the public about the risk in placing personal ads before the eyes of strangers.

I knew I needed to find an ISFJ as my soul mate, even though one ISFJ could be totally different from another of the same type. What I was seeking in the ISFJ was the idea of that personality type being the conservator.

## Seeing The Flip Side Of Your Soul Mate: His And Hers Blind Spots

The flip side of an SJ conservator is their inability to understand what they are doing to contribute to a marital conflict because they focus on complaining and whining about the significant other. They need to focus on the choices and decisions they have made in the relationship instead of blaming the partner.

All of these personality types will be explained soon, as well as all the strengths and weaknesses, and how each type acts under marital stress, but the point is, where and how can you find your soul mate? And once you've found him or her across the room some enchanted evening, how do you really know you've found your soul mate?

(If the word "soul" comes from the Greek word, "psyche," (meaning mind) you can use the word psyche-mate to describe your mind-mate, without the connotation of a spiritual aspect to the "soul" word in soul mate.

Can the term, "soul mate" be defined as someone whose character matches your personality preferences? To be a soul mate, the significant other and you should sit down and make a list. If you marry your "soul mate," then are Web ads for mail-order brides more like "soul bait?" Actually, before you can interest a soul mate in you, there must be some kind of hook or presentation that you leave as your first impression in order to allow the prospective soul mate to want to be in your company again.

That's why "soul bait" is another term for "buzz appeal." You need to put a "spin" on yourself in the eye of the beholder. Finding your soul mate is a public relations campaign. It's a production to sell you to the person you choose. You need to launch yourself in the other person's mind during your first five-second impression.

You are auditioning for marriage and so is the other person. Marriage is a stage on which you perform the hardwired acts of your personality. They call it the marriage game because the rules require fair play. Marriage is show business.

Marriage is publicity in the eye of your mate. If your mate is a private person and doesn't want outside publicity, the kind of publicity he or she does want is only between the two of you. The buzz appeal or "spin" that sells you in the eye of the beholder is the method you use to make the other person feel important and good about himself (or herself) in your presence.

No one wants to marry a partner who tells the other person what's wrong with him (or her) and how to improve. The reason why you marry, at the core level, is to find another person who makes you feel good about yourself, makes you feel important. If you wanted someone to tell you how to improve, you go to a coach, not to your mate. Marriage allows only so many critical evaluations and suggestions for improvement, efficiency, or perfectionism. It's not the role of the spouse to change the partner's personality basics. It's the role of the partner to make the other mate feel important and good about himself or herself.

If there are more positives than negatives about one another, does that make your significant other your soul mate? Isn't a soul mate supposed to be someone you'd marry over and over again in future lives as you did in past lives, in case both of you believe in reincarnation? Or is your soul mate simply someone who has the most similar personality style to yours? What if you hate your own personality type?

*     *     *

# Chapter Fourteen

## *The Smoothest Marriages*

Actually, the smoothest marriages occur between people who are more similar than different in outlook, interests, behavior, and goals. What attracts you to your soul mate is finding "an expanded hook" in your mate's personality type. An expanded hook is an immediate sense of having the same viewpoints in motion at the same time and similar reactions.

People who flock together in a work place environment or on campus and in various special interest and hobby groups have similar personalities, even in an environment where people of many different personalities work together. Personalities of a feather socialize together regardless of economic, ethnic, or religious differences.

The one trait you look for in a friend you want to be with is similarity of personality. Often, when the personalities are alike, so are the interests and conversation, even if the training and work situations are different.

Once you agree that you want to look for someone whose personality type matches and or complements your character, temperament, type, and style, the next step is to find out where you can find your soul mate. If you found someone, you can compare EEG brain waves to see whether you use the same neurological locations or positions in the brain to process information similarly.

If this is going too far, the most important point to look for is whether you and your significant other harmonize more than you conflict. Then recognize and accept each other's differences without trying to make over your mate in the image of your own personality type. The next step is to find out where do you go to meet your soul mate?

## How To Create Visibility For Yourself In Your Search

Where can you find Ms. or Mr. Right Personality Type? Chances are it's by creating visibility for yourself in your environment. Volunteer to be on a panel in the hobby or career of your choice at a conference or convention. Or make your hobby similar or complementary to the occupation or hobby of your future lover. Reach out to the environment of your intended mate.

Put a "spin" on your own personality styles and interests in the eye of your beholder.

Advertise if you're an introvert by building "buzz appeal" and launching yourself in the environment, at the trade shows, and in the newsletters of professional or business associations where your intended audience is present. If you're more of an extrovert, expand the ways you network and make face-to-face contacts in the places your soul mate would most likely be present. The more social you are at the moment, the more focused you can be as you really work a room at a trade show, professional association meeting, or convention.

## Which Personality Type Is Right For You?

The most frequently asked question at national and international marriage and singles conventions/conferences/trade shows, seminars, and courses is "What type of mate will I choose, and how do I know he/she will be right for me?"

The sixteen personality types (based on the Myers-Briggs Type Indicator ™) are not "a behavior." The types are based on a theory backed up by research-facts and credibility. Can the four letters of the sixteen types of the MBTI ™ or the four temperaments researched by Dr. Keirsey in his book, *Please Understand Me* or *Please Understand Me II*, help you determine whom you marry and how you work? Can other preference indicators do so also?

Choosing a soul mate according to your personality type is like choosing a career according to personality type matched to the character of any organization. How can you make the best decision about whom to choose for a long term live-in relationship or marriage?

The next few chapters will help to empower you with the facts you can use to make intelligent, logical, practical, and realistic choices based on solid research. You'll find no psycho-babble theories, no psychology jargon, and no far-out stuff. Only proven factual research made clear and simple to understand. Explained.

The information is useful and practical enough so that the majority of sensing feelers and thinkers in the world will be able to get a handle on these handbook rules of down-to-earth matchmaking. The intuitives can use this information to inspire and motivate them, to give them new ideas to expand upon and try out. Intuitives will see patterns.

Perceivers will see alternatives. Judgers will find quick strategies to make decisions and better choices. Thinkers will be able to check off lists of pros and cons about their soul mate. And feelers will be able to finally tap into romance as imaginations soar. How reliable is type watching when it comes to soul mate hunting-that is looking for a lifelong companion, spouse, lover, or significant other? If you take a personality classifier that is about 40 or 50 percent accurate each time, can you really rely on the findings to use when considering whether to marry someone of similar or compatible personality preferences and styles?

## What Are Your Preferences?

Most people continue to make these statements and ask these questions:

1. I don't know what my interests are.

2. I really don't know what I like. I've been doing what I've been told for so long, or did what would make money, or what my family told me to do, or what my school suggested was hot.

3. Now that I've decided to search for a mate, I don't know which one will work best for me, which will be compatible, supportive, enhance my self esteem, make me feel important, help me be more profitable, more human, act better toward people, and still let me enjoy the relationship.

4. What kind of mate is best for my health and will possibly extend my life span so I won't burn with resentment and frustration because of not being able to be the real me? Which partner will allow me to keep my health? How can I tell whether my soul mate is a pool of anger that will be directed at me after the honeymoon stage wears off?

5. What will I be happiest doing in the relationship? I want a meaningful, long-lasting relationship. I want to be enthusiastic about doing it. Will I become a sponge in the marriage, soaking up the blame and banked childhood anger of my spouse?

6. I want to live my dream in with a compatible soul mate, and make it real. I want to wake up eager get to work and eager to get. How can I find someone who will make me feel important and good about myself?

7. What will the character of my spouse be like? Forward-looking and visionary, or looking at the present based on past successes? How can I find someone who won't try to make my personality the same as his or her own?

How do you know what mate will work for you? How do you know whether you'll enjoy the relationship over time, and that you'll earn better health from it? How do you know what you are best at, what your real interests are, what you enjoy doing most, what's needed in your community that you will enjoy doing for a long time, over and over again?

Choosing a spouse according to your personality type eliminates the stress and exhaustion of working at a toxic relationship for which you have no natural aptitude or interest.

It's time to stop working at a relationship you don't feel comfortable with, working only to please others or only to earn a living. If your partner isn't working for you, choose the right partner according to your personality type. Personality type is biological and in-born, and only to some degree influenced by environment.

Certain types thrive in one relationship, and only cope in another until they burn out, sabotage themselves, experience a loss of self, a loss of power before they change to something more in line with their natural abilities. Some people don't even know they can change the type of business they operate and not suffer a loss in income.

Some people deal better with facts and reality. Others deal better with ideas, imagination, intuition, and global impressions. Some people are happier dealing with data or machines. Others like to be around people and activity.

Some spouses or live-in partners like to work alone at home. It drives them crazy when their mate is retired or at home underfoot and not at work outside the house. Others like to work at home with people around all day, such as in selling on the home party plan, daycare, teaching at home, phone fundraising, and investigating. Working at home in the same business with your mate can either destroy or strengthen the marriage bond.

There are artistic people, investigative people, people who like to organize and manage records and operate national clearinghouses or databases. There are those who like to deal with numbers and data, or scientific research, and those who like to craft things at home, such as designing lop-eared bunny dolls or creating hand-made violins.

There are people typing medical transcription records from their home, fishing work out to fifty other home word processors doing medical and legal transcription for one home-based cottage industry. Each marital relationship like each niche or cottage industry is unconsciously chosen according to the personality type preferences of each individual.

What do you look for in a soul mate other than someone with the same preferences? What if you're the partner who's tired of trying to change a spouse or lover to be more in his or her own image?

How your soul mate takes in information (concretely or abstractly) and makes decisions (subjectively or objectively) are two of the most important characteristics to look for in a potential mate. Two other are extroversion or introversion.

The last two are the need for quick closure versus the need to stay open minded longer for new information. Finally, look for a mate with a tolerance for ambiguity, if that's what you have and also want in a spouse.

\*      \*      \*

# Chapter Fifteen

## *Road Maps.*

Marriages are survival navigation games each person plays according to personality type when the going gets rough. The survival games we play vary according to our personality type. To survive in your business-based marriage, it's wise to have a road map. Your personality type affects the choice of a lover or spouse. Personality type, temperament, style and location in the brain itself are the bases of many theories that may determine the comfort level of your marriage along with other indicators such as similarity in beliefs, goals, and background.

Will your mate model behavior at home based on giant businesses where he or she mirrors their present successful strategies (the benchmarking mate)? Or are you or your lover changing, forward-looking, visionary, and full of ideas of alternatives, possibilities, creativity, risk-taking, and interested in forecasting future trends (the visionary mate)?

Will you search for a benchmarking or a visionary soul mate? Learn how to tell the character of the person's workplace and how it contrasts or blends with his/her personal character so you can later match it with your personality type and see whether it makes a comfortable fit.

## Your Niche

Each marriage is a unique niche. Position yourself first in your soul mate's mind. Find a gap in your mate and fill it. Love is a behavior you act out in front of an audience of one at a time. Love happens when the person you're with makes you feel important and good about yourself at the same time.

Marriage is an emotional business relationship between two people. They may look for what they wish they could be in one another (attraction of opposite types). Later, if familiarity breeds contempt, one partner may try to change the significant other to be more like himself or herself. The type hunter seeking a marriage partner asks: What personality type is best for me-my own, or a different type? Which types are compatible with my type? Which types have the least likelihood of constant irritation around someone of my type?

## Create Visibility

Use buzz appeal and put a "spin" on yourself before you choose your soul mate. Target your intended audience. Audition for marriage. The marriage game is show business and requires that you have a form of teaser or trailer to present to your intended showing the highlights of your personal "movie," which is about highlighting the events of your life and your personality preferences. Advertising, promotion, and communications techniques can be successfully used to search for your soul mate or a marriage partner according to your personality preferences. You are your own public relations director and marketing communications manager.

To find the right one for you, appeal to the types of audience, clients, or customers you want, attract them, and target their needs according to their personality types as a whole. You first need to find out what personality types you want to target. It's not so much sex appeal you need to find a mind mate and soul mate for marriage. It's buzz appeal, spin, and a good "press kit" to launch yourself in the media of your beholder's heart.

## Choose Your Marriage Partner/Soul Mate According To Your Dominant Personality Function

Get a map of the territory: Narrowing down your niche to a specific business. What's your dominant function? Is it extroverted thinking? Introverted feeling? Sensing? Intuition? Are you concrete or abstract in the way you take in information? Are you a thinker or a feeler in the way you make choices and decisions? Do you want to wait for new information to come in (perceiving) or make quick decisions and organize a plan (judging)? Are you so annoyed by popular psychology classifiers that you're ready to write a letter to a Web site? Or is hunting for self-identity a lifelong hobby or career? Do you enjoy exploring personality analysis? Perhaps you've had your DNA tested to find out your geographic origins 20,000 years ago. Chances are that you'd want to know what methods are flawed and what methods work for you when it comes to looking for a date or a mate.

Try the following game. Choose the right mate according to your dominant function. Your dominant function is one of the following: extraverted intuition, introverted intuition, introverted sensing, extraverted sensing, introverted thinking, extraverted thinking, introverted feeling, extraverted feeling.

Find your dominant function from your personality type as a result of the questionnaire. Learn more about your dominant function. Learn how the dominant function relates to your feeling of comfort, right fit, physical health, joy, optimism, enthusiasm, production and profit in the right home-based business. The connections between dominant function and natural at ease operation of a relationship. Enthusiasm for your marriage depends upon how it relates to your dominant function. Well-being is your goal in any relationship.

## How Others See the Flip Side of You In A Relationship Or Marriage. Are You A Whiner, A Databank, A Blackmailer, Or An Imposter?

Here are the types listed under the temperaments:

Key:
| | | |
|---|---|---|
| NF | Intuitive Feeling | Enjoys: Abstract theories. Decides by personal likes. |
| SP | Sensing Perceiving | Enjoys: Concrete details. Waits to add information. |
| SJ | Sensing Judging | Enjoys: Concrete details. Excludes information. |
| NT | Intuitive Thinking | Enjoys: Abstract theories. Decides by logic. |

## The Four Temperaments of the Keisey Temperament Sorter

(Take the *Keirsey Temperament Sorter* online at http://www.advisorteam.com/user/ktsintro.asp)

| NF | SP | SJ | NT |

## The 16 MBTI™ Types

Contact Consulting Psychologists Press for Information on how and where to take the Myers-Briggs Type Indicator. The company's Web site is at http://www.cpp-db.com/.

| INFP | ISFP | ISFJ | INTJ |
| INJF | ESFP | ESFJ | ENTJ |
| ENFP | ISTP | ESTJ | INTP |
| ENFJ | ESTP | ISTJ | ENTP |

**Key words:**

| | | |
|---|---|---|
| I | Introversion | Drained by people and too many activities involving people. |
| E | Extroversion | Energized by people and performance with people. |
| N | Intuition | Likes abstract theories and ideas of visionary imagination |
| S | Sensing | Likes concrete details and imitating successful giants |
| F | Feeling | Decides by personal likes and dislikes |
| T | Thinking | Decides by weighing pros against cons. Looks for flaws. |
| P | Perceiving | Waits for more information to come in before deciding. |
| J | Judging | Wants to exclude late coming information to make a decision. |

## Soul Mates For The NT Temperament (5% Of The Population)

>   INTJ
>   INTP
>   ENTJ
>   ENTP

## Soul Mates For The SJ Temperament (35% Of The Population)

>   ISTJ
>   ISFJ
>   ESTJ
>   ESFJ

In the business-based marriage, the number-crunching, logistics, accounting, programming SJ personality types loves getting the right things to the right people at the right time. These logistics-minded mates are right for SJ, sensing/judging people. They want to get the right things to the right people at the right time.

Major differences in the relationships will emphasize hardwired sensing or intuition. Sensors who enjoy learning the concrete details of situations usually have different interests or hobbies than intuitives who like the idea of abstract theories. Intuitives may attach their interests to matters that have little practical use in the eyes of the sensing beholder but find practical use in the minds of the intuitives.

Next in line of importance in a partnership or marriage are differences in feeling or thinking. Sensing, feeling people—(SF) mates like to be of service to others as in customer service, whereas ST (sensing thinking) people prefer to organize facts on paper or disk and make excellent trouble shooters and administrators who don't prefer direct contact with the public. The relationship and home as well as the business tasks may be extraverted or introverted, requiring lots of action and sales talking, or introverted working on long-term projects in isolation, as in accounting, tax law, and medical transcription, perfect for the ISTJ (introverted, sensing, thinking, judging) mate.

## Soul Mates For The SP Temperament (25 Percent Of The Population)

ISFP
INTP
ESFP
ESTP

The entrepreneurial artisan wants his or her own business and a mate interested in fun more than anything. These sensing perceivers want to be of service as long as their freedom is not curtailed. Where do you find such as soul mate?

Search the computer industry and its professional and business or trade associations where SPs are found as animators, technical illustrators, computer-aided designers, drafters, product designers, troubleshooters, robotics technicians, computer-aided manufacturing specialists, weapons masters and air controllers, and computer sales managers.

Sensing perceivers enjoy crafts and artisan works. This means down-to-earth projects with freedom and time flexibility. They also excel at producing videos on how to use the software. The SP play mate marries for fun, adventure, and travel. Freedom in the marriage is foremost.

## Soul Mates For The NF Population (Twelve Percent Of The Population)

The NFs are the most idealistic and romantic types. They write the romance novels and put romantic love, fantasy, and imagination first with emphasis on communication and a deep, meaningful relationship where only the soul mate is the ideal. They don't marry for practical reasons first, putting love first. Opposite of ENFP, for example, the most romantic and outgoing communicator, is the ISTJ, who marries, foremost for practical reasons, like real estate acquisition, money, security, financial stability of the partner's job, and to have a family and home ownership.

## Use Type Knowledge As A Map

How do you deal with your soul mate's darkest side under the most extreme stress? When manipulative, tactical behavior emerges as what psychoanalyst C.G. Jung called the shadow, also known as the inferior function of the self, how do you keep your cool? This is the time when it's most important to make your mate feel important and good in your eyes and in public. It's make or break a marriage time when your mate begins to feel loss of self esteem in your presence. Think before you speak about what your personality cries out for because your mate's personality may be so different, all the person wants is control over personal territory.

## Darkest Flip Sides Of Your Soul Mate's Preferences

Use your personality type knowledge as a map to identify the mate who's a blackmailer (SP), an imposter (NF phony or inauthentic), an SJ whiner (complainer), or an NT databank (robot/android). These are games mates play with new and older marriages without type understanding experience. What do you look for in body language, actions, speech, and work habits?

How do you see whether your mate and you will have clashing or conflicting opposite personality types that attract with that "I hate you, don't leave me feeling," or stay compatible even in the face of many family arguments? What living arrangement is ideal for your type, temperament, or personality style?

Living together intimately consists in interacting with a soul mate of one type, and possibly having children of many other types. Ask your local career consultant or adult education counselor to give you an official MBTI ™ questionnaire to compare with the other personality tests on the market. You may want to comparison shop.

Before you marry or move in, look at your mate's type. It's best to know as much as you can about your own preferences. Now let's take a look at what each of the different personality styles need when they form a relationship.

# Chapter Sixteen

## How To Be Your Own Marriage Broker

You know you have found your soul mate when in your partner's company you become more comfortable acting on your preferences. You finally give yourself permission to "act yourself" without hesitation and fear of your partner's reaction to the real you.

What do different personality types need when they form a loving relationship? Do you fall, leap, or grow in love? Who will be the best fit, the most comfortable, the easiest with whom to live?

You know you've picked the wrong mate when your partner puts you down to lift himself up. Would you like to marry someone who will shrink your world in ever narrowing circles? Or would you rather marry someone who supports your maximum growth potential in all areas of life?

Love means supporting your mate's personal, educational, career, and spiritual growth in a way that's best for your mate, including the freedom to move. In marriage, you always experience the upward gush of your own infancy. You'd rather your significant other would focus on the problem, the object, instead of always blaming you. Wouldn't you love to find a spouse whose personality "works right" for you-so you can say you married your best friend instead of the "takeaway monster?"

Would you rather see a marriage between two friends with similar ways of taking in information and making decisions about life? Or a marriage of convenience between a desperately dependent, avoidant person too scared to face financial and emotional independence in the outside world and a downwardly mobile corporate bully born with combat booties fighting the competition at home as well as in the office?

Most people want time-tested strategies that work to find the right mate. Only some of us see patterns in everything all the time, but many of us still marry at the level of our self-esteem of the moment. So why marry what you are (instead of what you wish you could be)? You marry in order to get or keep your self-respect.

We often marry a mate who has what we lack. For example, a person who failed math courses since the fifth grade might marry a mathematics or chemistry professor and complement the spouse's interests by going to the extreme other end and becoming an illustrator, sculptor, or musician so the mate will see math in forms of art and music and nature as symmetry.

Marrying your own or complementary personality type, temperament, and style helps you have greater self-respect for your partner and yourself. When you have greater self-respect, chances are you'll extend it to those around you at home and your co-workers in public as well.

In courtship, every partner is hypersensitive to the moods of the significant other. Your personality type determines how you respond to your mate's emotional reactions. If you're mismatched, you'll find your own emotional circuits overloaded and short-circuited.

You won't be able to deal with your mate's experiences and expressions. Communication will be cut. You'll feel as if you're trying to expand at the same time someone is squeezing you into the silver-plated corset of control.

If eighty percent of workers are mismatched in the wrong job, square pegs in round holes, how much more are soul mates mismatched in the wrong relationships and have the conversations of two alphabet noodles passing each other in bowl of soup? If only you were matched with a compatible personality type, temperament, or style, wouldn't you have similar tastes? Differences, yes, but at least goals and preferences in common. How you take in information and how you make decisions would be similar.

Whether you make decisions by thinking or feeling, by logic or values clarification and personal worth, by objective or subjective means, would be more alike than different. Some people want a completely different mate—at first. However, after retirement what would you two talk about when you're alone together?

Would he watch sports on TV at home with his buddies or alone and work on his computer or the house during his vacation because his introverted sensing needs to work out details within the walls of his territory? Would she travel alone to faraway places because her extroverted intuition continually seeks new people to meet and new places to see? Or would she remain by his side and write about other people's travels—to satisfy her need to express that extroverted intuition with big-picture ideas and theories?

If thirty-three percent of women are thinkers and sixty-six percent of men are thinkers, what chances do you have of making the right match? If thirty-three percent of men are feelers and sixty six percent of women are feelers, what chances do you have of finding a man and woman who are both feelers-so that they can make choices in the same way?

A thinking man or woman wants reasons for being asked to perform some task. A feeling person wants to nurture and please himself and still be able to please the soul mate and receive appreciation and recognition for being obedient. If he or she can't please himself first (nurture the self), the desire to please the mate freezes cold as a statue.

There's an old cliché that water climbs to its own level. Whatever the height or depth of our own feelings about ourselves at a given time in our lives determines who we feel worthy to meet, court, and marry. People tend to marry others similar in IQ, interests, and visible habits. The idea is to find something to talk about when the honeymoon stage is over and both of you are seventy, married for forty years or more, and sitting by the fireplace far from any places to go for entertainment. The TV is not working.

What do the two of you say to each other? Will you really have something worth staying together for in common other than your partner's money, free rent, or health insurance when the children have long since moved across the country and rarely visit or call? What will you say to your mate? Or will you, as many couples do, walk to separate rooms where he surfs the Internet on his computer and she on hers.

He's on the old time radio theater Web site and she's looking for pen pals in faraway places to discuss ancient history. How will your marriage play in its prime time? How will your marriage end?

## Do You Feel Worthy of a Great Marriage?

We ask ourselves these questions when we search for a mate or partner. Do we feel good enough about ourselves to deserve that person? Do we feel worthy of marrying someone in that occupation?

Are we feeling worthy enough to marry a man or woman of your own religion? Have your parents, your readings, or the society in which you live made you feel like it is not all right to be your real self, your original ethnic identity, or your parent's religion? Would someone of your own heritage accept you now that we have already married outside that group and, perhaps had children of a different faith or group? All these scenarios set the stage and measure how worthy you feel of marriage.

Not all people marry only for the romance of being in love. Some of us marry for reasons other than "love" that vary from fantasies of "gorgeous hunks" and "goddesses" of the cinema and novels to people we conjure out of history. Some of us visit past life regressionists to find memories of a true love in a former life. Others marry from fear of abandonment, or because they were rejected by members of a certain group, ethnicity, religion, income level, or junior high school sorority.

People marry out of fear of loss or to get away from controlling parents. Ask yourself all the reasons why you want to marry a certain type of person. Then ask yourself what it is about your background and thoughts that makes you want to marry this type of person from your culture or one so different it will never remind you of your own family. Why is it important for you to marry this type of person?

Will you feel the same way when you're sixty and your grandchildren's identity not only is different from your own, but your children forbid you to tell your grandchildren that you have the forbidden ancestry in your own family because it will bring dishonor to the family that will exist when you're long gone?

As an example, the case in point is the marriage of a Jewish partner to an Arab Moslem partner. The marriage fell apart in a few years. The husband divorced his wife and took the preschool children to his native country where they grew up nurtured in the father's religion and ethnicity. As adults they returned to pay a visit to their Jewish mother in another country, but kept their distance and forbid their mother to tell the grandchildren she was Jewish. The mother no longer felt worthy to marry in her own ethnicity, so she married a Christian man who couldn't have children.

Her dilemma is knowing that her children wouldn't want her to tell her grandchildren about her own Jewish parents who escaped the Pogroms of the Caucasus and Russia. So the richness of her ethnic heritage can never be passed onto her grandchildren or it would bring dishonor to the family of her own children, reared in Arab culture and religion to identify with Arabs and Arabic elementary schools. So who you marry at 21 because of a fantasy about the romance of one ethnic group can mean something different at age 60 when you have lost the chance to enrich the lives of your grandchildren with knowledge about your ethnic group, which they will never know about, even though they share a quarter of your genetic makeup. Keep in mind what will happen in the future when you marry.

How will that new person act toward us knowing we gave custody of our children to our spouse, or that our spouse took the children away to another land for the past fifteen years? So goes the way we question our own minds before making a choice about a partner.

Did we ever think of matching our personality type to the character of our soul mate? It has been said that the lower our self-esteem, the more we want someone different from ourselves in type and temperament.

You don't want to pick someone who will treat you with contempt, anger, criticism, and resentment. You don't want a mate who'll yell at you as you stand together in the romantic Las Vegas buffet line on your 20th anniversary, "Are you going to eat all that food on your plate, you pig?"

You don't want a mate who will encourage you to take a sudden interest in your Reeboks, as afraid at age 65 as you were at 35 that you'll say the wrong words to people when you're mate is around. If you have to walk on eggshells, be perfect, or change your basic biological personality, if you can't be the real you around your partner, grow, express your creativity, or do the work you love, don't marry that person. If you want to stay home and rear a family, marry someone steady enough to provide that opportunity. Don't marry someone who insists you go back to work right after childbirth and live on two incomes to make ends meet.

Don't marry your friend if silently, you long to be away from your partner so you can feel free to express your creativity without that feeling of being crushed silent in front of your audience. Or you feel the need to nurture yourself.

You pile the food high on your plate and enjoy, because there isn't a flicker of joy and optimism coming from your partner toward you after the first three months of marriage. And if your mate saw how big a portion you scooped, taking much more than you can chew, there'd be loud barks and disappearance from your side at the restaurant table.

The wrong mate humiliates you in public and criticizes you in private. The wrong mate calls you a loser. The word "stupid" soon replaces "sweetheart."

What does the right mate do? There's not merely one soul mate that's right for you. You may find a succession of soul mates in a series as in "series monogamy." These are people who have similar personality preferences to yours, similar interests, and may be in the same or compatible, but different lines of work from your career.

There's a percentage of the population varying from one percent to thirty-eight percent who's the same type, temperament or style as you from which to choose. Next time you look, try matching your personality type to the temperament and style of your partner.

Similar types work well together during a long relationship because they have similar ways of taking in information and making decisions. Opposite types attract at first, but wear thin over time due to differences in preferences.

Some types even help to provoke one another to violence or great anger if only because they emphasize radically different ways of taking in information or communication. For example, it's the introverted sensing man most likely to hit the extroverted intuitive woman when under stress rather than walk away to cool down. Later, more will be explained about the differences between sensing and intuitive partners.

A good example is in the film, "Blue Velvet." The introverted sensing male character was physically and verbally abusive to the extroverted intuitive woman character. If you ask an ISFJ male to view the movie, "Blue Velvet" chances are he will identify with the introverted sensing male lead character and cheer him, not being aware of how abusive he was, only feeling irritated by the antics of the extroverted intuitive female character who was abused because her extroverted intuition got on the nerves of the introverted sensing of the male character. Why this happens in a real marriage depends upon how each partner handles conflict in a relationship.

One of the worst mistakes some young women make is to marry men in medical school, work to support their husbands as students, and then get pregnant and have to quit work when a husband is dependent upon his wife for money and loans won't cover all expenses. It could backfire when the guilt he feels later makes him irritated at being around his wife.

If you're working to put your partner through professional school, ask yourself if when you're in his presence, whether he's reminded of the fact that you had to sacrifice your education to work at a low-paid job so he could become a higher-paid professional? The next step for him may be to find another woman he can impress after he's already successful, someone he doesn't owe and doesn't remember him when he was a poor student dependent on his wife or partner.

Turn the tables around with a man who supports his wife and stays home to take care of the small children while she goes to medical, dental, or law school. He may resent having to stay home and be a househusband. Or if he works, he may be called to work when his medical professional wife is in the middle of treating a patient and no sitter can be found. Stress erupts. At this time, the personality styles, if similar would both be able to take a step back and a deep breath. If the personality preferences had many differences, the dissonance could push the marriage over the edge or erupt in conflicts related to power struggles.

Find out how a man treats his mother or how a woman was treated by her father. A husband treats his wife pretty much like he treats his mother. There are exceptions, and there are men whose mothers are never wrong. If a man resents the fact that his mother was abandoned by her husband, his dad, when he was five, he could be fixated at the age of five when his father walked out.

When his wife frustrates him in a power struggle or when she seeks power over her personal space or resents his tight control over money, the man could explode in anger at his real problem, abandonment by his father. He may stay fixated on that abandonment fear and react violently or explosively with anger when he can't get his own way.

A combination of narcissism, low serotonin levels in his brain, a diet high in sweets or high carbohydrates, the tendency to fast for long periods of time, addictions, food or milk allergies, or the desire to "come on too fast" in a relationship, the will to control his wife, and a tendency to explode in anger all add up to big trouble in a relationship. Without anger management treatment and without a medical and mental health exam to find out whether he harbors any form of intermittent explosive disorder, you could be in the path of potential trouble. Some men may react to food with brain allergies. Steer clear of this type of partner, male or female (unless a food-based brain allergy is the only cause of the situation).

The issue of control could be the flashpoint in this type of relationship. Some men explode when all a wife says is "I'd like respect." It reminds the man of his mother talking to him and makes him feel like a child with loss of control he may over-react and double up on his control over you.

## The Goal To Is End Up Smarter Together

The higher our self-esteem, the more we want to marry and rear children with someone with preferences and goals like ourselves. Couples with greater self-respect for one another will stay together longer and communicate without fear of being verbally crushed or stifled. Depending upon how well your attitudes and preferences are matched, you end up smarter together or steering clear.

Let's look at a variety of ways we use personality to search for our soul mates. If you want to marry someone very different in culture and in the religion you choose for yourself in the present, look inside and find out what you're afraid of about the culture, faith, or identity with which you have been reared in your youth.

Did people from the ethnic group or income group you want to marry into reject you on your first attempt to enter their clubs when you were in your early teens? Before you decide on what ethnic group to marry into other than your own, even if you feel it's not okay to be what you are in public because of past wars, fear ingrained by relatives, or the way society acted toward you, look at the four temperaments. You're trying to see how the four different temperaments act toward each other living under the same roof. The four temperaments combine to make up the sixteen personality types of the Myers-Briggs Type Indicator ™.

## The Four Temperaments

In Dr. David Keirsey's best-selling classic, *Please Understand Me, (Character & Temperament Types*, by David Keirsey and the late Marilyn Bates, Prometheus Nemesis Book Company, Del Mar, CA, 1984 or *Please Understand Me II)*, four temperaments are discussed. These four temperaments are very important when you look at the business-based marriage or when you search for your soul mate, significant other, domestic partner, or spouse.

Many people are still marrying their opposites in personality. At the same time the divorce rate hovers between 50% and 58%. Are we corseting square pegs into round girdles? Are people as misfit in relationships as they are in the wrong job-because they matched personality type to the character of the wrong significant other?

As people have personalities, companies and schools have characters of their own that reflect the personalities of the people running the show. The character of your soul mate may be visionary or benchmarking, that is, emphasizing the changing future with vision (visionary), or imitating successful giants of the past and following tradition (benchmarking).

Your soul mate may look to change with excitement and feel in a rut when change isn't happening fast enough, or the person may stick to tradition and resent change as highly stressful because what worked successfully in the past will work in the future. These are two different characters that have a deep, almost genetic split.

Benchmarking soul mates even subscribe to different magazines than visionary soul mates. The publications that look to tradition and imitate successful giants of the past such as IBM are on the subscription lists of benchmarking soul mates. The visionary magazines and newspapers that target rapid change and looking to the future, going from project to project and changing what doesn't work good enough are on the subscription list of your visionary soul mate. A visionary soul mate is more likely to think abstract thoughts, look to the future for inspiration, live by imagination, and focus on change. Think of Microsoft as a visionary company employing visionary people and IBM as a benchmarking company employing people who bank on the successful traditions of giants of the past who are still very much growing such as GE and the shipping companies like UPS. Of course, not all the employees who work in visionary companies are visionary intuitive thinkers and feelers, and not everyone in a traditional benchmarking corporation is a benchmarking sensing judger.

What can you can take from these examples? If you're a visionary intuitive thinker or feeler looking to change residences, jobs, college majors, or the interior décor frequently and your mate is a benchmarking sensing judger that makes a decision and stays put, hoping to spend a lifetime in one career, will their be conflict in the marriage? Will you end up going your separate way?

Research also shows that long after the breakup of a relationship, people as often as not marry opposite types again. What would feel better is if they married their own type or one similar enough to theirs to at least have less conflict in preferences and attitudes.

There ought to be a computer that matches people by their type, temperament, style, and brain dominance. These four checkpoints will send up a database of red flags-warning signals or go ahead signals that the way each partner takes in information and makes decisions are similar enough to allow communication, maximum growth of each person, and a better way to solve conflicts and have fun.

Opposites attract, but also can physically and verbally abuse each other in a marriage or live-in relationship. Carl Jung said opposites fascinate each other because each partner sees in the opposite his/her own shadow of all that one has not been able to express, develop, create, or achieve in life.

Whatever we reject in ourselves, we are attracted to in someone of the opposite type because that person becomes all we wish we could be if only we could speak up in public and perform or achieve-or whatever else we lack.

That spells big trouble ahead, ending in violence. Stop searching for your other side in the opposite type and steer clear. Your own or a similar type can have you smarter together sooner. The trouble is, everybody's search for our opposite type (our flip side) is wired in our heads. The point of looking at personality in a marriage is to find a mate who won't abuse you.

What happens when we marry our opposite type seeking our other side in him or her is that pretty soon we end up trying to change that other person eventually to be more like ourselves in interests, attitudes, and actions. We always try to change our spouse to become more like ourselves. However, there's no way we can re-program our partner of an opposite type to be more like us without creating a rotten relationship and a miserable marriage. To review once more, look at Keirsey's Four Temperaments.

## Keirsey's Four Temperaments

The four temperaments are, according to Keirsey, as follows:

NF (INTUITIVE FEELING)
NT (INTUITIVE THINKING)
SP (SENSING PERCEIVING)
SJ (SENSING JUDGING)

## Which Are Your Opposite Temperaments?

| Your Temperament | Opposite Temperament |
| --- | --- |
| INTUITIVE FEELING (NF) | INTUITIVE THINKING (NT) |
| SENSING PERCEIVING (SP) | SENSING JUDGING (SJ) |
| INTUITIVE THINKING (NT) | INTUITIVE FEELING (NF) |
| SENSING JUDGING (SJ) | SENSING PERCEIVING (SP) |

## What's The Motto Of Each Temperament?

| Temperament | Motto |
| --- | --- |
| SP (SENSING PERCEIVING | Making an impact |
| SJ (SENSING JUDGING) | Protecting, serving, and guarding |
| NF (INTUITIVE FEELING) | Seeking rapport and reaching potential |
| NT (INTUITIVE THINKING) | Understanding and controlling nature |

According to the tapes and writings of Eve Delunas, Ph.D, author of *Survival Games Personalities Play*, (Sunflower Ink, Carmel, CA, 1992), a spouse's defiant behavior is paradoxical and tactical. It's a paradoxical and paralogical response to a paradoxical situation. If you want to understand by using the four temperaments why your lover's behavior is making you sick, look at your mate's payoff.

If your mate is complaining that you're the cause of your spouse's or lover's sick feelings, ask yourself what's the payoff of your lover's symptoms. Then look at the effect of your mate's symptoms on yourself. How do you feel when your lover acts up or acts out? What you feel tells you what your mate needs most and wants first.

If you feel angry, your mate's payoff is power. Your mate is probably of the NT (intuitive thinking temperament) whose goal in love is power through their own achievements. Achieving and achievements, including: Achieving control over nature through questioning all authority, being skeptical. NTs enjoy thinking and improving anything by finding flaws in studies and theories. The NT eye can find something wrong or flawed with research studies in various fields where the NT is knowledgeable. If it's not broken, then the NT might visualize breaking it in order to make it work better. Ideas are more important than facts because the NT can see patterns and branching pathways in nature and in everything else. The NF (intuitive feeler) also sees the big picture. An NF can see patterns and bring together two different objects, metaphors, or ideas to form a new picture, poem, idea, scientific finding, or object.

If you feel annoyed, frustrated, and tense, your lover's payoff is attention. Intuitive feelers (NF) want attention and rapport, to communicate intimately with you. They want to be the center of your attention. Achieving rapport is more important than power. Attention is seen as romance. They will go to any extreme to get attention so they can be authentic and real as in "being my true self, expressing myself creatively."

If you feel injured or physically hurt or abused, your lover is out for revenge. Sensing perceivers (SP) types take revenge when they feel betrayed, and often it's physical revenge done to you personally and to your property and possessions.

Sensing perceivers get mad when they are not getting enough play and fun out of life, not composing, performing, or getting hands-on experience in doing what they like to do.

If you feel hopeless, your lover wants exemption (getting out of responsibility) for duties. Your mate is probably a sensing judger (SJ) type.

Sensing judgers spend their whole life taking on other people's responsibility and duty at work. You react to the SJ by giving up. This SJ tactic is used when you ask more than the SJ wants to give, because the SJ already gave far to much at the office without appreciation and reward.

The SJ enjoys serving others so much, that when at home, the sensing judger wants to be served-and have exemption from responsibility. When overworked, the SJ responds by getting sick, tired, worried, or sad. Sometimes they get physical symptoms and retire to bed to be waited upon. They can also explode and throw objects at you when under stress. Sensing judgers get cycles of depression more than other types.

When well, the SJ's joy is in the work, not the relationship, although the SJ is least likely to want to make any changes or leave a marriage. After courtship, the introverted SJ isn't too romantic anymore. The extroverted SJ is more of a host to strangers.

When SJs seeks exemption, that means exempting themselves from meeting your needs, especially if you're a romantic NF needing to be the center of the SJ's attention, which you will never be. Work always comes first because it means security from scarcity.

The SJ makes you feel hopeless to prevent you from being homeless. Sensing judgers make you feel like giving up by exempting themselves from meeting your emotional needs. Therefore, to find out what your lover's greatest emotional needs are in the love relationship, write down how YOU feel when your partner seeks any one of these four payoffs: power (NT), attention (NF), revenge (SP), or exemption (SJ).

Quick-what's most important in your life-joy, duty, science, or spirit? When you search for your soul mate, consider focusing on the most comfortable, compatible temperament match in the long run.

Instead of fearing how much you don't like labeling people in little boxes, searching for a mate by compatible personality type will at least provide you with a person less likely to chafe you the wrong way all the time.

Do you want a supportive mate who will not crush your dreams or shoot down your ideas? Would you enjoy a type mate who could provide anchorage in reality so you can spend your time creating illusion?

Would you rather opt for power so your mate can live for freedom? Or are you about duty (leading to social status) seeking a mate who's all about spirit (self-actualization, having rapport, and making you drink your raw vegetable juices)? Would you like someone whose interests and goals in life are similar to your own-or different enough to provide you with anchorage or freedom?

Choose one of these four temperament categories: Joy (SP), Duty (SJ), Science (NT), or Spirit (self-growth), (NF). Worldwide, each person chooses one of these four niches that feels most comfortable. Each person emphasizes one lifestyle drive or temperament. Which type style is most important to you?

Can you say, "I'm all about finding joy and fun?" Or are you all about duty-being of service to people? Are you about science (power, controlling nature, and achievements) or about self-actualization and personal growth (spiritual values)?

Choose your soul mate/type mate by what's your most important and passionate life pursuit. What are you all about?

What would you like your type mate to be all about if you knew you could never change the person without destroying the relationship?

People fall into four lifestyle drives or temperaments-those who are all about **Joy, Duty, Science, Or Spirit.** Who will you choose as your type mate-the person who puts first in life spirit, science, joy, or duty?

From these four temperaments, form 16 personality types, based on personality indicators such as the Myers-Briggs Type Indicator ™, one of the world's most popular personality type indicators designed for normal people and not used to weed out emotional disorders.

The most frequently used inventory to uncover emotional disorders is the MMPI-The Minnesota Multiphasic Personality Inventory. There are thirteen personality styles described in detail in the book, ***Personality Self-Portrait, Why You Think, Work, Love, And Act The Way You Do***, by John M. Oldham, M.D. and Lois B. Morris, Bantam Books, NY, 1991.

The book, ***Personality Self-Portrait***, is based somewhat on the DSM-II-R. So if the DSM-II=R denotes 13 personality styles, and the MBTI presents sixteen personality types, and Jung wrote of eight types, and Dr. Keirsey's ***Please Understand Me*** describes the four temperaments which combine to form the 16 personality types of the MBTI ™, we soon find that there are four positions of preference dominance, a kind of mind mapping, classified according to mapped areas of the brain.

It's easy to divide the brain into two hemispheres as well as into four parts. One part, the cerebral cortex, could be for stating irony (NT), one part for metaphor, (NF), one part for reducing words to their briefest understandable meaning, (STJ) and one part for limbic area expression (SFJ) of emotions (extroverted feeling combined with introverted sensing and judging).

What type is brainiest? INTJ (Like physicist-cosmologist Stephen Hawkins). What type makes the best leader in technology or the military service? (ENTJ) (Like Bill Gates or General Schwarzkopf). What type is most creative with words and metaphors? INFP, like Shakespeare or most best-selling female novelists—Annie Dillard or Anne Rice or story writers such as Ray Bradbury. Most creative in art or music? (ISFP) (like Rembrandt). What type is most mathematical or analytical? INTP (like Einstein or the "My Fair Lady" linguist character, Henry Higgins).

What do the four temperaments want in a relationship? Those who apt for joy need the freedom to act and release from burden most deeply to thrive. Freedom comes first in their lives. If your type mate puts duty first in life, then life is all about social status and making decisions. Judgment is what this person is about. Following the rules is most important.

The type mate who emphasizes or whose niche is spirit seeks self-realization, self- actualization, rapport, and attention. This person focuses on self-development and human potential with the emphasis on being human and ethical, working with passion, and being all that one can be where spirit equals ethics. Type mates whose niche is science emphasize power and achievements as their foremost personal goal in life.

Each person eventually will rub you the wrong way and conflict will erupt. You can tell your type mate's temperament by the way you react to the person when the mate's need for joy, duty, spirit, or science is not being met.

To understand why you feel frustrated about the conflict with your soul mate, ask what is the partner's payoff? To find out what that person's temperament is, ask yourself: What's the effect of my partner's symptoms on me? What you feel tells you what your partner needs most.

Your *Joy*-seeking soul mate will apt for revenge when you crush the person's search for joy. You'll feel hurt or injured. Release-seeking "joy people" apt for revenge when you step on their freedom to act button, and they can't get any 'release.'

Your *Science*-temperament partner under stress will generate great anger in you. The science partner's payoff is always power. Most important in that person's life is achievement. If you feel angry, you science temperament partner's payoff is power. This is true in children as well as adults. Power struggles dominate the relationship.

If you feel annoyed, frustrated, or tense, your soul mate's payoff is attention. Achieving rapport is foremost for the *Spirit* temperament. (Spirit also can mean self-actualization, self-realization, and human potential building rather than spirit in the supernatural sense. Or it can feel more like a sprite driving you to act naturally as you do and realize it's a comfortable fit moving toward your goals.) The Attention-desiring person is all about ethics and being authentic.

If these *Cerebrally-Driven* temperaments are not being real, or being their true selves ("I gotta be me"), they will achieve rapport. When they're unable to have you're attention, they will annoy you until you tell them how much you love them repeatedly. The ideal relationship is what they're after. How these visionaries annoy you is by thinking about the relationship that they could have had which would have been deep and meaningful. Their payoff is remaining the center of attention in your life.

Your *Duty* temperament soul mate wants exemption and makes you feel hopeless when in conflict or under great stress. Do you feel hopeless around this person? This person of great responsibility at work now wants to run from responsibility at home.

The *Duty*-bound person's whole life is about responsibility to serving others in exchange for security and stability. Your-change-hating mate will become sick, tired, worried, or sorry when seeking exemption from responsibility to you in the home.

As the burdens grow greater at work, this withdrawing, withholding dance-away partner will force you to serve at home because the *Duty* person serves so well at the office and feels so unappreciated in both arenas. Yet *Duty* is your anchorage if you need an unchanging stability in your life so you can dabble in career diversity as long as you don't ask your partner to move work location with you.

## *How The Four Temperaments Combine To Form The 16 Personality Types*

Dr. Keirsey's four temperaments are included in the four letters of each of the Meyers-Briggs Type Indicator's (MBTI) ® sixteen personality types. The MBTI is one of the world's most popular personality tests for normal people, appearing in dozens of languages. It's used extensively by colleges, corporations, training centers, and by career counselors to find out general personality type preferences.

Here are the sixteen personality types of the *Myers Briggs Type Indicator* (MBTI) ® (a registered trademark of Consulting Psychologist's Press in Palo Alto, CA) as developed by Isabel Briggs Myers and Katharine C. Briggs who brought the theory of type to life and fact and to Dr. Mary H. McCaulley who helped to establish the credibility and careful validation of the indicator.

The MBTI™ is not a test. It's one of the most popular indicators of personality type in the world, translated into at least 36 languages. The MBTI shows, according to organizational development consultant, William C. Jeffries, in his book, *True To Type*, (Hampton Roads Publishing Co., Inc. Norfolk, VA, 1991), "how others see your orientation to the world".

Every year, millions of people take it at work, in school, and in career consulting and counseling. The MBTI only shows your preference in how you see and judge reality; whether your energy comes from being around people or from inside yourself when you're actively alone.

The MBTI shows preferences also in how you see your own orientation to the universe outside your mind. Keep in mind that there's always more than one soul mate out there whose preferences feel comfortable living with your preferences.

The strategy lies in finding what works best and knowing where to look to find a person most comfortable with your uniqueness. When familiarity doesn't breed contempt, you know your preferences match and blend.

Your soul mate is someone you'd want to be close to again in the next lifetime, in case reincarnation is real-because growing toward that person's love and light in this lifetime would never be long enough time. Your soul mate complements your preferences without conflict.

You know you found your soul mate when each partner's preferences harmonize at least five times more than they conflict. You know you have not found Mr. or Ms. Right Preference when a relationship slowly escalates to steadily growing anger, criticism, resentment, contempt, and abuse in the relationship because your preferences are so different from your mate's.

When preferences are so different, communication is different and difficult. You two are speaking at each other to different neurological locations in your brains.

Your intuitive theory may put your mate to sleep or distract so there is little listening to you when you don't give back practical, "useful" facts or skills. Your sensing partner's fact-finding may make you angry when you're listening for global impressions, ideas, seeing patterns, or waiting for rapport while your partner thrives on exemption.

The thirteen personality styles of the-DSM-III-R, are another way of defining your personality style. Finally, type also refer to the four brain locations which discuss the neurological basis of why people have different preferences and how to use these positions or locations to track down your soul mate-the best domestic partner or spouse for you. Frequently, several kinds of personality classifiers come onto the market, each marked to tell you your personality preferences and how to match them to the character of your next relationship, corporation, career, or contract. What signals are right for you?

## What The Four Letters Stand For: The Sixteen Personality Types

(Based on the principles of the Myers-Briggs Type Indicator) ™

| | |
|---|---|
| ISTJ | INTROVERTED, SENSING, THINKING, JUDGING |
| ISTP | INTROVERTED, SENSING, THINKING, PERCEIVING |
| ESTP | EXTRAVERTED, SENSING, THINKING, PERCEIVING |
| ESTJ | EXTRAVERTED, SENSING, THINKING, JUDGING |

| | |
|---|---|
| ISFJ | INTROVERTED, SENSING, FEELING, JUDGING |
| ISFP | INTROVERTED, SENSING, FEELING, PERCEIVING |
| ESFP | EXTRAVERTED, SENSING, FEELING, PERCEIVING |
| ESFJ | EXTRAVERTED, SENSING, FEELING, JUDGING |
| INFJ | INTROVERTED, INTUITIVE, FEELING, JUDGING |
| INFP | INTROVERTED, INTUITIVE, FEELING, PERCEIVING |
| ENFP | EXTRAVERTED, INTUITIVE, FEELING, PERCEIVING |
| ENFJ | EXTRAVERTED, INTUITIVE, FEELING, JUDGING |
| INTJ | INTROVERTED, INTUITIVE, THINKING, JUDGING |
| INTP | INTROVERTED, INTUITIVE, THINKING PERCEIVING |
| ENTP | EXTRAVERTED, INTUTIVE, THINKING, PERCEIVING |
| ENTJ | EXTRAVERTED, INTUITIVE, THINKING, JUDGING |

The sixteen MBTI ® types of Isabel Briggs-Myers are expanded from the eight personality types originally based on the 1923 books and theories of psychoanalyst, C.G. Jung. They have been statistically tested by the publishers of the MBTI ® and by users of the indicator worldwide.

There are sixteen different personality types found among all people in the world, according to the principles of the Myers-Briggs Type Indicator (Trademark). Based upon those principles and the theories of psychoanalyst C.G. Jung, here's a brief description of the heightened job and resume needs of each type:

| TYPE | IN LOVE |
|---|---|
| ISTJ | Organizers |
| ISTP | Tool masters |
| ESTP | Wheeler-dealing promoters, may gamble Loves freedom of travel |
| ESTJ | Household administrators |

|  |  |
|---|---|
|  | Organizes details or logistics well.<br>Outgoing concrete thinkers. |
| ISFJ | Dutiful to strangers and job first<br>Emotionally absent at home<br>Physically present at home. |
| ISFP | Most modest house spouse<br>Shows you how to feel |
| ESFP | Performer, making an impact,<br>Sunny fun seeker, card player |
| ESFJ | Persuasive host, needing friends<br>Great in sales and customer service |
| INFJ | Introspective teacher and poet<br>Answers correspondence, good with pen pals. Extroverted feelings in an introvert. |
| INFP | Writer/artist of entertaining fiction |
| ENFP | Rescuer of people and patterns<br>Must be center of attention in the home |
| ENFJ | Best public speaker or preacher |
| INTJ | Think for yourself-always. |
| INTP | Reclusive architect of change. |
| ENTP | Free thinking adventurer inventor Idea-bound. |

ENTJ             Uses visionary ideas to lead people.

What's the difference between your intuitive (N) and your sensing (S) dates or partners?

Intuitives and sensors take in information differently because intuition is located in the left hemisphere of the brain and sensing is located in the right hemisphere of the brain. This seems odd because we've been told that intuition (a flash of an idea, a thought or feeling about the future, a global impression, or imagination) is located in the right hemisphere.

We've heard that we sense facts from the left hemisphere because sensing deals with sequencing and chronological, linear events in the present. However, the opposite is true when type testing is done by mapping the actual neurological locations in the brain.

Intuitives see patterns in everything. What else will your intuitive lover always ask or talk about when you go for a walk in the moonlight together? Intuitives always ask "what if?"

## Intuitive

What if?
What if we wonder?
What if there's another way to do it?
What if we could dance ethnic to a different drummer?
What if we could sing a different tune with an optical disk?
What if we could grow stronger by listening to our inner selves or observing patterns in nature and applying them to literature styles or math formulas?
What if crop circles are mathematical equations?
What if we always ask "why?"
What if the real world isn't real or there are other people in other galaxies visiting us?
What if we ask more questions?

What if we change again and improve it?
What if we listen more closely or use music for healing?
what if we look at everything in a new light each day?
What if we wonder whether something's true?
What if we question all authority and think or feel for ourselves?
What if we look for something more in the relationship?
What if you're not my ideal soul mate and there's someone better waiting for me out there or inside myself?
What if we make sense of things through imagination?
What if we wonder about the far future today?
What if we explain what happened in a new way?
What if we ask if time travel is possible?
What if you're Mr. or Ms. Wrong Personality Type?

## Sensing

Let's live the best we can one day at a time.
Let's handle crises as they come.
Let's get things done by looking at all the facts.
Let's tell it like it is right now.
Let's deal with concrete problems using practical skills.
Let's be able to serve people with a smile.
Let's get rid of the theoretical, the abstract, and the conceptual because it's the biggest time waster and puts me to sleep.
Let's cut the excess and get to the point or baseline.
Money talks and bullshine walks.
What's your point?
No deskwork until the physical workout is over.
Patience is hard to find.
Create crisis to have something exciting to or otherwise make work by making lists.

Why write it down in a document when listening to it on tape is possible and saves so much time?
Let's listen to it while we drive or bicycle to where we're going.
Dealing with details and logistics makes me feel secure from scarcity.
Everything must have its usefulness and place in the order, or it's a waste of effort to make it.
Learn only what's practical because common sense is more important in a marriage than fantasy and escape.
Imagination must have its usefulness in entertainment or entertainment moguls would be poor as poets.
Starving artists should take up computer animation interactive multimedia technology.
Get a haircut and get a real job.
Shape up or ship out.

---

Now let's take a look out what you need most in a marital or loving relationship from each personality type or set of preferences using the MBTI ™ sixteen personality types. The idea is to have a good and lifelong marital not a combative martial encounter based on what you need most to do in a relationship in order to keep your health and at the same time make sure your significant other feels important and good in your company.

**Type      Action Verb      What You Need Most To Do In A Relationship**

ISTJ      Systematize      To organize, inspect, and control. To check for flaws in construction. To supervise accounting systems of large funds. To handle logistics and keep details organized in various systems. To run a marriage like the tightest ship in the shipping business. ISTJ's motto is "be prepared." The inspector of marriages will want a marriage organized systematically, methodically, and by plans and rules. This drive to systematize relationships may not be expressed so quickly in the marriage, but will come out during parenting and later in the marriage, depending upon the type of spouse, another ISTJ or ISFJ or the opposite type, the freedom-loving, extroverted, intuitive ENFP who wants rapport, new places to see, and more people around.

ISTP     Troubleshoot     Freedom in a relationship. Hands-on activity in the garage with tools, cars, planes, weapons, crafts, or product design or you could explode sadistically in a bad relationship under extreme stress. You could also implode into violence or abuse, but you're a great artist or draftsperson and a thinker. You could like cycles and fast cars, hot music, and being alone and free, even with that medical, computer, or engineering degree. Try animation or special effects to entertain your mate. To be a master of weapons or mechanical objects.

ESTP     Promote     To thrive on adrenaline, the excitement of variety bringing
shock and impact to the airwaves, even at home. Travel, adventure, great real estate, cops on the beat, promoting a practical game or stock market deal to test your spontaneity, looking for clues as a detective would do; vigilance.

ESTJ     Administer     To run the tightest ship in the shipping business-your home, manage an organization of children, like you would a corporation, to make decisions about people. You're an administrator using applied sciences. Computer security   and law is your niche inside your home and in family relationships. To teach time management and organize your files, lists, bureau drawers, closets, and things to do. To organize a marriage and prevent the spouse from succumbing to weaknesses. Read Ibsen's play, "The Doll House" to view one possible relationship between an ESTJ husband and an INFP wife. ESTJ is the opposite personality type to INFP.

ISFJ   Organize   To conserve and guard the family's finances and home by planning the home budget and taking care of other's needs. To save almost all your money for a rainy day and to worry about it, whine and complain under stress, blaming your mate with your extroverted feeling and keeping lists with your introverted sensing. You watch how much food your mate heaps on a plate at buffets and complain about all that wasted food uneaten, but you eat like a bird, except when it comes to sweets. You dream of a secure job and marriage with no changes.

ISFP   Compose   Nature boy. Nature girl. To compose computer music on a Midi-synthesizer. To extract sounds. To be out in the country and in tune with the animals with your mate and to be in tune with nature and remain modestly in the background of everything. To train pets or animals for performance in TV commercials or on the movie set.
To put world music on software. To design fashions using software. To ensure the well-being of many. To work in public relations as a flight attendant and come home to a traveling spouse. To work with color and texture. To produce films. To sell crafted pop-up books. To enjoy good living through the five senses-taste, sight, sounds, smells of honeysuckle and roses, and to enjoy and craft life like Hemingway, risking, leaping before looking, then being the househusband or homemaker, bicycle builder, animal handler/trainer or craftsperson. You like the zoo. To marry a news anchor person. To be a landscaper, decorator, or gardener.

ESFP   Demonstrate   To entertain or perform in front of friends.
Or to help the disabled. To get nicknamed Sunshine.
To use sports or games to make an impact. To make

anything fun to use in camp. To be a talent agent. To dance. To gather people around.

ESFJ          Host          To run a marriage in the most traditional way with children's activities foremost. To put on seminars, events or conferences. To be a people person or in sales or business training. To work in customer service with a smile and manage an office using word processing, records management, and desktop publishing. To run the sales department with an eye to meeting customer's needs and handling customer's complaints. To be a household administrator. To knit, sew, or craft for children and family or to cook for a large or traditionally ethnic family and join associations, houses of worship, or community organizations.

INFJ          Consult          To teach language, poetry, or savor art. To motivate and inspire small groups about one's personal theories and intuition about inner world issues. To be a psychic, poet, or oracle. To express feelings and be emotional about educating people about their press or their personality type. To complain about advertising in the media and to save the world from the living room couch. To chair groups on the protection of animals or run a talk show or shopping channel.

INFP          Write     To write autobiographical interactive fiction for CD-Interactive laser disks. To play at being a psychologist. To make work fun and fun work. To play cautiously.
    To be pure and immaculate in middle age and beyond. To be an Emily Dicksonian-type poet.
    To be monastic, reclusive, and dedicated to research in science, art, or creativity enhancement. To quest after self identity. To illustrate. To find ways of making money at home using imagination.

ENFP          Counsel      To solve human problems at home. To be a rescuer.

ENFJ          Train        To be a public speaker. To sell ideas and intangibles. To train and persuade. To preach. To train executives in conflict management.

INTJ          Structure    To be a systems analyst . To organize businesses, associations, or fund raising events. To import. To manage scientists. To explore artificial intelligence in the nursery, to work with neural network robots, and fuzzy logic stuffed toys, To solve marital problems globally. To drive the mate to work as hard as the INTJ. To control and commandeer from behind the scenes, to have inner visions and theories about what makes people tick, and most of all, to organize and conquer. To drive people to work harder and find flaws in theories through inner visions and realizations whereby the INTJ sees patterns in nature and organizes the patterns, applying them to other situations, data, or objects.

INTP          Analyze      To be the architect of systems built by the INTJ. To analyze securities. To apply artificial intelligence to global database management. To create computer models to predict the environmental changes well into the future. To design categories. To use programming in more flexible ways. To define and map matrixes. To design art using special computer effects or math fractals. To theorize, differentiate, evaluate, and critique. To design new software or invent better hardware. To become an administrative psychologist and run a type research corporation or create a publishing company to study type. To enjoy being a recluse. To be a math tutor. To get people to pay the INTP to sit and think in a think tank or make the home into a think tank and search for a soul mate where there's a meeting of the thinking minds. To be free to think openly. To think for yourself and question all authority in the home and in the office. To explore the mind and the future. To marry an INFP who looks up to you for advice. To emphasize intelligence, logic, and rational thought of abstract ideas and theories. To understand and control nature. To have power over nature, the market, the self, and the object of interest. To study law and serve in the Senate. To be the brains behind the show.

ENTP　　　　　Market　　　To invent and travel for adventure as a free thinker. To sell ideas and other intangibles. To run a technical marketing company. To be a freethinker at home. To produce videos. To publish books for entrepreneurs globally. To seek adventure and travel, sometimes with an ESTP there to promote. To import and export or translate. To market type through seminars and speaking. To counsel upscale people. To network with people. To link telephones, cable T.V. and computers. To report the possibilities and alternatives in the news. To do what a man's gotta do as a visionary interested in change. To make visual through photography or video. To break old rules that no longer serve and improve them.

ENTJ　　　　　Lead　　　To lead a lover or a firm into new ventures. To practice command. To raise venture capital as an investment banker or broker. To make decisions all day long. To manage or be an administrator in a company which combines computer systems with education. To seek closure. To ask for information from a spouse instead of a decision. To take command of an organization or army and lead through extroverted thinking and intuition. To look at the big picture from angles not yet tried.

　　　　　　*　　　　　　*　　　　　　*

# Chapter Seventeen

## *The Undeveloped Flip Side Of Your Soul Mate's Personality*

Everyone's personality has an underbelly, a side not shown in public that acts like a bowl encasing a quiet ocean. The flip side can expose your most ugly, combative, or frantic tactics. You make wrong decisions and take the worst possible actions or say words that bring others down to lift yourself up. These actions come out under stress and when you're burned out. The flip side is described as the "inferior function" because it's the least-developed function of your personality. It's different from what C.G. Jung called the "shadow side" of your personality. The flip side is unfamiliar and takes you by surprise. You can't believe you reacted that way or said those words.

It's an almost reptilian side you don't want videotaped and shown to your friends and relatives. It's like the flip side of a card that comes out in ways that are embarrassing. This other side could be an explosive volcano or simply an oceanic attempt to fix a situation gone awry by taking unnecessary action to correct a mistake. By taking that action, your attempt to fix a problem sinks you deeper into trouble. The result is you now have more people to contact to correct your mistake. You have looked at a small cavity and dug a big hole. Your actions could have been anything from using guerrilla tactics instead of winning strategies to acting in an opposite way from how you usually act in a situation.

In 1921 psychoanalyst C.G. Jung described eight preference types: 1. extroverts with dominant sensing; 2. introverts with dominant sensing; 3. extroverts with dominant intuition; 4. introverts with dominant intuition; 5.

extroverts with dominant thinking; 6. introverts with dominant thinking; 7. extroverts with dominant feeling; 8. introverts with dominant feeling.

Isabel Briggs-Meyers and her mother, Katherine Briggs, together expanded Jung's preference types into the sixteen personality types of the Myers-Briggs Type Indicator.

How you personally use the theory of type development in matching the personality type of your potential lover or soul mate to the character of your own preferences is up to you.

Be aware that you could always put down another type because it's the type you'd want to be under the best of circumstances, or you think you're supposed to act that way to win your mate or to position yourself first in a relationship, marriage, or in a job. What your preferences are depends upon how honest to yourself you are in reporting your real self, that is, how you'd act or react under stress, in courtship when you wear your mask of charm, and when you feel you are most like the real you under most circumstances of life.

Type development is about achieving excellence in the use of your dominant personality type and good development of your auxiliary or second best in the first half of life. As you get older, you tend to want to develop a little more and stretch your third function, that is, the preference letter opposite the second letter of your four-letter type, which will be sensing or feeling.

For example, if your second letter is N for intuition, then your third function is S for sensing. If you second letter is S for sensing, than your third function is N, standing for intuition.

It's only until you're over the age of fifty that you finally get in touch with your fourth or inferior function. It's your shadow.

It's also the dominant preference of the mate you're most attracted to from a distance because you are pulled towards your inferior function operating in another human being.

Your inferior function becomes another person of opposite type's superior or dominant function. It's that person's ruling preference used to make decisions or take in information.

Although most people do marry opposite types, it spells big trouble in many cases. With a west coast divorce rate of more than 58%, perhaps it's time to stop and take a look at your own or compatible types with similar extroverted or introverted intuition or sensing preferences and similar thinking or feeling preferences.

Perhaps the truer definition of a soul mate could be someone who is as intuitive or sensing as you are when taking in information. Your soul mate would use either feeling or thinking (whichever you do) to make decisions.

It's less important in a marriage success whether you prefer quick closure (J for judging preference), or want to stay open minded longer to wait for newer information to come in, or respond by being spontaneous to surprise situations (P for perceiving preference) as the last letter of your four-letter type.

To understand more fully how the preferences work when picking your mate, let's take a look at the dark side of each type first-how people behave under extreme stress in marriage. Later we'll also see how each of the sixteen types goes mentally ill in different ways, according to their type and temperament preferences. Picture personality preferences as a photograph. We'll now look at the reverse sides, but in this case, the undeveloped or 'flip' sides.

## Introverts: Their Flip Sides
## Enneagram Type One: Or MBTI™ Type: ISTJ: Introverted, Sensing, Thinking Judging Dominant Introverted Sensing With Extroverted Thinking

### The ISTJ Man

1. ISTJ, the controller-manipulator who monitors and critiques. ISTJ is always doing what other people say should be done. He'll succeed

in an introverted business or technical profession like accounting, tax law, real estate, computer systems, or engineering and be a good provider.

He won't make many male friends to bring to the house, and will monitor and supervise you and household cleaning until you strike back wild and crazy. As a good provider, you'll never be poor in your old age with all that real estate he'll buy for you and ask you to manage because he can't stand dealing with people face to face.

## Under Stress: The Darkest Side Of ISTJ In Marriage

These descriptions are not meant to generalize or label people. Types, styles, and preferences of personalities are people and will behave differently and have different degrees or scores of any of the personality traits. People act what their genes and environment suggest. And some people score as one personality type but may be another. These are meant as examples only of types with preferences that can be used as characters by novelists. Use these descriptions to get a very general idea of how the different personalities react under extreme stress, and hold in your mind that all these descriptions are only the author's opinion based on reading. So don't think that if you marry a specific type that the person is going to act this way. Everyone's going to act differently under different stimulus or stress and in different situations.

Marry him if you like doing tax returns for a living. He hates noise and action and won't let you entertain. Don't marry him if you're an extravert who likes people over on weekends. As an excuse he'll tell you he's ashamed of the house to keep people away.

He'll have his own bedroom with a lock on the door for introvert privacy. Don't bug him and he'll let have a good allowance. Better yet, have your own income and be glad you're also an introvert.

## The ISFJ Man

## Enneagram Type Two Or MBTI Type ISFJ:
## ISFJ: Introverted, Sensing, Feeling, Judging

## Dominant Introverted Sensing With Extroverted Feeling

2. ISFJ, afraid of men, but a tyrant with powerful women and loyal: ISFJ with his sense of duty and loyalty will tell you that the only reason he's allowing you to live in "his" castle is because he's a spiritual person and that another guy would have dumped you years ago. The ISFJ male's best experience of a day off from work to relax is watching the 1946 film, "The Best Days of Our Lives" alone, while his wife watches her favorite TV show alone in her separate bedroom.

He'll hesitate before saying "I love you." He might say instead, "I want you to be my wife." He might address you as "love" one second and the next moment demand that you open the window in your bedroom because the room stinks. He'll repeat his same commands to open your window every day after that, controlling your privacy. You'll wonder why he imagines your room stinks and what's on his mind.

Indirectly, he'll let you know he loves you by buying a four plex and telling you that it's yours when you reach old age so you'll have a pension. Then he'll sell it out from under you in job loss panic to get his money out when he's laid off ten years before he planned to retire.

His high sense of duty to work places other people's needs way above yours, but his need for harmony in the house won't allow you to state your needs in an angry way.

If you're afraid to work and pull in your own weight in salary to contribute equally to the household, he could develop an anger that lasts a lifetime. This long-burning anger will cause him to withdraw any trace of warmth and affection. You'll lose his respect forever by not going out and looking for a real job. If you're a creative artist type and not making money from your work, he'll seethe with resentment for burdening him with the hard work of supporting you financially.

If the respect is lost, it won't come back. He'll put you down at every turn, until you become more like him and start earning money from any real job he approves as legal and moral. Artistic creativity in you means nothing to him. Loyalty and hard work at any honest work is important. It's more important that you earn money doing the grunt work than living your dream and not getting paid enough to make you less needy of his paycheck.

At the same time, he will secretly look around for an underdog worse off or disabled to be of service to and help. However, once you don't need him to support you emotionally and financially, he'll lose interest, and you'll always thought what he really wanted was to make you independent. He doesn't want to be responsible for your happiness is what he'll tell you, but his body language and behavior says he's so fearful of abandonment, that he'll keep you financially dependent by encouraging you at the same time to do your idealistic thing, to live your dream.

It's so confusing for the NF wife of an ISFJ man. For the clear-cut ISTJ wife, she knows she can supervise him and he'll respect her authority in running the tightest household in the traditional family business. The ISFJ man often joins the military only to drop out later for a job with a big, security corporation when he's not getting a promotion from an ISTJ supervisor in the military. In marriage, the ISTJ woman provides a military atmosphere to the home commanding the ISFJ man's respect and loyalty. Since he's not asking for a promotion at home, he can live with her as his soul mate.

For the artistic INFP woman married to the ISFJ man, he only becomes her soul mate for his ability to hold the same job longer than most men and above all odds, if he can keep from being distracted by his feelings.

His extroverted feeling combined with introverted super sensing could make him rather short-tempered, explosive as a volcano, and angered easily like the ENFJ man, especially in the presence of women with extroverted intuition that is his inferior function. The dominant extroverted intuition of the ENFP or ENTP woman could rub the ISFJ the wrong way. It's because extroverted intuition is his inferior function and the ENFP or ENTP's dominant (best) and most used function and his least developed function.

If the INFP woman can get his financial support for the lifetime of the marriage, she can truly live her creative dream in spite of his calling her a loser financially. The ISTJ, woman, however works to hard and earns too much money or other reward. She earns the ISFJ man's respect because he can't find any names to call her other than impersonal. She becomes his supervisor in the home and he honors her authority.

It's important to note that the ISFJ man can become a suicidal wife batter with an idealistic enough NF woman who is totally dependant on his financial support and angry at his name-calling because he's frustrated at her desire to escape reality for imagination to give herself the nurturing he has withdrew in anger at her hatred for routine and repetitive hard work.

An ISFJ man and ISFJ woman would be ideal, but the ISTJ woman would find her soul mate in the ISFJ man or another ISTJ man as well. Since, in the best interests of all, we do well with our own type, in spite of the blind spots.

If you're not an introverted sensing woman, he won't respect you verbally and can be a hot verbal abuser, but he's forever denying it because he sees himself as a spiritual person who can only do good deeds for strangers. This lover will probably go impotent after a few months of marriage because of his anger at your not being his ideal in spiritual virtues.

He won't leave you, even though he might have affairs if he has the money. If he's poor, and ISFJ men may have low incomes in non-management jobs with large institutions or corporations, he may settle for picking up women and driving them home sitting next to you. He picks up women like strays on vacation with you and feels it's all innocent since you're sitting next to him in the car while he lends a helping hand to a single woman by driving her home. Meanwhile you wanted a romantic experience alone with him.

He will stick out the marriage long after the horse has died. If you try to beat the dead horse, he'll withdraw further into his introversion and talk loudly to himself but rarely talk to you except in commands. He's afraid of other men and will ask you to make some of his phone calls for him, (when he has to ask a favor) but he'll have no second thoughts about silencing you by turning up his radio louder. If he doesn't like what you did or finds it unethical he won't think twice about putting a gun at the side of your head to get your attention or spilling a cup of water in your face to make a point. Extroverted feeling rules this introverted super sensing man. He's concrete and interested in details and could laugh at you for being a loser if you choose a creative path. As a husband, he will neglect you emotionally when he can no longer be of help to you as you rise in your career. Often, he'll hunt for a woman with disabilities to help so he'll feel appreciated, especially if he doesn't get appreciation at work. He has a hard time saying no to being asked to work long hours on the job. This man may be highly dependent on his job, and when he retires will look for others to help.

He may be washed in vanity, narcissism, deeply concerned about his appearance or weight. He could fast for long periods of time and then toss a book in your face splitting open your lip if you make the wrong sound while stretching or yawning. This man is more concerned about getting facelifts for himself and hair transplants than he is about your emotional needs. He'll stop sex early in the marriage and retreat to his own room. If you ask him for a hug or a back rub or massage (forget sex) he'll tell you to wait until he goes on vacation, then promptly forget what he promised. He holds onto money at times and brings you down to reality. The ISFJ man is not a big spender on a vacation.

## Under Stress: The Darkest Side Of ISFJ In Marriage

This man thinks even children are too expensive to have, better put your money in real estate. When the miserly or tight-with-money ISFJ conservator/guardian man gets angry enough in the marriage that you won't do what he wants you to do or that you disagree with his views too many times, the first to go is sex and kissing.

He simply exempts himself from any need to give you pleasure. The more you love a big spender, the tighter the ISFJ will become doling out money and affection.

As an adult, he'll still give you an allowance of only enough food money to survive. You'll have to earn everything else yourself. He'll encourage you to ride the bus instead of learning to drive to save money. This man is afraid of scarcity and will often tell people you'll spend the money he works so hard earning only over his dead body.

It's important to have your own well-paying career with the ISFJ male. At the same time, he wants someone who's disabled or in some way an underdog so he can help you survive on a pittance and take care of you, as long as you don't become too much of a burden. He'll often call you a lazy loser if you're not working and pulling your own weight bringing home the bread and frying it up for him exactly the same time every day when he comes home from work.

He's guaranteed not to show you any form of body touching except an occassional simple hug in which his eyes are averted and his head turned away from you at a right angle watching something else-usually the television screen. If you try to talk, he'll stop allowing talking in the house except when he feels like asking you to do something around the house.

You talk and he turns up the radio louder or says, "Tune me out, I'm reading." Destroy the harmony in the home he craves and he'll shove you around. The only touching he's familiar with may be hitting.

However, if things go smoothly, he'll keep his distance, go to work, and give you just enough food money to keep you from starving, and not a penny more.

Many spouses of ISFJ men report having to take the price tags off all the groceries so there won't be a verbal fight. He'll usually ask how much anything is before you buy it for yourself or him.

Make sure with this man you have your own steady job. Keep your bank account in your own name and for your eyes only. He'll work forever at the utilities company at a routine job and love the security. When the ISFJ is under extreme stress, or you don't meet his picture of the dutiful woman, this man is perfect for the woman who loves routine, the simple life, hates changes and thinks sex is ridiculous.

He'll want you to work side by side with him in the garage holding a lamp or mopping the floor, just to put you to work because he can't stand your desire to only sit and think or create your dream. The NF or NT woman gets on his nerves. These intuitive women cause his temper to explode the more she extraverts intuition and imagination at the same moment he wants her to do some practical work around the house or get a "real job" that pays, like his.

He finds the NF not useful and the NT too arrogant for his strong extraverted feelings and fear of abandonment. He despises most of all a loud, pushy woman who refuses to work and pull her own weight around the house as well as outside it. The silent woman pulls him closer because he is usually silent at home himself to his wife. Yet the moment the ISFJ man comes home from work, he is most likely to call a co-worker at the office, and they will chat for hours. The minute he hangs up, he has nothing to say to his wife. He tells her, "tune me out, I'm busy. I have to study or write checks."

The silent ISTJ woman will busy herself. The similar ISFJ woman will understand, but her temper is shorter than his. She will turn to her decorating or flowers and introvert the anger until it hardens as resentment within her, finally causing her to come down with early signs of aging inside her body-or the most painful flare up of hemorrhoids. The ISFJ can be a real pain in the butt to any woman other than ISTJ or ISFJ.

The ISFJ/ISFJ bond in marriage is the least likely to divorce and the hardest to separate. They will bond the tightest and are inseparable. A high number of children from ISTJ/ISFJ marriages are rebellious INFPs. A high frequency of the ISTJ partners are in the military. If it's a soul mate you're after, it's best to know that ISFJ men really need ISTJ or ISFJ women for a long, happy marriage.

Otherwise, in the deepest throes of marital stress, the ISFJ male could hit the depths of depression and suddenly turn that anger out on the wife in one great explosion.

If not, over the mellowing years of the marriage, he can become so withdrawn emotionally, that the two will live alone in the same house for decades, until one partner dies, without ever having touched or spoken to one another except for the briefest of comments.

They may even go out once a year together, but sit in separate rows at events. If you're an NF woman in great need of nurturing, attention, and affection from your soul mate, sitting next to an ISFJ man at dinner means paying for yourself and having him comment on how much food you're putting on that plate that's going to waste and how he can't stand it.

You may never get love from an ISFJ man, but you'll get a house whose mortgage is paid off and enough of a vegetarian diet to barely survive. The rest is up to you earning your own way and finding other ways of getting your nurturing without learning to shoplift or secretly pee on your enemy's carpet or steal from your spouse's wallet each time he hurts your feelings with a comment of control.

So it's best for SJs to marry other SJs and be what they are: soul mates discovering pathways to keeping family secrets. The ISFJ man immediately will be taken for granted by his soul mate. Once the courting charm and mask comes down, he'll lose interest in his wife and take her for granted, too.

## The ISFJ Woman

**ISFJ: Dominant Introverted Sensing, With Extraverted Feeling, Judging.**
**Enneagram Type 2 With A 1 Wing Or ISFJ On The MBTI ™. Also, Less Frequently, (like the ESFJ) Enneagram Type 6 With A 5 Wing.**

The ISFJ under stress becomes an undervalued doormat who is taken for granted by her mate. She bottles her resentment which later causes symptoms like angina pectoris and related physical symptoms of premature aging inside the circulatory system. In this way, she is like the overworked ISTJ.

Bottled up emotion can lead to cycles of depression for the ISFJ woman, more frequently than for NF types. The ISFJ woman, like the ISTJ man, has a fatalistic outlook that increases under stress.

It's as if she's following a pessimistic script in life centered on saving and hoarding. Each member of her family fits into his and her place in a hierarchy. Only an ISFJ woman would put up with the SP mate hell-bent on freedom and adventure. It contrasts to the ISFJ woman's cautious behavior. Yet this kind of soul mate leads to her demise and suffering. Her play is catering to others and her mate wants her to cater to him. She wants to be liked by co-workers and neighbors and caters to them instead of to her mate. The SP seeks revenge on her.

When her SP mate acts out, the ISFJ woman goes into a deep depression and threatens suicide to manipulate her mate into catering to her needs to see her mate as a team player. He may be a loner. She denies her responsibility to her mate. She accuses him of abandoning him. Her greatest fear is of abandonment herself.

She plays the ISFJ game of whining and complaining. He belts her one for being a nag. Her health plummets from the resentment held inside.

Her day is spent speaking of the guilt she feels for imaginary mistakes made at work. She seeks exemption from burdens. For example, one ISFJ spouse was so upset that her INFP mate's children from a first marriage were returning to live in the same city after 20 years of living with their mother elsewhere, that she asked her husband for a divorce. When she found out the children were getting married and wouldn't ask her for money or to move in, she cancelled the divorce. She felt relief at getting back her privacy at home, after decades of living in a childless marriage.

The ISFJ woman, like the ISFJ man, feels guilt and remorse constantly for a series of imagined mistakes at work or neglect of duty at home. Frequent complaints about neglect of duty in many areas of life drive the mate up the wall, unless the mate is also ISFJ or ISTJ.

The anxiety expressed by the ISFJ woman coupled by depression, angers the optimistic NF spouse. The ISFJ woman thinks she's mother nature when she hunts for her soul mate because she has more SJ men from which to select. There are more SJ temperament people in the world than any other preference. Australia's dominant personality type of both sexes is the ISFJ.

The right soul mate for the ISFJ women is an SJ man. It's not a traveling SP man (especially not ESTP) who gives her a rush of adrenaline when she thinks of rescuing him from his freedom, fun, gambling, performing, and desire to get high, and not her opposite type whose gift of gab and smooth presentations excite her, the ENTP man.

She'll see the NT man as arrogant and snobbish. He'll make her feel dumb and slow to learn. The optimistic, joyful NF man will feel dragged down by her pessimism and cycles of depression. The melancholic INFP man has something in common with ISFJ woman-loyalty and commitment to the marriage, but he won't be in a secure enough job to ease her feelings of pending disaster.

Frequently ISFJ women end up teaching special education classes or managing apartment complexes where they meet ISTJ men who they train, who later become their supervisors. They begin to resent the fact that they are not promoted and at the same time fear promotion.

They see promotion as job endangerment and perceive the middle managers supervising them as being most likely to lose their job first because they don't do hands-on fixing anymore. The ISFJ woman sees husband hunting in the same light. They feel meetings are a waste of time, when doing the grunt work is more useful.

The ISFJ woman under marital stress becomes less verbal. Her silence may infuriate her mate because she's less likely to talk if the problem can be hidden and denied. She holds opinions made by established groups on one hand and fights for moral and ethical causes such as animal rights.

The ISFJ woman hates impulsive men. Her most hated of all is the mentally disturbed ESTP shoplifter or loud, swearing ENTJ commanding officer who uses "bad" words to push the little people around.

She hates the school, corporate, and military bully, yet so often timidly marries a man who bullies her. When she picks a place to work, it's usually in the school, large corporation, hospital, or military she serves with dutiful loyalty.

A woman whose life is so hard-working and routine an ISFJ, for example, could have an under aroused nervous system that needs to be stimulated by service to the sick, such as in a high stress job like nursing and teaching.

The ISFJ in her attempt to rescue a man she sees as a victimized underdog, or a helpless cripple, or a blind or deaf alcoholic, may marry the person and try to find him a job. An ISFJ needs to be shown that as much as she fears change herself, her attempts at finding a soul mate lie in the root of changing the other to be more like herself, an SJ. She is attracted to the excitement of the SP temperament that could be fatal to her when the SP strikes back after being manipulated by an SJ too long.

What she really is after is increasing her need to be needed. For only in being of service can the ISFJ woman feel securely wanted and needed. Her greatest fear is to be fired from her job that pays the bills to survive.

She feels that the more service and loyalty she offers, the more secure her job will be. The need to be of service is extended to a mate. Her husband has to argue that good financial planning for old age means having paid off real estate investments to live on when laid off the job at a stage in life when energy is winding down.

# INFJ

## Enneagram Type 4 With 5 Wing Or INFJ On The MBTI ™
**INFJ: Introverted, Intuitive, Feeling, Judging**
**Dominant Introverted Intuition With Extroverted Feeling**

3. INFJ, an inspiration if you look up to him. INFJ, ready to tell you how you can be better, but you're never good enough. INFJ is a most empathic lover. He's very aware of your feelings, but he won't do anything about them. INFJ majors in interpersonal dynamics. He knows you need positive strokes and to be told he loves you.

This poet, language teacher, or writer's extroverted feeling and introverted intuition with its inner visions will stress out the introverted feeling and extroverted intuition of the INFP wife, whom he usually marries for her interest in the arts and the way she inspires his creativity. Both share an interest in what makes people tick.

His ranting and raving in his flip side on why his wife won't answer letters or take action immediately may reveal the INFJ male's judging nature to come to conclusions and make decisions on plan and on track, whereas his INFP wife may want to wait until new information enters the scene. For an INFJ male, the ENFJ woman brings him out of his shell, even when he's in his flip side with his underbelly exposed and vulnerable. They make a great team—ENFJ and INFJ. Both have extroverted feeling and can be twin volcanoes working for a cause.

## Under Stress: The Darkest Side Of INFJ In Marriage

As an introverted, judging feeler, the INFJ male will have to be inspired before he'll say anything like those tender words. And inspiration day may be in the far future or distant past. He'll be a passionate lover only when he feels inspired, never mind your needs. You'll have to remind him to force himself to show affection, but if you're the same way, then two INFJ's may make things happen by attending marriage encounter workshops.

Make him trust you more and he'll open up, but he'll never be as romantic as an extravert. Then again, the extrovert likes people so much, that the chances he'll cheat on you are that much greater than with an introvert whose feeling is turned inward.

This is the guy who enjoys sex so much more by himself than with a partner. He's shy and critical, but he'll make lots of money with his writing to shower on his second wife. If you're an astrologer or professor, marry him because you'll go on great field trips together as anthropologists in New Guinea.

## The INFJ Woman

## Enneagram Type 4 With A 5 Wing Or INFJ On The MBTI ™.
## INFJ: Introverted, Intuitive, Feeling, Judging
## Dominant Introverted Intuition With Extroverted Feeling

INFJ, a communicator who studies communicators, a poet, artist, teacher, writer, or human resources manager who must have a steady job where seeing patterns in everything and bringing those patterns together to make a conclusion about people's behavior allow her to express her extroverted feelings.

Her inferior function or flip side is extroverted sensing. That's why she's so attracted to her opposite type, the restless ESTP promoter/wheeler-dealer. The ESTP will soon tire of her and leave her in a marriage when she becomes a rope around his neck and restricts his freedom to charm other women.

She may end up with the ENTP seminar conductor/speaker and entrepreneur, but soon find they can't work together because his dominant extroverted intuition tires out her dominant introverted intuition. It's her dominant introverted intuition that drives her to understand why people act as they do from the observation point of the newsletter publisher writing about life rather than out there in the action, living it, crisis by crisis.

It's the ISFJ or the INTJ man who will do more than sweep her off her feet. He'll sweep the marital problems of her loneliness and his withdrawal under the rug and sweep her back to reality and a steady paycheck.

The INFJ woman not only sees patterns in everything and ususally writes about them in newsletters and books about behavior and personality, but often is a gifted artist using intuition instead of sensing to capture a unique reality that sees everything in symbols and metaphors.

The INFJ woman can distance herself from a relationship within marriage as much as the ISFJ male, so they are well suited to each other in a dance-away marriage. The INFJ woman will give her husband gifts, cards, notes, or special foods, rather than tell him in words of her love and devotion, including self-sacrifice.

The INFJ woman's personality is totally about focusing on inner alternatives, possibilities, and patterns (spirals) in nature, including her own nature. She trusts only her inner images, not those of her husband. An ideal husband for her, the ISFJ, would trust only his inner sensing images that merge with her intuitive images.

With an objective, INTJ husband, she'll be driven as hard as he drives himself and criticized if there's any way he can find to improve her. The ISFJ man won't drive her as hard. They both share the feeling auxiliary and will walk a mile in each other's shoes, and show empathy toward each other in a way most feeling types do.

INFJ is not really interested in sex and sensation-seeking or physical touching when she's not in the mood. She may not like to be touched when she's meditating, or she may feel her husband's hugs hurt the arteries in her neck or are painful.

If she marries the ENFJ man who runs after her, they will find a great sense of humor together, including biting satire. He'll bring out the fun-loving laughter in her. However, his need to be touched and hugged is so great.

Her need to "dance away" from sensuous things when she's in the introverted intuition mode, is so driving. He would be the one to feel lonely and emotionally neglected in the marriage, in spite of the great business relationship ENFJ and INFJ have working together. When her extroverted feelings match the ENFJ's extroverted feelings, there is much in common. The INFJ woman has a choice, depending on what she wants from a marriage, to choose among the ISFJ, INFJ, INTJ or ENFJ mates.

The real soul mate depends on what she wants from the marriage: the introverted sensation of the ISFJ? The same type as herself-with perhaps, different actions as INFJs vary in score and degree, and can be very different? The hard-driving executive-type or scientific INTJ always looking at future trends? or the ENFJ smooth talking presentations man and trainer or psychologist whose dominant extroverted feeling harmonizes with her auxiliary extroverted feeling (the way she deals with the outside world).

He'll bring her lots of fun and joy, humor and laughter. However, the ENFJ male with the INFJ woman will soon show his two-faced, Jekyll and Hyde personality under stress. He could get hurt by her "don't touch me" chill when she needs to look inward to energize.

INFJ woman needs to be alone or work alone in order to focus on her inner visions. She needs a sensing man to market those visions or images in art, writing, or publishing, and create visibility for her. She trusts her inner insights will feed a great need in the community and make money for her. She needs someone to market her ideas, someone she can trust totally.

INFJ women make their mark on life by looking at love from both sides now-from all angles and writing about it or illustrating it. The will sell insight on your insight, if only someone extroverted out there could market their inner images for them in a practical, useful way appealing to the masses.

In the helping professions or in art or publishing, the INFJ woman, like the INFP, is a natural born psychic/clairevoyant. Her niche is foresight. If she can translate that intuition into trend forecasting and futurism, she has a niche market on which to make a living or a lovelife.

The INFJ needs to study trends. For that information, she often turns to the INTJ or INTP think tank director, involved in analyzing and forecasting trends of the future of labor, environment, health, education, psychology, or creativity.

Known as the prophet or psychic type, the INFJ woman is tired of being labeled idiosyncratic and filled with magical thinking. She's naturally into the expressive arts and creativity studies, but in a different way than the INFP. The INFP shares everything with her husband.

The INFJ will not share what goes on inside. The introverted intuition is an impression of an impression. The INFP's extroverted intuition is a database of networking resources, but the INFJ's inner impressions take in symbolic patterns and archetypes. This contrasts to the ISFJ's mind as an inner photographic plate that takes pictures. (C.G. Jung, believed to be an INTJ, shared with the INFJ, impressions of archetypes as symbols of human development.)

## INFJ: Under Great Stress: The Darkest Side Of Marriage

With enough stress, the INFJ could become convulsive when there is no underlying organic problem, or even become catatonic when actually mentally ill. She becomes that type of statue that won't move. And normal INFJ women, when they feel immovable, will become convulsive or twitchy, like the ENFJ under pressure, or tic-filled or shaky and not know why they can't stop shivering, shaking, quaking, blinking, squinting, or ticking when faced with changes or travel.

Like the ENFJ, under stress, the INFJ is prone to seizures and convulsing when there is no organic reason found for such symptoms. Her insights often cannot be brought out. They are not clear. To the INFJ they appear as impressions that can't be put into words.

They have trouble sharing their insights with the outside world, and live by leaps of faith in their inner impressions or visions. INFJs often say that they are channelers, mediums, psychics, spoon-benders, magicians, past-life regressionists, hypnotherapists, and UFO contactees. They find it hard to walk the gauntlet of the ESTP and ESTJ types who ridicule them in their most highly held inner insights.

Under stress, the INFJ woman might tell her spouse that she knows exactly what he is going to say next. INFJs always have "a feeling" and find that trying to share that feeling weakens and exposes them to the gauntlet. Under stress, the INFJ will interrupt her mate in midsentence frequently. INFJs have volcanic, extroverted feelings combined with introverted intuition that allows them to focus on inner visions. Often they become therapists or teachers and enjoy poetry or the written word and art. Their inferior function is sensing and dominant function is extroverted feeling with introverted intuition.

One INFJ woman walked up to a total stranger waiting at a bus stop bench and proceeded to tell the woman next to her what her ethnic origin and religion was, and what city she was born in. The woman was totally embarrassed-because she had guessed right-and because she thought the INFJ was putting her down by singling her out as looking like the stereotype of that particular ethnicity.

With strangers, the INFJ woman is the most empathetic of types and sensitive to other's feelings. However, with her mate, she is first to call her husband selfish when he doesn't do what she wants. She uses her extroverted feelings to complain to total strangers about the intimate details of her marriage, and then makes sure she never sees the same people again, once she's spilled her life story.

Under stress, the INFJ woman becomes even more stubborn than the INFP woman. She has strong devotion to her inner feelings, but can't put them down concretely and in simple words to share with the outer world. Instead, she turns her inner feelings into conflicts that turn into physical symptoms of pain, particularly ulcerated hemorrhoids.

Insight and foresight surround the life of the INFJ woman. Whenever there is conflict in the marriage, the INFJ woman uses insight and foresight impressions to grab onto the conflict and twist it into different kinds of bodily pains that seem to correspond to the type of conflict-at work, at home, with different pains in different parts of the body suffered in the presence of different disliked people or situations.

For example, migraines for conflict with the boss, chest pains for conflict with a spouse, and a prolapsed rectum for conflict with the children or in-laws. INFJ women consider conflict a sure sign that she's a defeated personality, that she's lost the battle to live by her inner visions.

Meditation and gentle Yoga, are usually recommended for the INFJ woman who tenses up on the telephone or in the presence of conflict or disagreeable people.

Under stress, the INFJ woman's speech becomes slower and lower-pitched, to barely a whisper. She bottles up her rage inside and turns it into her own bodily symptoms.

Stress to an INFJ woman means her inner needs and outer needs are being separated by her spouse or other relatives. Her judging attitude needs organization, orderliness, and planning-including making lists to please the outer world bearing down on her. Priorities rip her aparat.

She would like to get back into the womb and cocoon of her inner world. So she may turn to rebirthing techniques to achieve harmony. She keeps inner personal journals. Her inner needs focus on the opposite-adaptability, flexibility, freedom (like the INFP has in her outer world), and spontaneity.

Trouble in marriage comes from the man and/or children trying to pin down the INFJ woman. She needs quick closure, decisions that have been finished so she can go on to the next priority. She doesn't want any more commitments and responsibilities. (An ISFJ husband would take some of those burdens on himself as his duty.)

At home INFJ rebels and suddenly lets her house go to disorder and disarray, or she may wear disheveled clothing. Or she may go to the other extreme and run a shopping channel. She may write about designer clothing and cosmetic surgery. She tries to fool the world into thinking she's making decisions based on INTJ logic. She feels guilty about the masquerade, that she's not being authentic, so her volcanic temper explodes in blame on others on minute details, since her inferior function is keeping records of minute details or observing with the senses (extroverted sensing). She may focus on going back to check her bookkeeping again and again to correct errors, taking twice as long as an ISTJ would in checking details for flaws.

Instead of focusing on her outstanding intuition, she may try to excel in the world of logic. When she's steamrolled by the INTJ who may eventually want to conquer her and marry her, she feels he's there to make her his housecleaning slave. She begins to seethe with inner rage. She develops doubt in her own abilities, feels she's in the wrong job or wrong relationship.

Doubt about her abilities is the curse of the INFJ woman. Under stress, INFJ avoids the real world and at the same times realizes she has given little of herself to the world. She may withdraw even further. At home, she resents the overconfidence of her husband, or belittles him for his own self doubt, particularly if he's an ISFJ who puts himself down to show how great is his humility and humbleness. Often the INFJ woman teaches English or languages or writes poetry.

She may try to marry a rich, overconfident, or educated man to rise vicariously on his credentials and achievements, if she doubts her own abilities-instead of focusing on developing what skills and talents she has.

Her inferior function is sensing, the world of the practical, useful, detail-driven pragmatic realist. The INFJ woman feels a drive to avoid the real world. She looks for ways to escape, usually with a creative INFP pal at bookworm's conventions, where she keeps meeting ENTP men, particularly at science fiction and journalist's conventions, where she longs to meet investigative reporters using extroverted intuition in their research.

She worries that her own research will remain on the shelf without a way to make it of interest to the sensing type masses. Under extreme stress in the darkest side of marriage, the INFJ woman feels the urge to hoard and collect details in great piles on subjects she might need in the future for some job offer or project.

She will collect anything and everything. Newspapers can get stacked from the floor to ceiling. Nothing gets thrown out, if it could serve a purpose in the future.

The paper draws roaches, and her husband has a hard time throwing out the stacks of unrelated details she collects with no apparent goal or relationship of one detail to another. INFJ women do have goals, however. Their goal is to wonder if wherever they are in life, if it is truly the place that works for them.

It's not easy to find an INFJ wife, but they keep running into ISFJ, INFP, ENFJ, and INTJ men at personality type conventions.

INFJs, like INFPs, make up only one percent of the United States population. It's difficult for an INFJ woman to meet an INFJ man.

INFJ women frequently advertise for a relationship in the publications most read by INFJs and INFPs. These are the human resources management magazines, type-related newsletters and publications, journalism schools, the psychology and communications departments of various universities, English majors and teachers of English and anthropology in colleges, and writer's and artist's convention bulletins.

Many INFJ women and men work as human resource managers, career counselors or consultants and are in the recruiting business or in training. Like ENFJ men, they subscribe to the training magazines and join professional associations for trainers and counselors. INFJs join the clergy or take up religious pursuits of the intuitive kind, where they meet INFPs and ENFJs. INFJ women are also found at archaeology conferences, particularly Biblical archaeology meetings, and have an avid interest in reading anthropology books.

Under stress, loneliness is the biggest complaint of INFJ women. They are often desperately lonely, and yet prefer solitude above all other pursuits. The more stressed an INFJ woman is, the more she doubts she has any power to reach her potential, and may join a cult in order to find the right path.

Often, after broken by mental drilling, she comes out still vulnerable, disillusioned about how women were encouraged to be powerless about their own life plan. In her hour of acute stress, she looks to an impersonal INTJ man as her role model.

Instead, she should be looking inside herself to find her path-through healing others or writing about how others are healed. She could find happiness with an ISFJ man who respects her insight, symbols, and ability to connect patterns in nature.

The INFJ woman's insights are extremely subjective and personal. Under stress, she needs to turn to inner personal journaling and ask her mate to do the same with his dreams.

# INTJ

## Enneagram Type One With A Two Wing Or INTJ On The MBTI ™
## INTJ: Introverted, Intuitive, Thinking, Judging
## Dominant Introverted Intuition With Extroverted Thinking

4. INTJ is the most independent of all the males. If you're just as independent a woman, you'll demand the same in your mate. He won't give you support or assistance, and you wouldn't want him to because you're a superwoman, right?

This man will let you sink, so don't date him if you're trying to learn to swim. If you're an expert in his field, the two of you can make science together. Marry him if you want a partner with whom to win the Nobel prize.

## Under Stress: The Darkest Side Of INTJ In Marriage

If you have children with him, he might not lend a hand, and he could crush you when you go weak on him. He thinks he's invincible, yet despises weakness in himself and drives others as hard as he is driven by his need for perfection, efficiency, and improvement. He believes in the survival of the fittest and most competent. Make sure you're more of a man than he is before you bond with him. And don't ever get sick. He won't take care of you when you're down. This Caesar thinks he's a conqueror with inner visions of power, control, and megalomania. His reach for power is about understanding and controlling nature

You'll have fun watching him sink three times to learn to swim, but only if you're another INTJ, and he'll do the same to you. It's work at first sight. Both of you have something lovely in common that will make the marriage stick. You're both into taking charge of the abstract future and make a great team of engineers or scientists working together to build a family of robot visions with artificial intelligence. Under stress, he makes quick decisions based on the flaws he uncovers in other people's research, theories, or acts of creation.

He may think his inner visions reveal understanding that machines don't break, people do. He may be afraid what he is looking for has disappeared eons ago. Watch him perform his rituals as he organizes businesses, empires, or his animation hobby, usually getting highly creative people to do the work the way he has organized the plans.

## The INTJ Woman

## Enneagram Type 5 With A 6 Wing Or INTJ On The MBTI™

### INTJ: Introverted, Intuitive, Thinking, Judging
### Dominant Introverted Intuition With Extroverted Thinking

INTJ, a woman who also uses her inner visions to rule reality with an iron hand inside a velvet glove. The INTJ woman, like the INFJ, sees patterns in everything with her dominant introverted intuition. However, her extroverted logical thinking travels outward to be shared by the marketplace crying for a better mousetrap.

She connects the dots, sees the patterns, fills the void, puts the puzzle together, and makes the money. She won't predict the future as a psychic would do. She needs to use the scientific method to prove her hypothesis.

Once she is believed through logical validation, she scientifically forecasts future trends about anything that has a market. She doesn't channel feelings.

Instead, she uses a computer, market research surveys, or other means of audience and trend tracking to make money. INTJ, like ISTJ woman has seen evidence that people pay people more frequently to think than to feel in the laboratory or corporate world. (She believes only psychotherapists, nannies, and the clergy are paid to feel.) She takes the patterns she sees and logically markets them in the world of think tanks and brainstorming groups.

The INTJ's insights are impersonal and objective. She is a woman who needs to show the world her self-confidence as she makes her executive decisions. Her niche is in marketing or science research, and her soul mate is an ISTJ in experimental psychology or in the military.

The highly intelligent, intellectual (or would like to be) INTJ woman wants her soul mate to trust her logical decisions based on weighing pros against cons. Most men have a hard time putting that much logic in a woman's hands because of the old stereotypes about women leaders. The hard-driving, arrogant INTJ takes action to organize businesses as her mate begins to doubt the strong attachment she has to her intuition because she can't come up with the logistics of the long-term marriage relationship.

NT and SJ women are more likely to leave a marriage if they really have to with the confidence that they will not be a burden on society. It's the INFP and ISFP women who more often worry that they'll end up bag ladies, especially the INFP women with generalist, liberal arts educations who have trouble playing the corporate games.

She fears most her mate's desire to have children. Inside, she really doesn't want children to come between her and future on the career track- at least before the age of forty.

She has a deep fear that pregnancy and staying home with babies will "rot her mind," as the INTJ women of the late sixties put it. She'd sacrifice anything for a career-track job, or a doctorate in the field she loves to research. The INTJ woman wants challenge in a marriage. If she's not getting totally saturated with challenge in her job or education, she demands challenge in her marriage. INTJ rarely buckles under competition or runs to take cover under the umbrella of the first man willing to support her and pay the rent when the work place plays rough and tough.

INTJ will compete. She believes if she loses in competition to her mate, she will lose part of herself. Winning is everything to her. An ENTJ husband will challenge her. The ISTJ husband may continue to argue the fine points of logistics with her.

The majority of lawyers are INTJs. If she's an INTJ attorney, she could form a partnership in marriage and in law with an ISTJ or ENTJ lawyer and challenge him to a meeting of the minds at home as well as in court. However, her true soul mate lies in marrying not a lawyer if she's one herself, but a physician, preferably another INTJ.

Good marriage prospects for the INTJ woman are INTJ, ENTJ, ESTJ, and ISTJ. Her soul mate is, however, the ISTJ or INTJ man. If she needs a husband to run her business while she withdraws into the think tank research mode, the ENTJ will take over, while the ISTJ and ESTJ could run her corporation into the ground by arguing over logistics and details she'd rather delegate to the financial comptroller.

## INTJ: Under Stress: The Darkest Side Of The Marriage

She won't pay attention. Her impersonal mind is not on you, under stress, but on her introverted intuition. Such an inner force drives you out of her mind while she searches for patterns to connect, for symbols to market, and for trends to track.

What stresses her most is when her husband has no faith in her insights because they come from her innards. Each time she's not taken seriously, her stress escalates.

If she's ready to fall apart, she will not give a damn how you're affected by her actions. She'll always cut a man off in mid-sentence when her inner insights provide the right vectors to her destination.

Under stress the INTJ woman becomes a hard-driving, inflexible and obnoxious bully, including name-calling, belittling, and bullying other women around the office and bullying her husband for "not saying something logical-while she's thinking."

She'll give anything for a job that will pay her to sit and think. When she finds the information she wants, her inner reaction is that of a megalomaniac in battle. Whatever insight flashes on her, she lets you know she's right and must not be questioned, although she'll demand to be challenged scientifically.

The INTJ woman starts spouting how absolute her impersonal, objective truth really is when she's on the verge of falling apart with stress. The more the stress increases, the more she'll insist what she states is unchallengeable truth. She'll rip up all the logical data you give her. Her anger will explode if you disagree with her.

Only her insight counts, rigid as rigor mortis. It's got to be right, she says, because she's stepping out of her feelings like she would step out of yesterday's underwear. Once she's stepped out of her feelings, she believes her dominant introverted intuition can feed her only reality-simply because she's objective.

Under stress, conversation will be clipped and soon forbidden. The evidence the INTJ woman requests under stress, is soon ignored and takes last place to her inner visions.

The INTJ woman is the most skeptical of all the types. She believes nothing. She's a debunker of false prophets, magicians, psychologists, and scientists, and especially a debunker of men romancing her.

She's so skeptical, she really doesn't believe in Mr. Right. Her skepticism prevents her from believing marriages can be good or lasting (unless her parents had a good and lasting marriage).

She's disillusioned by dating. About men, she'll suspend judgment, unless under stress. Then she'll jump in with clichés about marriage, referring to a book of quotes on the institution throughout history.

The INTJ woman's soul mate needs to be a man who relaxes in the face of her intellectual skepticism. Such men include the ISTJ, INTJ, or ENTJ. A soul mate is a man who is relaxed, not challenged, by the INTJ woman.

Any man who seeks clarity from her could be Mr. Right. All she wants in a man is for him to seek her in order to receive understanding. It's impossible for the INTJ woman to suspend judgment without suffering a total loss of self. It's as if she lost the competition to her hated rival, or won the competition and had to see her best friend lose everything to restore the INTJ woman's power.

Power is what the INTJ woman is about. Achievement and power forms the basis of not only her career, but the core of her marriage. It's what she seeks in a soul mate. If she can't control her man, she won't marry him.

She won't fall in love quickly. Spontaneity is poison. It's the sign of the wuss or wimp. INTJ believes femininity is weakness or "chickenization."

An INTJ would be most likely to place the 1983 poem (by me) "The Chickenization of Women" on a wall plaque. It reads: "Have you ever noticed how often women are referred to as poultry? Young women are chicks. Married women cluck at parties. They egg men on. Mothers watch their broods. Child-rearing ends with the empty-nest syndrome. Husgands at home are henpecked by their wives. Runaway wives have flown the coop while stay-at-home husbands feel cooped up.

"The object of W.C. Fields' affection was 'My little Chickadee." Married women feather ther nests. She complains her alimony is birdseed, by her ex calls her a vulture.

"In Arabic, a beautiful woman is a fistoo, a piece of chicken thigh. Women are old crows, mother hens, or biddies. "She's no spring chicken," say men about mature women. To be feminine is to be a weak chicken. Is it just foul, or a coincidence that so many women's wages are chicken-feed?"

The analytical, disciplined INTJ woman is a commanding, demanding personality that dominates the commanding personality of the ENTJ male who flees from her into the INFP's arms. If INTJ woman thinks her soul mate is weak, she will offer him her sharp-tongued judgments.

If frustrated in her need for a leadership role, the INTJ will take the matter to the highest courts. She thrives on court battles, and is not intimidated by attorneys screaming in her face and pounding wood. Values and people can be ignored. She's no sensitive INFP or ISFP who will go to pieces if challenged.

The INTJ woman likes to point her finger at the audience when she talks, much the same as the ENTJ woman. She sees no people-oriented road to achieving her objectives. Under stress, INTJ keeps her inner visions to herself and her mouth shut, unless asked to analyze objectively.

Under stress, she is not balanced by the needs of the people around her. Her inferior function is sensing-dealing with real details, logistics. For help here, she needs her ISTJ soul mate to handle the facts and realities.

Without ISTJ, she has no factual basis for an analytical decision based on her logic or inner intuition. Here, intuition is turned inward, so she can't share it during a brainstorming session without a need to pause and write down her insights. ENTP can run over her during a brainstorming session using dominant extroverted intuition.

Under stress, the dark side of marriage makes INTJ go to extremes with facts, carrying details to an obsession-compulsion that gets on everyone's nerves. She'll check numbers again and again, feeling anxiety unless the numbers are rechecked over and over. You'll find facts and details piled from floor to ceiling, as with the INFJ under stress.

None of the facts will be related or have anything in common. Under stress, the INTJ woman can also ignore the facts as successfully as she can ignore people. Often she gets away with it because of her training or brilliance, or the fact that she may be paid to sit and think.

INTJ women often approach marriage with low self esteem. They may not have a good body image of themselves, and had to make up for it by developing their analytical skills. INTJ gets self-destructive in a marriage by using her inferior sensing to put herself down. Self-criticism coupled with low self worth combine to make her quit when she's no longer perfect at a skill or a subject.

She may use her inferior function of sensing in all its inferiority as a weapon to judge herself incompetent to be a wife, a mother, a professional, a student, etc. and fall into the black hole of self-criticism because of an incident involving the collection or arrangement of facts.

If challenged about how she handles logistics by an ISTJ, the INTJ woman burned-out and under stress, may use those facts to convince herself that she's unworthy or incompetent.

To find relief from stress and to succeed in a marriage, she needs to freely pursue her power-seeking. Marriage needs to be a challenging goal. When the INTJ woman writes in her honeymoon diary, "Today I died," her goal isn't challenging her. An INFP who wrote that then might have stayed in the marriage 40 years, and suffered resentment-built health problems, but not the INTJ or ENTJ woman who feels she can find a way to support herself even when she's too old to work for pay, almost never accepts that, and has made sure she can pay for help when she needs it.

Her soul mate must offer her a marathon race to run in courting and marriage. The ISTJ man can do that by offering her upscale action "on track" in lifestyle or career, not more ideas.

ISTJ really believes her ideas are a dime a dozen and action counts. She won't date a man who tells her, "I'm hoping something will break. Life's tough."

# The ISTP Man

## Enneagram Type 8 With A 9 Wing
### ISTP: Introverted, Sensing, Thinking, Perceiving
### Dominant Introverted Thinking With Extroverted Sensing

5. ISTP defines his self-worth by his ability or inability to perform some tool-wielding task at home or at work. He don't care as much to know what makes you tick because he's too busy finding out what makes some practical machine work. He won't stand for your analyzing him and trying to talk about it with him.

He's is a troubleshooter who loves putting out fires and crises symbolic or real on a moment's notice. He is ready to bolt, batter, hunt, and play with his weapons and cars. ISTP is so skillful with tools that he'll design weapons (or run an interior design and drafting company) so he can get his target practice and meet crises head on.

## Under Stress: The Darkest Side Of ISTP In Marriage

He'll learn it on his own hands-on, before he'll read the directions in some book. The ISTP male flies his marriage by the seat of his pants and often tries to patch his wife's needs like he does his symbolic tools and cars with a whack on the side a paper clip.

This man secretly loves his freedom and often dreams of racing cars. Sometimes, like the ESTP, he sees women as interchangeable as peripheral computer parts-waiting for the right deal or new variation on a theme-a different twist, a difference dance to a new drummer.

ESTP and ISTP men sometimes like artisan or intuitive, perceiving belly dancers and other performing women who work nights-where they can meet their girlfriends after the performance in her nightclub. After marriage, they may become jealous and possessive, make her quit her job, and then restlessly go on to the next woman entertainer-or lady mechanic.

This non-talkative tool man, technician/repairer, computer programmer, pilot, or weapons master is the man to fly off with into such projects as carpentry, kitchen remodeling, building fancy tables, designing the interior of big corporations which he sees similar to putting oil oil well fires, and earning a million as a contractor. He has lots of exciting ideas for useful things.

If you're interest is academic and work with people instead of being interested in how things work, under enough stress, he could say you're stupid, flighty, and impractical.

He's good at computer drafting, building weapons, piloting or driving vehicles, and helping architects. So you might want him as your assistant if you're an architect or interior designer because he's so good with his hands.

He works or builds by the seat of his pants on the fly rather than by blueprints and plans and makes a neat computer programmer. Too bad he won't use them on you except to whip you into submission if he senses you're a self-mutilating masochist under his strength. This freedom-loving, world-traveling hunter wants more of his excursions away from home. He's a thinking man as long as it's practical and useful in the here and now.

## The ISTP Woman

### ENNEAGRAM TYPE 8 WITH 6 WING
### ISTP: INTROVERTED, SENSING, THINKING, PERCEIVING
### DOMINANT INTROVERTED THINKING WITH EXTROVERTED SENSING

ISTP, a disobedient, insubordinate, optimistic woman, spending and shopping until it hurts someone else's wallet. She's a risk taking, impulsive "lady driver" who prefers action to sweet talk. She wants no obligations. She exploits and capitalizes on her lover's vulnerable points and on every opportunity to take charge of her man. Hers is a tool-centered marriage.

The ISTP woman is action-seeking, impulsive, and self-contained in her own world of purposeful insubordination. This women knows no fear, and will just as soon fly a plane around the world to break a speed record as pit herself against every casino in Las Vegas.

Her life is all about beating the odds, taking the risk, and thriving on an inner kind of excitement from sky diving to new product design. Her action-hunger gives her an explosive temper if she is not obeyed, particularly by an NF child. ISTP mothers have higher incidences of child abuse than other types, particularly abuse of timid and fearful INFP and ISFJ children.

Some mothers of abused children with multiple personality disorder and other dissociative emotional illnesses had ISTP mothers who tortured them, locked them in closets, etc. without even realizing how their punishments affected their children's feelings.

Impact-hunger surrounds the ISTP woman. To satisfy her thirst for making an impact on the world, she may go in for fast motion-in ice skating competitions, athletics, driving trucks or cars, or in any type of fast-moving competition with men or other women equally athletic or technically artistic.

ISTP women also make the best computer programmers, provided that they are dealing with concrete programs and not abstract theoretical analysis. Each day, the ISTP woman needs to get high on excitement of some type. Many become ski instructors or work with dangerous tools, or get a job washing high-rise hotel windows.

ISTP women frequently compete for jobs as firefighters or apply to work on the police force, or like ISTJ women, seek a military career, although rules bother them, and they may soon leave the military to open their own appliance repair business or go into computerized drafting careers or robotics technology.

In husband-hunting, the ISTP woman is a risk-taker, moving in the fast lane among the ski instructors, or others who need a faster pace to tune up an under stimulated nervous system.

Tools are what is most often found in the ISTP woman's hands. The ISTP woman knows by the time she's in elementary school what kind of a soul mate she wants and what kind of work she will do.

The kind of man ISTP woman wants is a male ESTP or ENTP, an adventurer and a promoter of her dreams. She may become a lady trucker, steer her tugboat, or drive her bus all day, but the man she comes home to must offer her adventure, excitement, and risk.

The ISTP woman with a high degree of intelligence may become a surgeon and wield a scalpel like a warrior, fighting a battle against disease. She is a virtuoso in whatever she uses to get high-a career as an orchestra conductor, technical artist, or world-class ice skater.

Every man she meets is bent to her impulse as if he were another tool she wields to manipulate her world of chance and game. She could be a sharpshooter who finds her soul mate in a promoter, bounty hunter, or a physician asking her mate for separate tours on her honeymoon so she can indulge in her desire to roam free.

She tires of a man quickly, even after marriage, and grows impatient with her children at times, if she sees no way to find excitement in them. Her search for the right man is performed as if she was an intelligence agent or spy, and often, she is. She's most likely to join the FBI and hopes to find her man there, or in some substitute but similar organization.

Her pride is in her daring, bravery, and exceptional skills with tools and mechanical objects. This does not make a woman feminine in many men's eyes, except in that of another ISTP or ESTP, who will promote her skills.

The best man for her is the restless ESTP or her own type. This man plays on her impulse to take off with him for Katmandu or Peru only because she needs to scratch where it itches to travel.

The ESTP man and the ISTP woman will both seek to get "high" on the excitement of whatever impulse of the moment titillates their prowess to manipulate some tool, design, plastic product, or weapon.

The ISTP woman can be found as the single mother of five, who at any age, stands in line all night to be first in putting in her application to work as a high-paying earthmover or crane operator. She's first to seek nontraditional work and nontraditional men.

She also can be an artist or sculptor and seek her soul mate in her male model. After all, Michaelangelo and Leonardo Da Vinci have been said to display all ISTP characteristics.

If she works with computers as a graphic designer or programmer, the ISTP woman is first to sell modems to the man she's romancing on her computer screen. This woman frequently seeks a mate through electronic bulletin board correspondence groups.

She looks to join groups where all her extroverted needs are taken care of. The ISTP woman, like the ISTJ frequently joins the military to find a husband.

She feels somehow the military will issue her a husband or make it easier to meet Mr. Right Personality by providing electronic mail penpal clubs or job assignments where she'll work with a male partner.

She frequently signs up to be trained as a helicopter pilot if she joins the military forces. Or she may work for a radio station as a co-pilot in traffic news broadcasting where she won't have to speak, only drive the plane for the announcer.

The ISTP woman if stereotyped, is the Harley-Davidson biker, the crop duster pilot, the gun collector or instructor of firearms safety, or the female hunting and fishing enthusiast, fencing teacher, coach, or zoo breeder. Her life is all about seeking thrills and chills in dangerous play. Any man "man" enough for an INTP woman needs to be able to meet her challenges and need to put risk and danger in playful fun.

She's a mountain climber because it's there. Her soul mate needs to be able to match her, maybe take her up Everest or Anna Purna while both are young enough to do the climb. Whatever she does during the day-from physician to deli-girl, on the side she'll seek out thrills, risk, and danger fearlessly.

She needs to meet her match and her challenge to keep her interest. An astronaut is about fine for her, or her equal in an adventurer. She's a loner who secretly sidles up to her own kind at the bar, at work, at play or at a sporting event, choosing the man who can move with her flawlessly through the tools she wields, with a minimum of small talk.

An ISFP man is also appealing to her because he communicates more through action than words. He shows her rather than tells her where the action is. Forget the verbal approach to this woman.

Her man is as silent or as restless as she is. When she does talk, the conversation will be to the point and mostly about the tools she uses in her work, hobby, or interest.

She also succeeds with the ENTP male, perhaps an archaeologist she can team up with to work on finding the missing link or a geologist or petroleum engineer she can work with out in the field. Let the ISTP woman lead with her realism. She seeks a soul mate who will join with her to seize the second and exploit that moment for whatever treasure can be squeezed out of the find.

The intelligent, trained ISTP woman makes a fine statistician, mathematician, or computer consultant dealing with practical matters. Her soul mate usually comes from the ranks of her job environment. Or she meets him on a climbing, surfing, or ski vacation.

The ISTP woman waits until her man has served out his usefulness to observe how useful he was to her. She has no time to figure out what makes her man work or what makes people tick.

She's a smart sportswoman playing at her game. Love is a floating crap game. The ESFP's belief in Lady luck has nothing to do with it.

ISTP's skill in manipulating people the same way she wields her toys determines who wins the competition. The ISTP woman must position herself first in the mind of her mate.

She uses her eye-hand coordination to hunt for a husband, responding to the lover immediately in front of her. She doesn't look to the side through the corner of her eye to see what else is in the room at the moment that's better as the NF would do in search of the ideal relationship.

## The ISTP Woman Under Stress: The Darkest Side In Marriage

Insubordination is the ISTP woman. She'll kick up a crisis, a fire to put out, if there isn't one available. She'll create a crisis in her love relationship so she can jump up, solve the problem, and take the credit.

If she's working in a hospital, there's the possibility she'll conjure up a crisis so she can get the credit as the heroine who saved someone's life, who responded to the crisis in the nick of time and saved somebody or some equipment. The normal ISTP won't go out of her way to hurt anyone, but she's always looking for that crisis so she can jump into action to put out that fire on the spot and take the credit. She'll even start the fire so she can put it out, figuratively, if normal, or if disturbed, literally.

Heaven help her if she's married to a cautious ISTJ or ISFJ man who needs to control her and keep her reigned in tightly to his rules because he fears abandonment or loss of security in the home.

She can quickly turn into a sadistic, weapon-wielding male-batter or child abuser, if stressed beyond her break-down point. This woman fights dirty. If she's a martial arts expert, she can use these skills with deadly force against any man.

If she's petite and demure, she can use vandalism and physical brutality to extract revenge on those who wrong her.

This woman is not above using physical torture on any man who hurts her, or destruction of property as a revenge technique. She's out to hurt and injure if she's hurt. She lives dangerously on the edge in her thrill-seeking play, and uses play as work.

Under great stress, the ISTP woman reacts like the ESTP man. The older she gets, the more she resembles the ESTP, and may even study to be a private eye in middle age, eventually using the techniques against her man or relatives that hurt her.

In her younger years, she may appear to be like the ISFP woman, loving to be out in nature, training animals, practicing her art and design or working with tools, perhaps as a sculptress. As she gets older and more hardened to a life of dangerous risk taking, she uses her introverted thinking to plan ways to seek more thrills, to test her mate to his breaking point.

The optimistic ISTP woman, when put down by a pessimistic and controlling ISTJ or ESTJ mate, seeks her freedom, but not before the cat-and-mouse game commences. She's a great spender getting even with a tight-fisted, miserly spouse. And she will get back at her SJ spouse first through his wallet, then as an avenger.

ISTP woman lives to break the rules because they restrict her personal freedom and thrill-seeking. Any man or child who gets in her way becomes a rope and heavy stone around her neck to be discarded figuratively or literally.

The game takes precedence over life itself, over the tradition of home and hearth.She's a hungry huntress on the prowl, the cat-lady in a Batman-like movie out to defy her soul mate at every turn, except if he offers her the excitement and challenge of a new mountain to climb in the relationship and in reality.

With an ESFP man, she can create the special effects he needs to perform before an audience. Her good cheer, when not emotionally disturbed does not portray the possibility of sadistic anger and unbridled rage lurking deep inside. She needs a man who's her equal in order to have any type of loyalty.

Love for her is a behavior consisting of having no obligations or laws that can't be bended or broken on impulse. Under stress, she will quickly leave the SJ man who confines her to duties.

The ISTP woman makes no promises to her soul mate that in any way restrict her freedom or make her feel boxed into a corner. Her life needs no man to complicate it and no complications coming from a man or children. However, as a mother of the family she plans and wants, the ISTP woman is trusting and generous, and in good cheer. She is receptive to friendship, as long as her soul mate gives her the longest rope ever woven by man.

An ISTP woman is shy and insensitive to her soul mate's emotions. She is not aware of how her actions are affecting her lover' feelings. Her undeveloped intuition pushes her to test her mate to see how he'll hold up under the mass of facts and clues she has gathered about him. She's not so much cautious as she is ready to punish herself for not measuring up to her ability.

An extroverted man is seen as so prying and nosey, he gets on her nerves when he pries into her secret life of risk and dangerous moves. She holds back many secrets from her lover. Yet, the extraverted sensing man, an ESTP may be just what she needs to promote the visibility of her powerful inner strengths.

It's hard to get the ISTP woman to share her thoughts with her soul mate. She doesn't want him to judge her by her declining ability as she matures. She's so impersonal in love, that it's hard to tell when she's ready to walk out or about to begin a new, exciting phase of the relationship with action in another direction.

Usually, Enneagram type 4 with a 3 wing, also found in type 2 with 3 wing and type 6 with 7 wing or ISFP on the MBTI ™ (fun-loving artisan or outdoors person and gardener at heart).

## ISFP

## Under Stress: The Darkest Side Of ISFP In Marriage

### Enneagram Type 4 With A 3 Wing Or ISFP On The MBTI ™
### ISFP: Introverted, Sensing, Feeling, Perceiving
### Dominant Introverted Feeling With Extroverted Sensing

Trying to get him to act on his affectionate impulses only results in a quickie under the boardwalk. Marry the ISFP only if you're ready to try any texture, tone, or mood once for art's sake.

6. ISFP, a bucolic artist in the woods who can't hold a job, unless you find him one in the zoo, a poodle-grooming parlor, or in a guide dog

training school being close to animals. He could also be an artisan, artist-craftsman, or racing bicycle builder or shop owner or clerk.

ISFP is so artistic that he'll go into sculpture just to restore concrete gargoyles on medieval European cathedrals or become a composer and orchestra conductor for an opera company. He's the ultimate artist or musical composer who rarely speaks. Words are cheap; a picture is worth a thousand words.

If you think a word is worth a thousand pictures, then the two of you will create great comics together. The ISFP artist is just the right partner for the INFP writer. Together they'll make graphic novels.

He may be a chef, landscape designer, animal trainer, or ice skater, a ballroom dancer or cartoonist who won't say he loves you, in so many words, but instead will bake you a cake with your portrait painted on top in colored sugar crèmes. Love is expressed with food. He'll grow rotund with you and bring you flowers from the country all the time.

This silent man who hates to write or speak will say it all in pictures. Harpo Marx's mute character was the epitome of the ISFP silent male who says it all with music or mime, or by making the finest violins. Hemingway was the ISFP who said it all in Spain in the dust and under the sun, using the ISFP concretization of words.

## Under Stress: The Darkest Side Of ISFP In Marriage

The ISFP male sees his woman in caricature and may even draw her by emphasizing and exaggerating her features in caricature. He lives in caricature for the humorous effects. He's a natural mime. When he runs out of alternatives—and patience, he needs to be told more of the possibilities, or he'll start swinging his fists or his dancing feet. Don't depend on him as a good provider. You do the providing, and he'll take care of the kids and design the most wonderful teddy bears with lop ears. If you want money, you'll have to promote his designs with your verbosity and business skill.

He's less likely to batter you than the introverted sensing judgers (SJs), but when he runs out of words, he's still the third most likely to get on the band wagon of the abusive husband. Don't expect him to run out of steam when he is at a loss for metaphors.

He will make his impact on you in a bold way and may want revenge. This nature-loving animal trainer only wants to communicate with the animals. So you may have to learn to speak his non-verbal language with the right communication signals. Watch how he trains his dogs and cats.

Don't expect him to be the greatest conversationalist. If you want conversation, try an ENFP or ENFJ. Don't expect him to share much talk. Like the ISTP, he's the silent type who really wants to make you laugh by his actions or bold compositions. Let him draw his feelings on greeting cards, and you add the tender words to his true colors. You'll have to walk his talk.

The ISFP male may resent your interest in theoretical or academic subjects if he's artisan enough to savor the concrete detail of any story or portrait he'll express. Picture him as a Picasso of his craft or music. He needs to express his feelings for you in a modest way and may shun the grandiose. Find out how he intends to make his bold impact on you so you'll remember him as the music man or crafter of dream catchers. His fantasy as a film producer will propel him to the top in real life if you can walk with him in his concrete boots. Look for the details in his craft, as it is his life's work. Picture the ISFP man, not as a gardener, carpenter, or chef, but as a great film producer on par with a Spielberg or a Streisand. That's how he sees himself in his goals, however modest he may act.

## The ISFP Woman

### ISFP, Introverted, Sensing, Feeling, Perceiving
### Dominant Introverted Feeling With Extroverted Sensing

ISFP, an indirect, freedom-seeking woman who will act first rather than try to explain. This dancer, skater, athlete, illustrator, or craftswoman and quilter/potter, is way too modest, preferring homemaking and crafts as long as it's done with the free spirit.

Never attempt control. Like risk-taking Hemingway (ISFP at least in his novels), the ISFP woman tries leaping before looking, sometimes taking risks with her body. Your marriage will be about colors, music, and textures, tastes, and foods. Above all, there's a delight cooking and eating (at home or in restaurants) with all the senses tuned inward to nurture the self or punish the self through the senses, while preferring to be out in nature, hiking, and getting closer to the animals. She will practice variation on all the themes of freedom-seeking.

The playful ISFP woman will let her lover know of her desire to play the game he commands her to play. Or if she's not willing to play at whatever role in life assigned to her, she will use revenge to avoid playing such a game. She won't make the first move in approaching a soul mate.

Who ever appoints himself as her director will find the ISFP woman responding to the role in positive or negative ways. She won't speak to her lover first. He will have to approach her and start the conversation to become acquainted. The joy-seeking, optimistic ISFP woman with her extraverted sensing and dominant introverted feeling wants to do favors for her friends. She needs to respond positively to her friends. It's just so hard to make friends in the first place!

The ISFP woman is the epitome of the professional stage dancer, a sole ballerina, a belly dancer who really gets into the folk music of the East, even to the point of donning blue chin tattoos and ancient wigs. Or she retreats into her introversion to design and sew costumes, dance slippers, racing bikes, or ice skates.

The ISFP woman loves to cook creatively, often going to chef school abroad, or opening her home-based catering business. She is most likely to be a musician virtuoso, or in some way engaging in colors, textures, sounds, or tastes in her hobby, home life, and occupation. Some INFP women become textile artists and team up with husbands who run weaving cooperatives with them in Central American Indian villages or work together in importing of textiles, foods, or musical instruments.

In marriage, the ISFP woman's life centers around amusement. She could be the high school student who worked summers in the mobile carnival or circus and who today, still hangs around or works in amusement parks. Life is so much entwined with amusement, that her children will be encouraged to draw cartoons or interact in some way with amusement characters. Harpo Marx was the epitome of an ISFP in his silent film character mime roles.

The ISFP woman's desire is to tickle your amusement fantasy, to entertain, by remaining as invisible or alone as possible, yet still amuse you in a way that does not require her to carry on continuous conversation. Her body is her tool, whether in dance, ice skating, mime, or in creating cartoons or comic book art.

She is happiest married to an INFP or ISFP man, although she's more closely like the ESTP man. With the ISFJ man, she'd be happy. However, he would try to control her showmanship.

The ISFP woman is the least competitive of the types. She does not want to win any ice skating competitions for speed. If she performs, it will be solely to amuse. Or she'll play an instrument to put on a performance only to show what she composed.

The ISFP woman designs and collects dolls, or secretly wished she could if her family wouldn't call her names for thinking how good it would feel to design costumes for dolls. In her showmanship, she wants to excite her audience, and hopefully just one significant other by her performance.

Anything abstract will be avoided. The ISFP woman will not tolerate theory or the abstract psychology that the INFP man loves to weave into the conversation. Yet, he will find so much love and companionship and a long-term marriage in common with this very different woman. She's rational with her dominant introverted feelings-the way she decides by her likes and dislikes and inner personal values.

What she does in her life with her lover or with her children must be concretely useful. In this way, she makes the ISFJ the most practical wife. She can choose successfully between the ISFJ, the ISFP, and the INFP lover with almost equal harmony. Yet each of these men will assign her different roles to play in life, and this joyful entertainer will adapt to each according to her hobbies and interests. Each man will empower her in a different way.

With an ISFP like herself, both will have the same blind spots, but both will spend a lifetime finding everything that's useful in life. Married to the ISFJ, the ISFP woman will be bossed by the whining, complaining utilitarian realism of the ISFJ man who insists on efficiency and utility from his wife.

The ISFP woman isn't interested in the ISFJ efficiency. She is about utility and will rebel against his insistence that she clean off her desk or arrange the kitchen counter tops clear of appliances when he gives the command. He spends his life telling her how he wants the housework done and the appliances arranged in the closets.

With the ISFJ man, he will bond to her and put up with her disorganization as he will with the INFP whom he will torment and bind in an iron corset of control. Yet with the ISFP woman, her showmanship will free her from his withdrawing, dance-away anger, if she can stand the lack of warmth and affection that comes after the first three months of marriage and remains for decades.

With the INFP man, the ISFP woman will show her lover the use of everything she grabs. What actually happens is what the ISFP woman is concerned with, whereas the INFP man is concerned with discussing psychologically why it happens.

The INTP man will be concerned with why it happens biologically, scientifically and mathematically. The ISFP woman doesn't want to hear why from either man. Still, she will listen to the INFP man because he talks empathetically about people's feelings. They both have in common dominant introverted feeling.

The ISFP woman will play without a stop for the sake of playing itself, and nothing will stop her-whether she's playing cards, an instrument, her body, or whatever her game is. Her life is her sport or performance. She can perform alone or in front of an audience. While she's performing, she's alone up there in the spotlight, extroverting her sensing, not her feeling.

To the INFP man who is most likely to want to marry her, the ISFP lover is a hedonist. While the INFP man seeks to please and nurture himself with pleasurable experiences of the intellectual kind, such as wandering through an art museum, the ISFP woman, just as artistic but in a concrete way, seeks a life of pleasure.

She is the ultimate of hedonists. Pleasure is what she lives for in her particular form. This could be anything from designing dolls for children to anything else that gives her pure joy without end. She must have fun at any cost. The ISFJ man will crush her fun with one swift kick of his need to put her to work doing routine household chores and his insistence on her earning money for the household.

The INFP man will adapt and join her in having fun, as long as it's the kind of fun that has a healing influence on the body, such as meditation, raw vegetable juicing, walking two hours a day, and no smoking anywhere in sight. The ISFP man, like herself, will join her in the kind of fun she wants with no questions asked. They have in common the desire to have concrete, utilitarian fun without end. This includes useful fun as a paid occupation as well as after working hours as recreation.

The two could succeed working together as recreational therapists, or outdoors as forest rangers, or in an entertainment theme park or outdoor zoo theme park. The ISFP woman considers anything immoral that does not lead to useful fun.

In contrast, fun for the INFP is writing a series of psychothriller novels under contract, that is creative expression as fun. For the ISFP woman (and the ISFP man) fun must have it's usefulness.

Fun must be practical and concrete, such as teaching finger painting and dance to preschoolers or creating electronic or make-up special effects, dinosaur sculpture, and monster faces for science fiction feature films and animated cartoons. An ISFP must have created 'Toon Town.

This woman needs her own fun house to run through to keep her marriage joyful. She's the type who will dress up as Santa Claus on Christmas, or don a clown's costume, go to the park on Sundays, and make money painting flowers, hearts, and kitten-whisker faces on kids. ISFP must make an impact on her lover and on anyone else watching her one-on-one show.

If she can't make an impression on you, she will find someone else who enjoys her performance. She is compelled to perform, even in a silent, introverted way. She is a modest adventuress, but will seek any adventure that randomly occurs, regardless of the risk.

## ISFP: Under Stress: The Darkest Side Of Marriage

When life's stressors hit the ISFP woman, she turns her anxiety in on herself. Stressed-out ISFP woman are the head bangers and the women who cut themselves up with razor blades to feel pain in order to let out the emotional pain inside bottled up. She's more likely to hurt herself under stress than to vandalize or hurt another, the favorite revenge technique of sensing perceivers.

Under stress, the ISFP woman ignores pain and exhaustion. Her extroverted sensing combines with her dominant introverted feeling to produce less awareness of the pain and fatigue wracking her body.

If she's a musician, acrobat, ballerina or skater, she'll ignore the pain and keep on performing the show. Later in life, she'll keep on doing the same repetitive movements to do her work without realizing she's developing repetitive movement injuries such as carpal tunnel syndrome or violinist's hand and jaw problems.

The ISFP woman gets caught up in the show or storm. The activity puts them in a type of hypnotic trance where they can't stop practicing the movements of the dance or composition. She's wearing "the red shoes" (as in the fairy tale and film), and those dance slippers won't let her stop dancing no matter how fatigued she's getting.

The extreme, but hidden, risk-taking for adventure increases as stress increases in the ISFP woman. Her freedom means everything to her, and she will take her children with her when freedom calls.

She performs or runs away or mutilates herself to release emotional pain for the thrill of it. If she is drowning in household or workplace routine, she will begin a thrill-seeking adventure hell bent on having fun without planning for the future.

The ISFP woman is the epitome of the waitress character in the film, "Thelma and Louise." Under stress of routine and lack of fun, she will "flip out" or "crack" and take off for the adventure of a lifetime-risking everything for a moment of thrills and chills, for fun in the most playful sense of the word.

Under stress, she will hunger for taking chances. This stress-detour in her life doesn't require a lot of pressure before it occurs-merely too much routine in her life. Without time to play each day in her own way, she will create her own "variation on a theme," as Dr. Keirsey describes the SP temperament, and create her own variety in life's pleasure and leisure.

The ISFP woman describes herself as a woman of "leisure and pleasure." She will break all the rules. And in her modest, silent way, she will use her extroverted sensing to have fun in the most useful way she can create. At work, under stress, she will break the rules and do the task her own way-varying the way something is supposed to be done.

In the home, she might pull her child out of school and take off for exotic places to do something more fun and more useful to her lifestyle. This ISFP woman in her home and among her children and family, as well as in the presence of her lover (or new lover) is the most sensation-seeking of all the personalities.

As an introvert, the way she seeks sensation will be hidden behind those feelings inside her. As an extroverted sensor, she will seek until the ends of the earth to quench her hunger for sensation as play, and sensation-seeking as a full-time paid occupation. This is not bad, immoral or unethical.

Sensation-seeking for fun and money usually means opening a small one-woman business she can run alone her way, or working in an entertainment theme park in a resort city, such as Las Vegas or Atlantic City.

Typical examples of ISFP women "exploding" in an act of sensation-seeking under stress, include quitting a bookkeeping job to open up successful workshops manufacturing cute stuffed animal toys that people find irresistable, or designing and illustrating special effects at gigantic entertainment theme parks around the world.

Some ISFP artists/artisans can pick out one color variation in a thousand, and some ISFP musician/composer/orchestra conductors can hear one wrong note in an entire symphony. Examples of such possibly ISFP artists include Rembrandt and the musician, Toscanini. Hemingway, as an ISFP novelist, described the senses in utilitarian words, not abstractions or metaphors.

When the ISFP woman cracks under stress, her dark side in marital stress consists in dealing with minute variations of sights, sounds, motions, and colors. Stress may turn her inward to mutilate herself with razors and bang her head against the wall under mental illness, if mentally ill. However, if not, if she's a normal ISFP under stress, her darkest side will move to restore harmony to her senses.

Her whole life is about touching, tasting, smelling, seeing, hearing, moving together. She will work to restore her senses to move together in harmony and serenity. She grows more masochistic under persecution from the ISTP man, who could, under great stress, sadistically abuse her at a time when her masochistic reactions put her in a trance so she stays and takes it "like a soldier."

The ISFP woman has been described as "color-crazed." Under stress, she's waiting to hear one false note in her lover's words or promises. As stress increases, making her marriage more painful, her awareness increases. She must fly far above convention.

At all costs, she is driven to "slay convention." She must resist tradition, especially the tradition of the ISTJ, ISFJ, ESTJ, and ISTJ mate or employer. Under more stress, she extends this "must kill convention" attitude to institutions, including the institution of motherhood and marriage, or family, and patriotism.

She is now totally pitted against anything that's "standard." At any risk, she must find out what on earth she must change in order to survive and renew her self, to start a new life.

The darkest side of marriage creates in the ISFJ woman under stress a desire to pay the penalty first, and then make the big change with optimism and joy. She's not bringing together like the INFP catalyst does under stress. She's flying apart and loves every minute of it.

Under stress, the ISFP woman becomes even more optimistic than the ENFP woman, who is often billed as the ultimate optimist. It's the ISFP who is the most playful optimist under stress. The ENFP collapses with bad health (ignoring their bodily sensations due to inferior sensing until psychosomatic sickness, or physical symptoms and a breakdown hits them).

The ISFP woman's health is better because she believes in having a lucky day, not in the NF's belief in personal growth. The ISFP woman believes she is Lady Luck. The higher the stress, the more lucky she feels. She may become a compulsive gambler, losing everything. Yet the next game will provide a win, because in the mirror, she sees only a lucky lady.

The past is forgotten. ISFP women use the cliché, "don't cry over spilt milk," frequently. Under stress she could split on her husband and five kids because they soon become "water under the bridge." She lives for clichés that swarm her conversation, clichés about forgetting the past and moving on to the next lucky day.

She's not a depressive type under stress. Usually, the cheerful, joy-sprinkling ISFP woman marries by grave error, the ISTJ or ESTJ man (usually for his secure paycheck), and then rebels against his tight reigns and short rope peppered by cycles of his depression at her strong "chomping at the bit" attempts.

Under stress, she feels like a harnessed workhorse under a control freak ISTJ male, and she must flee and take everything with her she can carry-in order to get back to her cheerful self again.

No matter what she does, she will always believe "be happy, don't worry," even while she's cutting her ankles up with razors and banging her head against the wall to release the pain. She's in pain because her kindness has been ignored.

The ISFP woman, even under the most horrific marital stress offers unconditional tenderness to children. She feels everyone else's pain and responds to their needs. If she can, she'll take her children with her when she leaves. However, if her children show the least bit of controlling SJ behavior with her (which she sees as abuse), she will leave them with their father (who may have the better-paying job).

If her husband is abusive, she will take her children with her, and find work around small animals, small children, or any other place where luck and good cheer are bound to show up the next morning. She is little

Orphan Annie singing, "the sun will come out tomorrow." She does this under heavy stress and in the face of loss and grief.

The ISFP woman finds joy in the faces of preschoolers or helpless baby animals. This work relieves the darkest kind of stress that could befall her. The harder she's hit, the kinder she acts, the more generous she is to herself and her children.

She may dye her hair purple, join a punk rockers grunge group at fifty, pierce her nose, put five earrings in her lobes, pierce her navel or tattoo her body to make an impact. Inside, this act of setting herself apart from the society that has caused her pain and persecution is done to make an impact, a statement about how she feels inside.

She may run with the earthy crowd, but she's looking for a way to show how kind and generous she is on the inside toward those who need her love. At the same time she's full of cheer, joy, and optimism, her belief in "have a lucky day" (rather than have a good day), creates the most cynical woman towards marriage of all the types.

Under stress, the ISFP woman becomes vigilant, cautious, and cynical towards love, men, and marriage. She knows her lover has shallow pockets, clay feet, and a whipping hand. She knows she's been used by a man for what he could get out of her, and she's mad as hell (and won't take it anymore). As the ultimate cynic under stress, the ISFP woman thinks all men are narcissistic pigs.

She is not under any kind of illusion. There's no INFP mask in her. She doesn't dissociate or step away from her identity and become someone else. She expects men to treat her lousy.

She knows "all men are out is to get more than they give." Living with this kind of cynicism while under stress, the ISFP woman will fall in love again, but always think the man is there for what he can get out of her. She'll never trust 100 percent again, but she'll always believe in Luck.

Under stress, she'll tell her lover he's just another "John", another "Trick"-if only to make an impact on him, to let him know she knows what he's up to. She knows he's there to clean her out and discard her when she's useless to him.

She expects her new lover to be like the last. Under stress, she looks in every garbage can, seeks out every thrift shop or garage sale to see what lucky piece will surprise her. This is literally what she does, and scrapes the bottom of the barrel for people as well. What she's looking for are useful objects and useful people who will give her what she needs at the moment.

The highly intelligent ISFP woman, in all her modest silence of voice, under stress will use a whirlwind of activity to save her mind. She will scrounge anywhere to create a new home that she can turn into a sorority house of sorts.

She'll join a commune or rent her house out to a horde of room mates. In spite of her introversion, under stress, she will create a mobile homestead that moves quickly with her. She needs a "nomad" type of caravan with freedom-seeking people who can be of use to her, not take from her.

ISFP woman is the ultimate flower child of the sixties, the epitome of hippie. She avoids the SJ hierarchy of the paternal, traditional family as if it were the Bubonic Plague.

Freedom seeking under stress and in the darkest side of marital troubles is what the ISFP woman creates in her caravan. She will do what she wants when she wants it, or she promptly runs away.

The ISFP teenager who runs away from the rules, chores, and traditional, hierarchical family life of ISTJ/ISFJ parents to get married to an ISTP or ESTP biker is the typical example seen repeatedly on the media tabloid talk shows.

Under stress, the ISFP woman uses defiance and rebellion to seek her freedom and regain her cheerfulness. Family rules are there only to be broken. The ISFP is the most likely type to marry outside her religion, ethnicity, race, or nationality in defiance of tight family rules of tradition.

She gets her way by defiance. Sometimes revenge is carried out-such as vandalism-if defiance doesn't work.

It's emotionally upsetting for an ISFP woman to see the older male in her family getting the money for college or the full inheritance. She will fight for equality, when equality means freedom.

Sadly, under stress, the ISFP woman tends to marry again to an ISTJ or ISFJ man. It's the ISFJ man who runs after her to marry in order to help her by controlling her, by tightening the corset.

He marries her to supervise her and tell her what she should be doing right. He thinks he's giving her economic anchorage in a safe harbor of love by making her a landlady. What he's really giving her is a rope around her neck weighted down by a heavy stone. He sees marry her as giving her security. She runs to the financial security, blind to the way he will check the labels on each grocery item to see whether she's spending too much money on her favorite foods.

The ISFP woman will find, taking her ISFJ man shopping with her, that he'll lift up a ten-pound sack of pinto beans and move it into the cart with the statement, "Look how much food we can eat so cheaply." She'll find herself standing in surprise as he takes her favorite tin of gourmet love-food (her senses can't resist), out of her hands and puts it back on the shelf as he says, "It's too expensive."

She could respond by shoplifting it when he turns his back to give herself that little food pleasure. She may become a closet eater in response to her SJ husband's monitoring, inspecting, and supervising her every twitch of freedom and pleasure seeking from material items like food, comfortable shoes, and her hobbies.

She's charming, so charming when she wants money from her lover, that she will pretend to overlook his need to control his spouse. With an ISFP or INFP man, there won't be the control, and there may not be financial security.

With his last cent, the INFP or ISFP man will indulge in that expensive gourmet ice cream with her, but make sure it's nonfat, nondairy, and sweetened with pear juice concentrate instead of white sugar. Unlike the ISTP or ESTP man, she won't feel she's being used, and he won't feel exploited. She may feel the INFP's restlessness as not having found the ideal relationship, but he may not move on if he could lose the economic harmony he has set up in his search for serenity.

What ISFP woman wants when she's under stress, is for Mr. Right Personality to do her a favor, to make her day. She will charm the skin off a snake. The ISTJ man will see what he perceives as the vulnerability and weakness of the ISFP woman, his perfect victim.

He will not realize he is destroying her by inspecting and supervising her negatively until she has a stress breakdown and is no longer able to work. He picks on a woman because he's afraid if he did it to a man at work, he'd be challenged, fought, and defeated. He believes the ISFP woman can never defeat him, so he lifts himself up by putting her down.

Driven to masochism by the browbeating inspections, the ISFP woman will turn wayward and defiant until she meets her soul mate, the INFP or ISFP man who will match her optimism and cheerfulness with his desire to let her be free to be who she is.

She's frivolous. This attracts opposite types. The opposite of ISFP is ENTJ. She is drawn to his combat boots and dominating style. Soon, he makes a fool of her behind her back in front of the people he gives presentations to at work. He puts her down, says she gives information when he wants decisions, as he puts down the INFP as well. Still, he pursues the ISFP woman as does the ESTJ male.

She gravitates towards her opposite to find stability. She won't find economic stability with the ISFP or INFP man. The ISFP bicycle shop could close. The INFP minister/counselor could remain unemployed for years unless he finds work where he can "live his dream and passion." The INTP or INTJ man laughs at the ISFP woman frivolousness.

Under stress, the ISFP woman runs away when she is concretely aware of her bodily sensations. She needs stability in her life, but finds most men too impatient with her child-likeness.

The inner child inside her wants to roam. What man will let her go free? Who will realize that if you love someone, you set that person free? If she loves you, she will come back. She sees herself as a pet bird flapping her wings in a gilded cage.

To stabilize herself under stress, the INFP woman in love needs to show people how to do concrete and exciting things. If she finds excitement, she will stay and earn money having fun.

Marriage is a way the ISFP uses to entertain by using concrete motions and variations. She needs to move parts of anything and anyone around in her environment until they fit the puzzle spaces of her lifestyle.

The ISFP woman uses guerrilla tactics to get what she wants from a relationship. Love is variation. Life is a game. Play a lot. The male or female ISFP can carry on the same poker or pool game for weeks. Marriage can also be played like a game. Under stress, the game becomes a challenge. In the game, it's the ISFP woman who hates competition, because playing should be fun.

As her stress increases, the normal (not emotionally disturbed) ISFP woman will join as many groups as possible to help herself. She's not joining for the inspiration that NF seeks. She's not there for the rituals that SJ wants. She's there to join in or by entertained by the festivity: the color, sounds, and food. That fiesta atmosphere brings her to the group where she can seek help.

If you want to draw the ISFP woman to therapy, you need festivity and celebration to satisfy her incredible hunger for frivolity under stress as a way to relieve the pressure. The more useful fun she has, the more she can help herself stop blaming others.

Under stress, the ISFP woman will deny anything is her fault. She'll start up her favorite game of revenge. She'll pee on your carpet and defecate in your kitchen. She won't take responsibility for her retaliation.

She will punish her lover by mutilating her own body in some way that leaves scars. Sometimes, she'll say PMS made her cut up her arms with razor blades. Other times, she'll blame her family.

What she's trying to do is restore the excitement to her life by punishing her lover. Since she won't physically strike him, she will abuse herself in any way that will leave a permanent mark.

Excitement is hers by divine right, and she will destroy herself in order to bring excitement back into her life. She will also get revenge on those around her. The ISFP woman, silent and modest in normal mode, is likely to create violence (or self-abuse) in the workplace if mistreated there as she is at home.

ISFP is a masochist under stress. The more insecure she feels about the strength of her impact on her lover, the more she will abuse herself, not so much to hurt her lover as to bring excitement back to her lifestyle.

She needs at this point to be directed into composing music or songs, or some better way of making an impact than cutting herself or drug-taking, or banging her head against the wall.

She needs to get back to practicing her performance or composition in whatever field interests her. Her lover should give her songs to write about the stress in the marriage or relationship. With an INFP husband or lover, she can team up with him to write love songs. She needs to create excitement in her life. He needs creative expression.

She's a performer and a composer, however introverted, and in many walks of life, not only in the arts. She can create a mobile aerobics or gymnastics class for preschoolers. He can create her visibility and write about her, increasing the excitement in her day.

Under stress, the ISFP woman increases her rehearsal of whatever she does over and over. She can take up pottery making or weave wall hangings or exotic clothing. She can get into sports or together with her INFP husband who writes, write gags for stand up comics. One of the best ISFP gag writers was Jack Benny.

Overlooked in the "silent" ISFP woman is her writing ability. Hemingway broke through the NF (intuitive feeling) communication monopoly by using his extroverted sensation to write concretely instead of the INFP's and ENFP's extroverted intuition used to write more with metaphor. (Most full time freelance writers are INFP, INFJ, and ENFP.)

The fun-seeking ISFP can write jokes and gags because gag comics need to be very concrete. It's in writing gags that the high stress suffered by ISFP in the throes of loss, grief, pain, marital woes, children's problems, and work pressures, can be reduced. If she's having fun with the gags and they act as a catharsis to release her pain, then write gags. It's much better than using acts of self-abuse to punish a lover or family member.

Under stress, the ISFP woman becomes more private. In normal times, she's the most private of private people. She's not going to give speeches, but she can write gags for stand-up comics. If she writes, it's not for the sake of writing words, but only to keep her eyes on where the action is.

She won't talk about something if she can get involved with the action of it. She'd rather be a travel agent than a travel columnist.

Under stress, the closer she becomes involved actively with reality, the quicker she'll feel better. The ISFP woman must compose songs. So why force her to compose screams?

## The INFP Man

### Enneagram Type 4 With A 3 Wing Or INFP On The MBTI ™
### INFP: Introverted, Intuitive, Feeling Perceiving

### Dominant Feeling, With Extroverted Intuition

7. INFP, his dominant introverted feeling is directed inwardly. Unless you make him feel good about himself, important, talented, and

creatively expressive, he may be unable to show affection (except to himself), but wants you to perform kinky acts on him.

The INFP man needs your respect when he is unemployed, which could be frequently until he finds his heal-or-save-the-world niche that grants him respect in the world of work. At home, he cares so deeply about having loving relatives to support him emotionally and financially when laid off from his job, but he can't express it because he's so shy and secretly wants to nurture and please himself first.

INFP men and women are often the last hired and the first fired because their preferred work is so creative, idiosyncratic,

and non-routine (e.g. screenwriters, ad copywriters, freelance reporters, work-at-home entrepreneurs, creativity teachers, newsletter publishers, magazine illustrators, clergy, counselors, UFO researchers, psychics and astrologers, and non-degreed hypnotherapists).

The word "kook" and "flake" is harshly applied too frequently to the sensitive, avoidant, and often dependent INFP male as well as to the INFJ male idiosyncratic type who professes his psychic ability too loudly in public and then pulls away from people in introversion.

The INFP male uses his extroverted intuition to deal with the world and earn money or court his future wife. He's so non-directive, his gift for helping people understand their feelings and feel good can help you. However, he's a born rescuer looking for a victim to save, much like the more extroverted ENFP male in some ways.

The INFP male will "dance away" from people because they drain his energy, making him shake and shiver on the inside which he tries to conceal by speaking faster. His ideal, the ENFP male, will dance towards people, making rapport with less caution and fear of being "hurt" by people who may disagree with him.

Don't go near him if you're co-dependent. He'll end up as your persecutor. If you're pretty stable and had a loving childhood, the INFP male will be of help to make you feel good about yourself. Take his advice, consolation, and appreciation.

He's an introvert and will work well with a female introvert. Let him write those way-out novels and screenplays. Don't ask him to fly if he has a sensitive nervous system, panic disorder, or agoraphobia. Let him take the bus if he is too nervous to learn to drive. On the other hand, he may have tired of his profession and would enjoy working at home coaching others in how to research quality of life issues. The INFP male focuses on giving information, background, and history on a wide variety of subjects or an in-depth resource in one area.

The INFP man can be a writer of mystery novels, a clergyman, a teacher, a psychiatrist, social worker, journalist, or artist. He's fluent in languages, and may end up as a self-employed consultant in some esoteric field like translating Tibetan scrolls or writing books on the paleontology of human consciousness or bicameral kingdoms in ancient Sumeria.
You'll find him at a lecture on Egyptology or at a holistic health convention.

He doesn't have the guts to ask for money. So don't marry him if you're looking for a good provider to shower you with jewels, minks, and homes in Beverly Hills. If you can provide for yourself, you'll have a fascinating man with an imagination that could turn out a stream of novels and a need for romance.

## Under Stress: The Darkest Side Of INFP In Marriage

He may be an eternal boy going from job to job looking for independence from supervision. If you're a thinking-type woman who knows how to make money, this romantic man will create visions for you and write the most imaginative novels and plays. You have to be the patron of his art, though. Or he may be a middle-class psychotherapist with a tenured university job and a stream of steady clients. He may be the perfect mate for a steadily-employed social worker or tenured English teacher of the same type.

He may not have confidence in himself that he ever helped anyone or that anyone took him seriously, even if he's a psychiatrist. The INFP male may not offer you appreciation because it's hard for him to express emotions.

He is looking for perfection, and you can never be the perfect wife. Also he may feel incompetent when under stress because he can't find perfection within himself. If you want such a man who can express passion, then look for an ENFP, the extraverted version of a feeling, perceiving and intuitive man.

## The INFP Woman

### Enneagram Type 4 With 3 Wing, Sometimes Type 4 With 5 Wing Or INFP On The MBTI ™.
### INFP: Introverted, Intuitive, Feeling Perceiver
### Dominant Introverted Feeling With Extroverted Intuition

INFP, this woman shuns reality and dissociates in order to escape the cold, cruel corporate world and the commandeering world of the abusive, dominant husband. The worse thing an SJ husband could do would be to give her orders on how to clean the house better, command her, or try to dominate her.

She must be encouraged to create and to express her creativity in healing, writing, art, counseling, or teaching. Otherwise, the INFP woman will seek a passive/aggressive secret kind of revenge on you in order to please and nurture herself.

If she's verbally abused or put down at home so you can pick yourself up, the INFP woman will do a sit-down strike against the powerlessness of women. She will dissociate and act out the ultimate in feminine stereotypical behavior.

She might become agoraphobic, or prone to panic disorder, or forgetful. She could, if prone to agoraphobia, under stress, become housebound without knowing why she's housebound, a type of Emily Dickenson.

The INFP could become reclusive if disappointed in the way people treat her. She needs respect. When there's no longer respect in a marriage, the INFP will become physically ill with a variety of symptoms involving high adrenaline and insulin levels in the blood.

INFP women frequently marry ESTP or ISTJ men and then become battered wives. They can also become avoidant/dependent and stick by a bad marriage out of fear of going to pieces under the stress of a real corporate job outside the home, preferring working alone inside the home instead.

Often, INFP women will give up the chance to earn enough money to make them independent of their abusive husbands in order to stay at home and express themselves creatively in work that pays too little to allow them to leave violent marriages.

In a choice between working at a routine secretarial job or remaining under a wife batterer or verbal abuser offering little but emotional neglect and criticism, the INFP will choose to remain at home to write or illustrate for no pay, rather than leave a marriage gone sour and work for another authority figure.

There is often great fear of father figures or authority figures in the corporate world-and a history of abuse by ISTJ and ISTP fathers and weak, usually ISFJ mothers who were beaten themselves. The INFP woman will go to great lengths to find ways to nurture herself and find the space for creative freedom.

She will use the power of introversion against a verbally abusive husband (one who puts her down to pick himself up). This means turning into an ice statue, preferring no one if she can't have true romance.

She can live monastically as a recluse telecommuter if pushed around by enough disappointing relationships at home and bad jobs at the office. Frequently, she will insist on having his and hers bedrooms for her privacy. She has trouble relaxing and is startled easily.

As a dominant introverted feeler, she appears cool-headed, but introverts her feeling where it creates too much and too often of the flight syndrome and concealed fear inside. Direct work with people and family is exhausting.

Indirect contact is energizing. INFP loves to let you do the talking, but often marries introverted men and has to end up doing all the talking in the marriage, and feeling exhausted. Often, the man in her life is a move-away lover, a Mr. Takeaway man, someone who is cold and withdrawing when asked for affection. Sometimes, the INFP woman will feel too weak to fight her husband for custody of her children. INFP women may marry abusive men, usually sensing types, who attack her for her weakness. To escape, she may run from reality and delight in fantasy, becoming a recluse for the sake of art or research.

The INFP woman will demand a relationship so much she'll fight for it verbally. Then, when battered by a more nonverbal (ISTJ, ISTP, or ESTP man), she will hear the man yell, "Give me a break!" She'll often reply, "Not until I have a connection."

Early in the marriage she will pound on his separate bedroom door for affection and attention. He'll slam the door in her face or come into her room and beat her up verbally and/or physically. From that time on, she'll turn to a statue and avoid further contact with all men, finding nurturance in fantasy, imagination, food, literature, and art-but she'll stick in the marriage for decades out of fear of being on her own. If given a choice, the INFP woman would prefer to be 12 years old forever.

The uneducated INFP woman finds creativity in desktop publishing jobs as a way of escaping the secretarial pool without leaving the world of computers. No matter how many degrees she gets, the INFP may truly say that the only skill she used for survival was what she learned in her $7^{th}$ grade typing course.

The educated INFP usually wishes for a doctorate in counseling, and then becomes a writer of psychology text books or a novelist. ENFP women write romance novels. INFP women write mysteries and psychothrillers or historicals.

Worse off is the INFP humanities graduate, usually with a master's degree in English, who can't find a writing job paying a livable income and is too anxiety-wracked to enter teaching. She takes a low-paying clerical job to survive and then looks for a lover who has a steady job, usually an ISFJ, who will see her as needing his income to support her creative pursuits at home. As soon as she's found her sugar daddy, she will stay home and clean his house, if only he'll let her write or paint, or read her esoteric books on Jungian psychology. However, he'll demand she pull her weight in salary at any menial job.

As his lack of interest in her creative projects increases, she'll develop physical symptoms that will grow worse with age. She'll think about why after writing 75 books, her husband still belittles her for not earning a salary in a real job.

Nothing she can do to live her dream could please her SJ husband. She won't give up her creative expression that earns her very little in money. He punishes her by providing only what she needs to survive and not a cookie crumb more. He also picks the cheapest house in the highest crime neighborhood to live in so he can walk to work.

Her resentment grows and she turns it inwardly and begins to describe herself as physically disabled to get people to feel sorry for her when she feels that are about to compete with or judge her. What she doesn't realize is that she makes the best possible text book writer to train teachers of creativity studies-with or without a degree.

## INFP: Under Stress: The Darkest Side Of Marriage

Agoraphobia could strike the INFP woman under extreme stress, especially if she's genetically prone to panic disorder. Chronic anxiety plagues the dominant introverted feeling of the INFP under stress, particularly if she's not paid for creative expression in a career, and at home she's a battered wife.

She will be torn between leaving an abusive, celibate marriage where she's browbeaten, hit, verbally put down, or emotionally neglected-but gets three hots and a cot (three meals a day and a room of her own) and the chance to do her unpaid creative expression-art, writing, reading psychology books, anthropology or archaeology research, etc. Or leave the marriage and be forced by the "wrong liberal arts degree and no doctorate" to work in a secretarial job doing routine typing all day.

In many cases, under stress, the INFP woman will remain as a martyr in an abuse marriage for decades-well into old age-in order to trade off the freedom to express herself in her art or writing, usually paid too little to support herself financially, independent of her husband.

Why she chooses to stay in a marriage where she is totally neglected goes further than her low self esteem and low social needs. Her dominant introverted feeling takes over and as if in a trance, "forces" her from inside out to value her quest for writing, art, illustration, or other research, above any other need outside the home.

As long as her abusive husband (or unfulfilling relationship or marriage) provides her with enough food to survive, a free bed, and enough clothes to go outside, she will ignore her physical surroundings and retreat as a recluse would, inside her head to practice her creative expression in whatever form it takes.

Usually, it's in writing. Under stress, the INFP woman becomes self-absorbed and writes the same ideas over, repeating herself all throughout her books. Her redundancy infuriates NT readers. She needs to beat the same point into the minds of her audience and imprint them over again with the point she needs to make on her quest.

The INFP woman under stress becomes even more monastic. At times she takes on a mission and crusades for her cause. Then, defeated in trying to motivate and inspire others to her personal cause, retreats to the reclusive life of the monastic. In her home, like poet Emily Dickenson, she prefers the escape quality of her workroom.

If her husband or lover intrudes in her room where she creates her projects, or tells her to clean up her messy desk, the intrusion disturbs her third function, her introverted sensing. She is immediately thrown off balance, and feels off-center for a long time after. She's unable to return to her work and concentration.

This stress makes her even more afraid to relate to people in the outside world and draws her further into her imagination and own reality. The ISFP woman can extrovert her sensing deal with the outside world, and feel at home in the world of quilting, sewing, and crafts.

In contrast, the INFP woman using extroverted intuition to deal with the outside world, can only sit and write about her dominant introverted feelings, her likes and dislikes, in her inner personal journal. It is only when she truly learns to extrovert intuition and not feed it back into her introverted feelings that she can become a resource person.

Using her extroverted intuition, she can conjure up hundreds of ideas and resources to bring people together, to connect people to places where they can find the information they want on any subject imaginable. Introverts use their second (auxiliary) function to deal with the outside world because their dominant function is introverted, remaining hidden and used to make decisions or choices in life.

Under stress, the INFP woman in love or seeking it, transfers her urge to make the world a gentler and better place to pleasing herself. She wants her life to be about an endless search for self-identity and for the deepest possible meaning of life.

As the stress and pressures increase, she finds there is no way to uncover what her own deepest meaning is on earth, because, obviously, it's out there on other galaxies only to be found among more highly evolved space beings who have been here billions of years longer than ourselves.

So she focuses, instead, on developing human potential to the fullest while at the same time avoiding face-to-face contact with people.

Being around people too much makes the INFP woman sick-exhausted, hypertensive, shaking with adrenaline from the flight response of stress.

She needs a week to recover and recharge after speaking in public. In fact, she hates having to teach or speak before a group. Yet, she is pulled into inspiring and motivating people in jobs more suited to the ENFJ or ENTP, making presentations. She'd rather say it in writing. She has entered teaching or the speaking circuit against every fiber in her body which cries out for introversion, from moving away from direct people contact. She's entered this field as the only realistic alternative to secretarial routine.

If she stays in the secretarial routine, she works at home as a medical transcriptionist, competing with the ISTJs who can do that work better, but she really hates routine, repetitive clerical work even more than she hates public speaking.

With enough stress having to talk in public, physical symptoms arise to make her quit and return to creative work inside the-home-writing, magazine illustration, book indexing, or organizing other people's files. Only the disorganized, messy-desked perceiver, the "P" will meticulously study books on how to organize files and eliminate clutter. There is no better cluttered woman than the INFP, with the ENFP almost an equal in disorganized, creative, and messy desks and closets.

For a fee she'll tell you how to organize your files and manage your records, meanwhile inside hating every moment of such obsessive behavior about files. She'll get fired from job after clerical job, driving the ISTJ clerical supervisor nuts or making mistakes in detail on so many jobs that they ask whether she had spent time in a mental hospital if she should work in a real estate agency. No, she hasn't. She's a square peg in a round hole. She needs to work on creative projects to lessen her stress.

In a marriage, under stress, the INFP woman seeks a man to whom she can devote her gifts and talents. She won't waste her energy on a man who will be controlling. She's after his wallet.

Only in finding a man to support her financially can she realize her dream of sitting like a kitten on a satin pillow and writing her series of psychothriller novels featuring radio talk show psychologists as detective characters-women who talk fearlessly on the airwaves, sending shock waves across America, brilliant ENTJ women leaders.

INFP woman under stress becomes Cinderella. Inside she hates authority figures. Outside she needs a husband to be a patron of the arts. She seeks a husband to sponsor her, to financially support her, so she can stay home and practice her artistic personality-whether or not it earns money for her.

At the same time she craves attention, rapport, and recognition, fame from the public for her art, she needs to maintain her privacy from intrusion.

As stress increases, she takes the phone off the hook and leaves it off for days at a time. She wants no one to crack her monastic reclusive life. As a recluse, she can outdo the INTP recluse. The INFP woman seeks solitude to get away from people causing her to feel anxiety by their demands. She sees people asking for money or favors as exploitation.

INFP woman is interested in what makes people tick. She writes about it or illustrates it in art every minute of her day.

She is flexible and adaptable. Under stress, her own high standards hurt her and make her more ill than her husband ever could, regardless of the names he calls her. She's attracted to the ISFJ and the ESTP man. One of them will physically beat her, maybe even kill her, if given the chance under the right circumstances. The other will verbally abuse and emotionally neglect her.

As a perfectionist, the INFP woman under stress measures her marriage against everyone else's standards of perfection. She seems never to find romance outside a novel. Her idealism causes her downfall because she needs to have everything about her lover just right.

No man can live up to the standards of perfection of a romance novel character from her imagination. No soul mate can give her the freedom she wants and at the same time allow her to control his actions as she controls hers-even though she's not a judging type.

It's not compulsion that drives her to control her mate, it's the need for idealistic perfection. The INFP woman's control-needs-her need to control every movement of her mate are enormous. That's why with an ISFJ male, his attempts at controlling her in the typical ISFJ fashion are timid compared to her control needs with her soul mate. Not finding perfection in the marriage is the cause of her stress.

She will control her husband, trying to make him fit her ideal of perfection in love, but never being able to show her feelings of love which remain introverted-until one of her values is violated.

Under stress, she will halt the process of adapting to her mate. There is no more stubborn woman than a value-violated INFP.

Her inferior or shadow function, the fourth function of her four-letter type is extroverted thinking. It's what is least developed in her personality. She won't even get in touch with it until she's more than fifty years old, and even then, it will be child-like and feel undeveloped or new.

She won't make impersonal decisions that will cause conflict. She's afraid of conflict. She'll let an angry, violent ESTP husband take away her cash, car, house, and children before she'll subject herself to the anxiety of fighting him in a courtroom or facing the cruel, cold, corporate world trying to find a grunt-work job to support herself and her family.

Under stress, her inferior function, as C.G. Jung puts it, or flip side kicks in, so that extroverted thinking is inferior. She will scream at her husband, analytical judgments that are not really logical or true, but dogmatic and prejudiced. Facts are hotly misquoted. Emotions show extreme verbal hostility, with rapid speech. Whatever is analyzed is viewed with haste. Her decisions are value and person-centered. Under the shadow side, the inferior function of extroverted thinking appears hostile to the listener.

If she's angry at her mate, the vocal side of her high verbal intelligence becomes hostile. She will argue with an ISFJ man until this normally timid man cracks, and in a flurry of anger and blame, and beats her up physically and verbally with words like "loser," "friendless," and "job quitter."

Blame takes over the relationship, and then contempt. The resentment grows, and the contempt and criticism increase until the couple are shrouded in a marriage based on anger.

INFP women tend to become locked into their least developed side, which is extroverted thinking, when under stress in a love affair or when in a job they no longer enjoy. In love, the INFP woman uses her inferior logic as a weapon against herself, preventing her from entering into what could be a good marriage.

Low self-esteem is the cause of why most INFP marry down instead of up as most women want to do. They don't consider themselves worthy to marry a man of the rank they fantasize about in their dream of what a good marriage should be.

For example, an INFP woman married outside her religion and had her two children kidnapped by her former husband, a foreigner, (and also a wife-beater). She felt unworthy after the divorce to marry a man of her own religious and ethnic background.

In her second marriage, she chose a man with just as little education as her first husband. He also abused her.

This man also was of a different ethnic and religious background as her own. Her second husband often expressed negative words and bigoted attitudes toward her ethnic heritage, yet she remains married to him for several decades "taking the abuse" because of her fear of financial problems in her old age. She hasn't worked outside the home or earned money of her own for more than two decades and has less than $500 in savings in the bank.

Under stress, INFP women put their work down, saying they have accomplished nothing worthwhile in their lifetimes. The INFP woman drowns in low self-esteem created by her own introverted feelings that dominate her entire being. They complain of being strangled by the men who narrow their world to the threshold of their homes. They speak about battling the "upward gush of their own infancy."

INFP women speak and write in metaphor. They worship those who show them irony, usually NTs, and humorous NT men and women who present their humor in biting satire are their idols, but the INFP woman fears the NT's logic and criticism. She fears the NT man will see everything possible that could be criticized with her and proceed to criticize her in order to improve her.

She worships her own inferior function or shadow function, the fourth letter of one's four-letter type on the MBTI (extroverted thinking) in any man. She reads the ultimate NT magazine on the future of technology and science. She writes science fiction.

It's the ENTJ (dominant extroverted thinking) man she idolizes, but it's the INTP, Albert Einstein's picture (and the logical, Spock character from "Star Trek") whose photos are on her wall. However, she wouldn't go near a real INTP for fear of criticism and distance from emotions. She doesn't feel worthy (with her low-self esteem and self-criticism) of an intellectual NT man who could find a redundancy or other fault to criticize in her work. (She'll do it by herself.)

She avoids the NT skeptic when she is an NF believer in the leaps of faith when praised and the encouragement of the human potential movement. She can't take a mentor because she has a need to be one. Her low self-esteem makes her afraid of watching the competition.

Too often the competition is from a younger, NT job. More than loving him, she desperately wants his job, is jealous of it, and at the same time feels in love, she would be totally dependent on him financially.

Under stress, her need for privacy from her mate and from anyone else grows. She would rather improve herself through personal growth experience involving praise, not criticism. If a writer, an editor's criticism will be put away for a decade before read when her self-esteem improves.

Under marital stress, the INFP woman gives no man any power over her, yet she is afraid to learn to drive or to venture across the street.

Agoraphobia often takes hold at the point when stress overtakes her body and powerlessness appears to be unchallengeable.

Under the worst of stress, the INFP remains the most idealistic of all women, carrying the Cinderella story to its epitome. It's not beauty that wins the prince in the INFP Cinderella story, it's creativity and intelligence.

The INFP will see people's most positive potential and most important value. Through the written word or illustration, she will try to develop that potential and value. If the INFP man succeeds with an ISFP wife, then the INFP woman thrives on the stability of the ISFJ soul mate.

INFP woman judges herself more deeply than any INTP man judges himself critically. She also heals herself-alone and undisturbed except by nature and the life force. She must pursue ideals as the ISFP woman pursues play.

INFP women have a low social need to meet new friends, unless those friends can find them a creative job that pays well. When stress is gone, she becomes more extroverted, often taking on acting roles, different identities, pretending to be people of different nationalities to develop her ability to create characters for her novels or artwork or counseling skills.

INFP woman is a catalyst, bringing people together for a common interest to learn about how to improve, find a better job, or learn how to express themselves creatively. Under stress, she will write about her self and her mate more, as in a diary or autobiography.

Then she'll turn the autobiography into a film script and seek a producer. In her need for both recognition and privacy, there is a tendency to write many books under as many different names.

She will disguise herself, wear wigs of different colors, change her eye color with contact lenses, or travel incognito to be left alone, except by those with similar interests.

She advertises for a soul mate in specific trade magazines or scholarly journals in esoteric subjects such as publishing, writing, archaeology, anthropology, psychology, illustration, genetics, ethnic studies, or creativity and the expressive arts.

Her soul mates are ISFJ, INFP, ENFP, and any other man terribly serious about life and making the world better and healthier. Under stress, the INFP woman needs to be taken on a trip where she can create her own reality and escape for a short time to relax her chronic anxiety and fear that people are going to harm her. Her biggest complaint is that she doesn't feel safe around her mate. She needs a safe house.

# INTP

## Enneagram Type 5 With A 4 Wing Or INTP On The MBTI™
### Introverted, Intuitive, Thinking, Perceiving
### Dominant Introverted Thinking With Extroverted Intuition

8. INTP, will solve any problem, but too busy collecting facts to show you passion. Give him clarity or give him riddles to solve.

INTP is the most logical-also an analyst, architect of ideas and models as well as a skeptic. If you want someone like Star Trek's logic-wracked Spock or an Einstein type, than look for this arrogant, reclusive, and intellectual snob (worshipped and followed around by INFP women) who uses his thinking— pure logic—to express love. ESFPs might call the INTP male "an academic blowhard." It depends upon prior experience with this male who finds research studies flawed and reports in writing on the flaw. You may not measure up to his analytical façade. He's a tough act to follow or to top.

The meaning of his writing may be lost in verbosity. He'll put you down for redundancy, but rarely will he strike you. More likely, he'll go on strike. He won't tell you he feels love. He'll only say he understands love to be a remnant of the bicameral mind of three thousand years ago and before, when men listened to auditory hallucinations of their dead kings and had to obey the cold commands of the hallucinated speech of their idols. He won't tell you to go to hell in a hand basket.

He'll point out what went wrong and analyze why. This cold, INTP Einstein of a man wants to be alone in his room so he can watch his equations squirm up the page. Don't let him watch you squirm. Merely tell him you're too intellectual to fret. The best way to outsmart him is to tell him your motto is "be prepared," which is the motto of an ISTJ logistics maven. The INTP's world is theory, analysis, and research, not development, but systems and architecture. He'll build you a matrix when you want a mattress.

If you want to get concrete with details, the INTP will tell you which securities he analyzed using neural networks, heuristics, and artificial intelligence applied to the stock market, or you can watch him predict weather patterns a century in advance on his computer. For best results, interest your INTP in computational linguistics and watch him try to find a subject in common with you.

If you're an INFP woman, you can learn a lot. He may lack confidence in himself. So if it's advice you seek, turn to the INTJ. And when the INTJ starts to extrovert thinking at you, and your mind goes blank, return home to your INTP and listen to his research. The analysis will make you aware of what you have in common: extroverted intuition and a bounty of research and resources on the subjects you enjoy most. INTP and INFP have a lot in common such as a mutual interest in archaeology, anthropology, and finding out what makes people behave as they do.

Picture an INTP professor who is seduced and brought down to ruin by an ESFP lover in a movie such as "The Blue Angel." When opposite attract, the shadows that draw out the reclusive INTP may pose a danger of pulling the absent minded professor type into a vortex where the dominant introverted thinking function isn't in touch with the partner's dominant extroverted sensing in the case of an INTP man and an ESFP woman. When the tables are turned, and it's the INTP woman looking at her ESFP lover, she sees in him the confidence she lacks in performing in front of large audiences. However, INTP women usually are drawn to ENTP men who spend their time inventing gadgets. When INTP marries, most often it's with an ENTJ leader in business who gives her a private space to do her analytical research and writing.

## Under Stress: The Darkest Side Of INTP In Marriage

Under stress, INTP will become reclusive, avoiding people in order to sit and think. If you want the epitome of a scientist-researcher who collects facts and shelves them, marry the INTP logician.

He may be a math major, a scientist, researcher, historian, or academic. He's perfect for the imaginative INFP woman who needs facts from the past or from research to write a historical novel about the age of auditory hallucinations from speaking gods in ancient Mesopotamia.

This wordy man will hook onto the creative and imaginative INFP woman like glue and remain loyal. In bed he'll woo you with accounts of ancient history, Greek mythology, and his theories of the origin of the universe in mathematical formulae or his infinite vocabulary of words you'll need a quintessential dictionary to find.

The INTP man or woman hates redundancy. So say it only once.

Someone will always want to hire him for his competency, which he will always be seeking to improve. Everything needs to be improved in this man's eyes, even you. He'll never be poor, but don't mess with his computer.

# The INTP Woman
# Enneagram Type 5 With A 4 Wing Or NTP On The MBTI™
# INTP: Introverted, Intuitive, Thinking, Perceiving

## Dominant Introverted Thinking With Extroverted Intuition

INTP, an indifferent-to-reality woman, can find her soul mate in the ISTP male, who's fed up with the real world of present-day facts. He hungers for adventure and excitement with a female analyst of securities, trends, science, and the future.

The INTP woman's soul mate is a companion who can think along with her-the ISTP in his utilitarian way designing products, the INTP in her in her philosophical, abstract way-designing computer languages, number systems, or ideas in philosophy or psychology.

If both ISTP and INTP work in the computer field, they could find a strong common bond from their different corners. She's there for the intellectual challenge, he for the excitement of creating computer games, special movie effects, or useful products like designing the faces on phones.

In her search for clarity, the INTP woman sees patterns of evolution in each man and in every individual marriage. She sees patterns that she hopes to connect and collect, label, and classify as Darwin classified different species in the throes of evolution.

Everything in a marriage is to be classified according to labels, types, styles, temperaments, species, formulas, equations, models, or tables. There's a name for everything in the INTP's search for clarity. In the meantime what could be a simple fact is made complex by abstractions and irony.

Her soul mate is the man who can make simple and concrete what she has made complex and theoretical. Her marriage reads like an advanced computer manual she thinks she has clarified. She's turned life into a puzzle. She may grow more reclusive with less self confidence, yet become more analytical as she grows older. She's searching for a laid-back type of power seeker who can tell her how to get important people to help her without having to socialize and make small talk.

The INTP woman seeks charisma in a husband. Her brilliance in the intellectual world demands a tight metal corset, a heavy anchor to weigh her down to earth without enslaving her.

It's a fine line to straddle, so she balances on the edge, forever seeking a soul mate who has both charisma and economic stability without the boring emptiness of the SJ controller who to her focuses on conserving the petty details of life.

She swims upstream against the prospect of motherhood in the full blast of its sacrificial martyrdom. Like the INTJ, she dreads having to give it all up to stay home with the children when they're small, fearing she'll never get back the credibility and power she had. She left her achievements in midstream because they crashed against the glass ceiling.

Her soul mate needs to be a man to whom tradition isn't important, but intellectual precision is-in a woman. What this female Henry Higgins wants is a man she can analyze like she would in her ideal job as a securities analyst. Her silent ISTP Eliza Doolittle may do little for her in the economic world, but with his tool skills, can bring out in design what's in her mind.

The image the INTP woman has in her mind of her ISTP soul mate is a flight captain, designer of planes and space ships, an astronaut or weapons master who uses his thinking to put to paper when she can only philosophize about in the abstract. INTP woman uses extroverted thinking to deal with the outside world.

She needs an ISTP man who also uses extroverted thinking to deal with the tools in his hand and head as well as the three-dimension models he creates on his computer or in bold sculpture. It works the other way around also, an INTP man (analyst, self-publisher, professor of philosophy, math, or psychology) married to an ISTP woman (robotics engineer, pilot, physician, or technical illustrator). He can work on his complex, abstract thoughts at home while she goes out with hard hat and builds the robots, flies planes for her own clients, examines patients, or drafts water-saving toilets for a plumbing company.

The INTP woman is one big concept seeking clarification. She needs a man to provide her with the conclusion to her life's search. That man is the ISTP, INTP, or ENTP. The ISTP and INTP soul mate are a match for her. She will reduce the ISTP and INTP to a concept.

The ISTP man wants his freedom and his space more than anything else in the world. The INTP woman wants her own physical space where she can sit and think out her puzzles more than she wants power. They will give each other the freedom both need.

## INTP: Under Stress: The Darkest Side Of Marriage

Reducing her mate in her mind, judging him incompetent is easy to do for the INTP woman under stress. She needs intellectual rapport with a mind that stimulates hers. If she leaves her ISTP, it's usually for financially irresponsible INTP. She will take charge of her own corporation and seek out extroverted business partners to make presentations with or for her-usually ENFP men.

Under pressure, she goes blank and loses the ability to speak in public. She withdraws and falls silent as a fossil's hoof mark in sandstone. The higher the pressure, the more disorganized and absent-minded INTP woman becomes.

She criticizes her mate freely under stress, moving her spouse or partner from one intuitive, abstract thought to the next, until she runs out of ways to improve her mate or he falls asleep, not listening to her any more because he doesn't understand the symbol to which she's alluding.

She uses big words when simpler ones would do, showing her arrogance at her sensing mate's plain and simple tastes, unless she finds a renowned scientist to marry. Her arguments are complex enough for her mate to tune her out or turn up the radio louder when she opens her mouth. As a result, she withdraws into silence.

INTP manipulates people by distracting them. Under stress, she confuses her mate or children by using big, meaningless words to frighten her preschoolers as in, "If you don't clean up your room, I'll send you to the curriculum."

When dealing with her sensing mate's issues, the INTP woman acts bored. She hates the realities and details of being married. Even more, she hates shopping, cooking, cleaning, and mending. Anything mundane dealing with the cold facts of life are disgusting.

If she makes a mistake, she'll give herself a verbal whack before her mate can blame her. Boring details drive her into further reclusiveness. She'll do anything to work alone, to gain the solace of solitude.

Under stress, the shy INTP grows even more shy and reclusive. It's up to the mate to make sure the details presented to her deal with extroverted intuition and alternative solutions or possibilities.

INTP has great stress meeting people for the first time and will fall silent or shun social meetings and conventions other than giving a business presentation. If stopped, she'll usually shy away saying, "I don't have time to chat."

Don't force the INTP woman to attend parties, unless the discussion is on a topic she's researching. Under stress, the INTP woman feels betrayed by society. She's not supposed to be a "thinking woman" without being punished by men and traditional, ESFJ women. She's cautious and guarded about people who tell her what she should do.

If she says, "I love my career." And the next words out of an ESFJ woman's mouth is an abrupt, "Who takes care of the children?" The INTP woman will snap back, "What children? I don't have any. Why should I have kids when I don't even like them?"

The conversation will go downhill from there on. The more stress is put on the INTP woman, the less she will be aware of how her words impact other people's feelings.

INTP as a teacher won't give you a bathroom break. It's a favorite slip of memory to lecture complex, slow-moving and esoteric subjects until every one's attention span has drifted off the subject to a trance state.

As a wife or soul mate, the INTP woman won't make decisions based on any personal value, like or dislike, without thinking she has just blurted out an epithet of bigotry. Low self-esteem plagues the INTP woman, no matter how many college degrees or how prestigious her job is.

As her marriage sours, low self-esteem hits suddenly. She falls into her inferior function, introverted feeling...and behaves like the worse side of an INFP. She'll make really bad subjective decisions. She'll put herself down before anyone else can take a shot.

Anger takes over the life of the INTP under stress. She withdraws from all social contact, screams at store clerks, or goes blank in public when she has to think and speak. Under stress, the INTP woman will avoid with great fear doing anything requiring touching machinery, mechanical objects, handling equipment, or learning any new subject (like music) requiring sensing.

She fears she will not be perfect. If she can't be perfect, she won't embarrass herself by making a lot of mistakes while learning. To be a beginner in learning a new skill is dreaded with shame. She's afraid she'll be laughed at for her beginner's incompetence. So if she can't do something well, she won't try to learn it at all.

Marriage is one other conceptualization for the INTP woman. Under stress, she will not speak to a stranger first to introduce herself. Human relationships is her weakest point. She can use the help of an ISTP soul mate to excite her enough with his very different concrete thinking. Concrete thinking can help her put aside shyness. A soul mate to the

INTP woman is a companion willing to trade the energy behind crises tactics for her intellectual gifts.

# ESTP

## The Male Extroverts: Their Dark Side
## Enneagram Type 8 With A 7 Wing Or ESTP On The MBTI™
## ESTP: Extroverted, Sensing, Thinking, Perceiving

### Dominant Extroverted Sensing With Introverted Thinking

9. ESTP, full of restless drama—he looks for clues all over the world, taking in details about people you wouldn't always want to be remembered. ESTP, under the best conditions is a publicist and promoter. Under extreme stress, this man can be the most unpredictable womanizing, globetrotting sadist, possible kleptomaniac, and foremost wife-beater, a wheeler-dealer promoter ready to drop you if you mention his girlfriend. This man's an extroverted sensor.

He'll observe detail about you and tell others in front of you that you pee standing up and condemn you for it in front of mutual friends. The revelation will be sudden and in public, and you wonder why couldn't he have mentioned what he observed to you in private. This is a man who enjoys observing details about you and broadcasting those details publicly, usually when you have several guests in your home. It's his way of telling you he's angry because he wants to be free, and you're a stone around his neck weighing him down to hearth and home. If he leaves you, he'll take the children and then dump them on his mother to rear so he can be free to travel, meet more women and find out what they can give him. If he's new to your nation, he may want to marry you so he can get a card to work in your country. Keep your garage door closed when he's around, as he may steal what's inside, thinking if you're dumb enough to leave the door open, then you deserve to lose your valuables.

He could be the guy who looks at what works and then moves on to something more exciting. If bored with you, he can become in a year or less, a cheater who will in his faked sociopathic way travel to the ends of the earth to follow his impulses and affairs and never stick to anything long enough, but just could promote something into millions but only for the moment. He fakes being sociopathic to enjoy his right to take what you left unguarded, from your property and real estate to your citizenship, children, or community property.

He's truly a man who could hate women under the right circumstances if you're the right masochistic ISFP or INFP woman who loves him for the excitement he generates, his charm contrasted against the simple life he abhors, and your arts and crafts or music he is eager to put his foot through.

The ESTP man in his possibly kleptomaniac way, longs to break the rules of love and marriage as he breaks the rules at works and aims to be his own boss. He'll do you in first, and worry later about which rules he broke on purpose to satisfy his need for excitement and action.

This man won't go past his baseline, but he's not above kidnapping your children to a foreign land to be raised by his mother without answering your mail until the kids are old enough to come around asking for college money from you. The ESTP man is the toughest bureaucrat in your bed who will split the second someone who looks like you offering more excitement or money comes along. Sometimes, he may think if your stupid enough to marry him, then you deserve to be lied to. That's only when he's feeling down on himself and wants to pick himself up by putting you down.

He is a man of action, and he'll leave rather than continue beating you when there are ESFP women to watch performing that he can follow around. He'll attach himself to an ESFP woman, usually a dancer or performer and follow her at all hours of the night to clubs to socialize.

If you complain about his girl friends, you'll be slapped down again and your children will be swept away from your custody so he can boast, "I don't want my kids on welfare." He won't hang around too long, but he will send his mom money to rear them. What he really wants is to charm rich, prominent women into making him the center of attention. If his business is slow, he needs to promote something he values. The best cure for his kleptomania is to make him the host of a national radio talk show.

This may never happen, so he will keep on traveling and meeting wealthy women to sweet talk. He may buy a restaurant or nightclub to socialize with new people, but rarely will take the time to learn how to manage the business by the book. He runs his business by using people around him to do the physical work so he can talk to customers and impress them with his tales of adventure. He will fake almost anything to get by or dress up in costumes to impress and fuel fantasies.

The ESTP must have an outlet in marriage for excitement, whether it's a mistress who dances exotically, a few nights a week at with the boys at topless bars, his own nightclub and restaurant, a real estate agency or any business that deals with the public in exciting ways. The ESTP is the essence of the dramatic.

Marriage, like work, means variety at a fast pace. This man makes an excellent stock broker who thrives on adrenaline and calling people all day, or waiting on tables. Or he could be a genius who grabs the moment from some business enterprise and creates visibility in a concrete way, like running a circus or casino.

The impulsive ESTP man marries for the electricity so he can improvise his way through a relationship as well as a job. Sometimes his impulse control can get so low, that he'll shoplift because he saw something exciting lying there. The ESTP man may not have any awareness of his impact on your emotions.

He won't sit back and let poverty wash over him. He wants the great life, not only the good life. He's a gambling risk taker who loves places like Las Vegas, if only to go there with a girlfriend who's in an exciting or entertaining job herself. The ESTP man is the world's best hustler in any relationship or business deal.

If this man is no longer the center of your attention, or if you no longer are the center of attention in his life, he's out the door, sometimes with all the money in your joint account and usually with your children too.

ESTP doesn't care about how you feel unless how you feel about something makes a big difference in something the ESTP wants from you. He's not above cancelling a divorce until you sign the house over to him, and then starting the divorce up again as he kicks you out the door.

No decision the ESTP makes are centered on people, other than himself and his children, placing them above the wife's individual feelings. The ESTP man needs the practical. If it's not reality-based and practical, it will never make sense. Don't bring up the esoteric, theoretical or metaphysical with this man, or risk being called a flake and a kook if you're into self-actualization, personal growth, or the world that can't be touched with the senses. He does not believe in invisible realities, except a superficial programming in his religion.

This man doesn't think in terms of values clarification. He's not concerned with personal values of yours unless it affects his well-being or goal. As the ESTP gets older, he may get in touch with his intuition more. In youth, getting in touch with his intuition means sometimes reading science fiction or watching science fiction on television.

This man is not going to stay in school for long, unless there's the type of hands-on, fly by the seat of the pants activity that he craves, such as being a radio talk show host or running a restaurant, machinist's shop, or supermarket. He has to see a practical use for any course, game, job, or relationship. If he's bored, he'll be bad. The ESTP man, when depressed, gets angry at himself and often gives up his fight to live. He withdraws and thinks negatively about everything, including how to get revenge on you and take something away something from you that will hurt you where you'll feel it most.

Action makes the ESTP stronger-getting involved with the risk and excitement of action. This man won't share his inner fight with you. His temper is usually very short. What the ESTP man loves most is total freedom to come and go as he pleases. You become a rope and stone heavy around his neck when he's tired of you, which is usually about seven years into the marriage or less-and two preschoolers later.

He is unpredictable and loves his freedom to travel in order to meet new people. Each new person he meets can serve him, give him something, and make him freer. He doesn't want a rope around his neck, which could be the same wife for many years. There are too many other women he'd like to meet and greet, women who can give him money, a passport, or prestige.

He likes getting the adrenaline pumping in tense situations of work and relationships. He's not for the romantic woman. He's for the fast, restless ESTP or ESFP woman who challenges him and can find new relationships when he's gone. He's for the woman who's a beautiful entertainer with a day job in real estate, for example, who doesn't need him for financial or emotional security because she has her investments in many accounts and owns her own home from a previous situation, a home he can't touch, should he depart and ask for the house with which to buy a business.

The ESTP can never be tied down. Give him challenge. He leaves the woman when family life becomes mundane and work becomes routine. He needs room to roam around the world many times with an adventure buddy, preferably an ENTP. Women attracted to him are other ESTPs and ESFP entertainers, dancers, physical therapists, skiers, or other athletes.

## Under Stress: The Darkest Side Of ESTP In Marriage

Marry him if you want excitement and passion until he's sidetracked by something with a fresh angle on his news. This adventurer, real estate promoter, or talk show host is restless to start new businesses and new relationships. He's tired of sitting back and letting poverty pinch him. If you have the money he want, he'll go out of his way to court you. When he gets what he wants, he'll move on to the next way to make a living promoting himself. He's a social climber without much preparation, and he'll fake being impressive if he has to in order to gain the hand of a rich woman who can give him what he can't give himself—status and class, even though he's an extroverted charmer to the public. He looks for short cuts to wealth and fame.

He's a charmer in public, but can toss the vase in your face across the dinner table. Watch out for his sizzle and tool-wielding abilities as well as the way he waits on tables with that ESTP Rhett Butler smile. Frankly, my dear, when he's restless for fun and adventure abroad or on the air, this freedom-seeker doesn't give a damn! The most he'll want you to be is not a stone around his neck when he's ready to move on to run his own gig.

ESTP is the most unpredictable ultimate realist of promoter-wheeler-dealers who'd make a great companion for an ESFP belly dancer at three in the morning when she gets off work. He loves excitement, travel, surprise, and variety.

He'll cheat on you left and right. He'll never be on time or hang around when you have babies and come down with postpartum agoraphobia. That's when he'll split, when you're at your lowest point and get boring.

He's the most likely to become a misogynist when the chips are down. This promoter can promote your business to high heaven. He's a con man who'll make you rich quick by any means he can, even devious methods.

He invented the sting operation. He'll also import a product and gain the rights to distribute it in some other country and make a million, but lose it just as quick. He won't show respect for family traditions. If you have children with him, he may take custody in a divorce just to flout tradition.

If you're that ESFP performer, personnel director, athlete, coach, physical therapist, nurse, teacher, dancer, or other entertainer, he can be the ESTP promoter you're looking for to sell you to the public in a flash and be gone an instant later in his search for variety and excitement.

Don't expect him to buy local real estate with his money so you'll have security in twenty years. He'll rent a night club for three years and then split to a third world country. He lives for the moment in concrete, practical reality.

## The ESTP Woman

**Enneagram Type 8 Woman, Usually With A 9 Wing, Lower Score On Sensing And 7 Wing For Higher Score On Extraverted Sensing Or ESTP On The MBTI ™**
**ESTP: Extroverted, Sensing, Thinking, Perceiving**
**Dominant Extroverted Sensing, With Introverted Thinking**

ESTP, a woman of action who won't sit back and let poverty wash over her if a tycoon can help her find a more exciting life using her spontaneity to meet crises. The ESTP woman wants to fly by the seat of her culottes. She puts out symbolic fires in the oil wells of men's hearts.

In any marriage, when an ESTP woman walks into the room, the game of entrepreneur happens. She's the goodwill ambassador or diplomat, the promoter, and negotiator. She will sell you real estate on Mars.

If the male ESTP is a wheeler-dealer, the restless female ESTP is the conciliator. A resourceful ESTP woman will negotiate a job contract or a prenuptial agreement better than the average male executive, even if she's a high-school dropout.

Paired with her soul mate, the ENTP male, the ESTP woman becomes a negotiator par excellence. She can take almost any man away from his wife, if he has enough money and charm to make her world exciting. The man hunt is her game. She must make things happen in a relationship. It takes her about seven years to lose interest, unless there's something else she wants from the game, like property.

She's fun, above all, with the ESFP man, who often becomes her lover, when marriage to the ENTP man becomes too abstract and boring for her concrete tastes in fun. She isn't after power like the ENTP is. She's after fun, games, change, and excitement. Most of all, she's out to manipulate her external environment as much as the men in it.

In marriage, the ESTP searches for the dramatic "in the activity of the moment" to promote about a mate. Her personality is a dramatic, impersonal, analytical, and concrete. She lives in the moment, not for the future. Her soul mate is a partner who would above all, give her the freedom to move at will, to travel.

Her life is hell bent on adventure and travel. Her headquarters is Las Vegas or Hollywood. Only the ENTP adventurer/producer, another ESTJ, or an ISTP tool-master or pilot can give this restless roamer what she needs to use her practical thinking abilities in a relationship.

In marriage, she will break all the rules. Her goal is to make the relationship work while it excites her. Nothing is sacred and nothing forever, except her need for excitement, fun, and thinking on her feet.

She makes a good match for an ESTP or ENTP diplomat traveling in the foreign service who prefers not to put down roots anywhere for many years, or for a radio talk show host, who travels from station to station to make an impact sending shock waves over the air. She needs to be around her own kind of fun-seeking, game-playing, straight-talking people, outgoing people who think dramatically for a living before an audience of pragmatic realists.

The ESTP woman believes in never asking for marriage advice, never going to a "shrink" and never going to an attorney, until you know exactly what you want to hear from the so-called expert.

She knows how to negotiate a prenuptial marriage contract by asking the type of questions that elicit the positive answer she wants. This natural negotiator will keep her bottom line in her head. She'll walk out on a marriage and on a whole series of jobs or business deals if asked to make the wrong decision for her lifestyle of the moment.

Making impersonal decisions about facts is the way she runs her marriage. Either a love affair works or it doesn't.

She never says she's sorry, and she never reflects on the road not taken. There is no usefulness to looking back when moving on up in love or business.

ESTP women are tough, blunt, and resilient, and sometimes find themselves surviving well in prison, literal or figurative. She will dirty her hands and work well with the ISTP using tools. As a radio talk show hostess, she is paid for being to the point and obnoxious. As a skeptic for pay, she can debunk almost as well as the INTJ. Any idiosyncratic behavior in others, such as belief in invisibile realities, or magical thinking is dismissed as crazy.

She hates men who are dreamers and loves men who take action. She'll jump right in to everything from a marriage to a venture capital deal and decide immediately what she must do to get her share out of the experience.

Life is a game of variety called crises. Marriage is a variation on a theme. In love, she'll go for what's quicker. This woman loves to handle crises by the typical "SP" temperament "expedient guerrilla tactics" rather than "NT" temperament strategies of logic and analysis, such as the typical ENTJ solution of C3 I, Command, Control, Communications, and intelligence.

In fact, what the ESTP woman hates most in a man is his NT use of the "military shorthand" C3 I that NT mates love to use to control their SP wives.

NT men, especially ENTJs, use a system on SP wives, (especially ESFP and ENTP freedom-loving women seeking to put out symbolic fires in the home and everywhere else) by using a system of command, control, communications, and intelligence to insure that the commander is able to communicate and receive intelligence from his units in the field. Thereby, the commander can retain and execute control of a situation.

Using C3 I on a mate results in a bi-directional flow of information. That is, communication goes both ways. NT husbands use this strategy on their SP wives. And SP wives use tactics to get even with their husbands. Particularly, the ESTP woman adapts her NT mate's system to her outgoing, social battlefront.

Revenge is the ESTP woman's way of not feeling vulnerable about survival and endurance under the crushing corset of an SJ or NT male. However, the ENTP male, is less crushing than a rule-rationing SJ would be with a wayward artisan ESTP woman.

She's impatient with the NT or NF mate's theory. She runs with open arms toward the mate who can offer her immediate, useful, and practical solutions in her love life or in business. More often than not her love life results from success in her work life. She meets her mate most frequently at work.

She's not above taking away another woman's husband for her own, even if it doesn't result in marriage. She seeks what usefulness the relationship has to her social climbing. The man she's most likely to leave is the mate who offers her only alternatives and possibilities. She can't see them other than the products of useless fantasy.

ESTP won't trust her mate's hunches. They waste her time, and she won't try to conjure up hunches of her own. Usually they're all wet. Her inferior style is introverted intuition. She could wreck the married life of the INFJ man who feels drawn to her for the excitement, adventure, and exotic travel she offers.

Extroverted sensing is the realm of the ESTP woman. It's her best shot. Extroverted sensing is about finding all the clues inherent in observing details about objects or people. She makes a good detective or private eye, and is not above checking out her future mate as a private eye would. She notices every detail about her mate.

Introverted thinking is her second best style. She uses it in practical ways to find what's useful to her in a man. Her third function is extroverted feeling. She can be charming and warm when she needs to in order to attract the man of her dreams for her immediately practical use.

## ESTP: Under Stress: The Darkest Side Of Marriage

When she's pushed to her outer limits, the ESTP woman can become violent or threaten her mate by throwing objects around a room. She's likely to spit in his face, to pull his hair, to shove him out of a moving car, or to have affairs under his nose without trying to cover up the affairs in the least. At lunchtime, her mate will see her openly having business lunches with men who will see her most charming smiles and warm feelings if she thinks she can use them to rise up in social class, income, or lifestyle.

Under stress, she will use harsh words to people for making mistakes that cost her money. She gets angry when people have too many children and can't support them at middle class levels, or if she loses a client's money. ESTP woman makes an outstanding and formidable stock broker. She thrives on the adrenaline of calling people or of promoting the sale of financial investments or real estate, like her ESTP male co-worker.

Under stress, the ESTP woman's need for activity increases dramatically. She needs to put more excitement into her dramatic lifestyle. She's the type most likely to quit school to make lots of money as quickly as possible and move on to new interests and people using her sharp thinking skills.

She will lose interest immediately in any person she has no practical use for, and any mate not contributing to her goals will be seen as boring. She will leave and take the kids, house, car, and all the money in the bank if she can get away with it by saying anything to calm her spouse at the moment.

Truth is not one of her virtues in a marriage. The ESTP woman was put in a marriage only to disrupt it. In school, she's the most likely type to also disrupt classes ruled by ISFJ and ESFJ teachers.

Under great stress and pressure, the ESTP woman will spend time alone. She'll withdraw from people. She'll spend months wallowing in self-pity and act helpless, crippled, or sick to make others feel sorry for them. She's not above cooking up a scheme to sue stores by pretending to slip and fall in public, making sure it's videotaped, when she's in need of money and too stressed out to think up ways to earn it.

She's not good at thinking up possibilities or alternative ways to earn money once she loses the business or the job. It's far easier for her to find a wealthy or financially solvent marriage partner than to ponder possible new business to open. She usually sticks with what business is familiar-real estate, selling stocks or commodities, promoting other people's business, radio broadcasting, managing restaurants, sales, or meeting other business's crises.

ESTP women work as policewomen, detectives, firefighters or are in the some unique form of foreign service, perhaps as hostage rescue commandos or soldiers of fortune. They don't like to follow the military's rules in the traditional "ISTJ and ENTJ" military service. Stress comes easily to the ESTP woman's marriage. She seems to bring it on by her frequent need for action and excitement. ESTP women usually are married more than one time.

Under stress, the ESTP becomes unpredictable, irritable, moody, and negative. She puts herself down instead of becoming involved in anywhere the action is. She withdraws the more pressure mounts. Her temper is hair-trigger short. The freedom-seeking ESTP needs a soul mate who can give her the outlet for action she needs.

Her life is based on handling tension and crises outside herself. Being tied-down stresses her out. It takes another ESTP man or even an ENTP to present her with one challenge after another. This lady needs running space in a marriage. Routine is her downfall in love.

## The ESFP Man

## Enneagram Type 7 With An 8 Wing Or ESFP On The MBTI ™
## ESFP: Extroverted, Sensing, Feeling, Perceiving
## Dominant Extroverted Sensing With Introverted Feeling

10. ESFP is a big spender and more generous than a movie star on awards night. He'll meet the needs of many people, but be a stranger to yours unless you fight the crowd for his attention. Marry him if you want a man who's sidetracked by every passing stranger who needs to be rescued by him. He'll go in a dozen directions at once without focus.

He believes life is not a dress rehearsal, that you only go around once and there's no reincarnation. He's a performer looking to impact you with his big noise. He's the typical performer in Hollywood looking for a break, the male version of a chorus girl. He'll never meet your "routine" needs to have all his attention all the time. In bed he'll perform and watch himself in the mirror, not your reactions to him.

He's busy watching himself make an impact on you (sending shock waves across the airwaves). If you don't react to him so he can watch himself grow bolder at your reaction to his impact or performance, he'll look for someone else to be his groupie. If you have children with him as a parent he will promise one kid to be picked up at the same time as another and then leave his wife cooling her heels with a ruined dinner that he never got around to coming home to eat.

## Under Stress: The ESFP's Darkest Side In Marriage

ESFP, is the epitome of the radio talk show host who feels before he thinks, an actor and performer, a sports fan who has impact hunger for you. If he can't make an impact he'll go on to another venture where he can help someone less fortunate. Like the ISFJ male, when you don't need him anymore to depend upon, he'll lose interest and look elsewhere for somebody else's body to build. If he has the chance, he'll look around for someone to take care of who he feels "really needs him."

He's capable, in spite the feeling used for decision-making, of domestic violence towards his wife. He's capable of physically hurting you for revenge. He's also capable of saying, "See what you made me do? Hit you! See what you made me do? Become an alcoholic or addict!."

ESFP is known as the addictive personality when under high stress. This type also becomes bulimic. He uses his threat of becoming addicted to something-anything imaginable, not drugs, cigarettes, sports, alcoholic, food, etc. in order to make you do something his way.

He'll often marry an ISFJ woman who wants to change him, and end up abusing her in the worst ways imaginable while she becomes physically ill-tired, sad, angry, and sick. Some of the hardest working ISFJ nurses are married to rebellious, alcoholic or other addictive ESFP and ESTP men who wreak havoc and revenge upon them in the most wayward ways.

Other ESFP men are having multiple affairs in the marriage or are devoted to men's night out and sports to the total neglect of their hardworking SJ wives who complain, whine, and try to change or control them to make them toe the rules of the marriage vows.

He'll crush cans with his foot to make a loud noise to startle you, beep his horn as he drives by to force you to look up from your bus bench and notice him because nothing's going on inside him. He wants to send shock waves over the air and over you.

The ESFP addictive personality can't resist a quick fix, a high, and whatever else feels good for the moment without thinking of the consequences of the future. He's an exploding star that burns out early, but he'll shower you with his sunshine while he glows. He can make it rich quick, but chances are when he's rich, he'll switch.

## The ESFP Woman

**Enneagram Type 7 With An 8 Wing High Score Extraverted Sensing And**
**Lower Score On Feeling. Enneagram Type 7 With A 6 Wing For High Score On Extraverted Sensing And High Score On Feeling, Or ESFP On The MBTI.**
**ESFP: Extroverted, Sensing, Feeling, Perceiving**
**Dominant Extroverted Sensing, With Introverted Feeling**

ESFP enjoys being on stage and admired by onlookers. She's a natural born performer, physical therapist, trainer, and party woman who must perform and socialize at the same time. She would make a great real estate sales person. The epitome of the ESFP is the movie star who gathers facts about people to gossip. The right mate for ESFP is someone who is aware of who's doing what at the moment. ESFPs, like ESTPs, represent about 13 percent of the population of the United States. She is best mated with another ESFP or an ESTP who employs her on his team. The ESFP woman showers people with her sunshine and giggle, but really wants a large group of friends to be with her when she can no longer serve others. Her forte isn't service with a smile in the same way an ESFJ would organize an office. Instead, it's through making an impact in a bold way on an audience. In her young days, the ESFP might have waited on people or danced on stage. As she matures, she wants to sell real estate or luxury items to the rich and famous. She will always be a performer at her core, regardless of whether she works in a medical office, a nursing home for the aging, swims in a theme park, or sells fixer-uppers.

The mate the ESFP woman will pick and love will be like a movie camera sweeping over her constantly, a romantic who will make the marriage a costume drama in the particular time and setting she selects for the day. She is like Elizabeth Taylor in the 1964 version of the film, "Cleopatra," waiting for her "Antony" to keep her busy with what is.

This romantic, practical fun-loving woman seeks action in the physical body, such as skiing, swimming, or sports with spectators watching her perform. She may work as a nurse or a physical therapist, a teacher of preschoolers, or an event planner, but whatever she does in the mundane world, she will perform to an audience.

ESFP is generous with money, a big spender, and the most generous of all female types. Her gifts to men are exquisite and expensive. Usually, she finds her soul mate in a roving, ESTP adventurer.

Like the ENFP, ESFP is charismatic and fun to be around. She is the life of any party. Her soul mate is another ESFP, an ESTP, or an ENFP who appreciates the freedom-loving aspect of her performance for the sake of performing.

If she marries an ENFP, he will perform to enhance the personal growth or self-actualization of his audience. She will perform to excite and entertain, for fun, because she needs to be the life of the party, the center of attention. Her ENFP mate will need to be the center of attention for the sake of being loved, rather than for the excitement. If she marries an ESTP, her marriage will live as long as the excitement of the attraction.

The ESFP woman is the most passionate performer in bed of all the types, matching the ESFP man in displays of dominant extroverted sensing. It's not extroverted feeling she's exuding when in love or in passion. It's sensing. The ESFP's auxiliary feeling is introverted. Extroverted thinking is her third style, and her inferior style or function is introverted intuition.

She's keeping a record of every detail about the person she's with, about her lover. And she will throw it up to you, every detail, every fact, in an argument. Her life is about collecting any facts about people she can observe and using it to enrich her life for the sake of fun and excitement around people, not impersonal objects.

Her game is extroverted sensing. That's her idea of fun. She uses people to sort out the facts of her life. To stay married for long, she needs variety and action. Her soul mate needs to be subjective, a feeling man. Love must cling to reality. The ESFP woman looks to have fun and a good time in a wide variety of ways from owning a fashion, jewelry, cosmetic, or floral boutique, restaurant or night club to teaching belly dancing classes in community centers. ESFP does not like theories that put her to sleep. She's concrete and deals with tangible objects she can work with, whether they are fabrics or costume designs, houses or imported tile.

## ESFP: Under Stress: The Darkest Side Of Marriage:

Chaos in any form excites her. The more stressed she becomes with the loss of her loving friends, the more chaotic her life becomes. She's the most impulsive of all women, sometimes with very low impulse control.

Under stress, the ESFP woman will go to any extreme to get attention, competing with the ENFP male's need for attention. Her extremes will be further out, dangerous, and exciting, like an acrobat choosing to perform on the trapeze without a net in front of the roaring crowd.

If you've wronged her, she'll punish you by saying you made her addictive to something-alcohol, pain killers, drugs, surgery, food, sweets, or whatever it is she's going to be addicted to. ESFP women frequently go bulimic under stress, prone to binge eating and purging to stay normal weight.

When unhappy, she'll gain weight rapidly. It's hard for her to make any objective decisions about herself or the people in her life. She decides by her likes and dislikes. Under stress, the ENFP woman refuses to deal with anxiety. She wants a fast-working pill to kill emotionally painful feelings fast.

Her thoughts are extreme, dealing with negative possibilities in unreal ways. Depression is frequent, but not in the way it affects the SJ temperament in cycles. The ESFP under stress is the addictive personality type. Under stress, she will ignore trouble and put on makeup and a smile for her audiences, who could be anyone from store clerks to party friends.

Under stress, her shadow side takes over, which is introverted intuition. As pressure increases, ESFP will focus on the meaning of the rest of her life, and it will come out negative because she's in her shadow function under stress.

She withdraws from people and focus on her lack of alternatives. She sees no alternativs, no way out other than suicide or divorce. ESFP sees exciting alternatives for all their friends, and a blank wall for themselves. If her lover puts fun back in her life, if her mate shows her how to make things happen, she will snap back to her friendly, outgoing self, the quintessential party girl.

ESFP puts bright lights in everyone else's life using fun, pranks, and entertainment. Under stress she doubts herself and falls apart easily. ESFP learns best through entertainment, and the living room should be the center of learning while she's stressed out. The wrong mate shortchanges the ESFP. It's not the SJ mate for her. That's depressing, pushing her into addiction or alcoholism. She doesn't need rules to obey or to be controlled.

ESFP needs a soul mate who can add cheer and sparkle to her freedom-seeking pursuit of fun and excitement from being around many people. She needs a variety of sights and travel, foods, music, and entertainment as much as possible, in a positive atmosphere.

She doesn't need the smoke-filled nightclub type of entertainment when she's stressed out. Or the abstract grunge and punk lifestyle of purple hair and rebellion. ESFP is too cheerful and concrete.

She needs practical, concrete, people-oriented experiences where she can help others more needy than herself at the moment-such as studying physical therapy or raising funds for a worthy medical cause by contacting entertainers and planning events, parties, and other fund-raisers with top performers.

ESFP woman needs more confidence in herself because of her strong tie to the practical pitted against the abstract world of higher education. Life must be oriented toward action for her.

ESFP relieves her stress by teaching the world how to enjoy life. In marriage, ESFP needs action, joy, variety, and people. She has no tolerance for anxiety or being alone.

Under stress, she grows more unpredictable. She ignores the dark thoughts until they break through, then becomes more vulnerable to temptation than any other type, including temptation to have an affair with those she works close with or meets at parties.

An ESFP wife will cause extreme tension and anxiety in mates that are not ESFP, ESTP, or ENFP. Her adventures will force her lover to live on the razor's edge, never knowing when she'll stray to someone more exciting. She's a good-time person, sweeping problems under the rug, never discussing them, even when forced.

ESFP loves without expecting anything in return. The ESFP woman is the most easily seduced-either psychologically or physically. If her lover becomes sick, she will want to leave to find a man more fun to be around. She's not the type to want to take care of a sick man in old age, although she will take care of strangers in her job as a nurse or physical therapist, for example.

ESFP goes on her route, seeking activity. She's a natural in the public relations business or dealing with people in any way. Under stress, she relies on her personal background of collected facts about people to make decisions. Her lover must have immediate use for her. Marriage is to the ESFJ like selling tangibles.

Under stress, she seeks drama in a love affair or in a more exciting job. The ESFJ likes working with people in crisis, but frequently walks out on a crisis when her own lover becomes ill. All she wants is to thrive in the spotlight.

When the stress is ended, her search for a soul mate will be for someone who also thrives on the excitement generated by her contact with a continuous variety of fun-loving people in search of a worthy cause.

She excels in raising funds by entertainment, sparkle, and public relations. If ENFP has charisma, ESFP has glitz. Her objective is to make an impact on your memory so she is not easily forgotten.

The fun-loving ESFP wants you to show her a good time. And a good time usually is some form of travel and entertainment that allows her to use her fine extroverted sensing. She'll look for textures, colors, tones, moods, and objects of beauty in nature and in interior décor.

The darkest side of an ESFP woman's love life is that she's most likely to take away the husband of an INFP, travel to the ends of the earth to perform her dance or act for him, and end up selling real estate not realizing that her ESTP lover really wants to be free.

The ESFP woman will spend long hours working at in a gym or taking care of her body so it can be shown to the public on stage. She doesn't take it lightly when she loses her attraction and may run for plastic surgery. When's she's through taking away the husband and even the children of another woman, she may realize that he's no longer interested in her. Who fears the ESFP woman most? It's her rival, the INFP woman, whose ESTP or ESTJ husband and property she covets.

# ENFP

## Enneagram Type 4 And/Or 6 Or ENFP On The MBTI Also Type 4 With A 3 Wing And Type 6 With A 7 Wing

### Enfp: Extroverted, Intuition, Feeling, Perceiving
### Dominant Extroverted Intuition With Introverted Feeling

11. ENFP, the restless revealer (hankering for a new and more ideal relationship) who can't keep his mouth shut while he listens to your problems. He's your rescuer or therapist who flirts with every woman and believes in touchy-feely encounters, hugs, and wringing life dry with strangers. He's the type of guy who talks to you for ten minutes at a party and walks away with the excuse that he wants to circulate. But he's ready to take off for Peru to look at UFO hot spots if you want to travel.

Unfortunately, he can't find a job he likes and has so many ideas about his need for constant change in career goals that he can't focus on one long enough to earn any money-unless he becomes a therapist or counselor with a tenured job. He could be a burnt-out stockbroker who gave his job to an ESTP who thrives on adrenaline. After forty he stops wandering around looking for or to be a Guru. He ends up going back to school to become a new age counselor, rehabilitation therapist, or psychologist who has trouble finding clients or work.

He's a good speaker, as long as it's on something not practical like past life regressions. Yet, he can do anything people-oriented and extraverted-until it bores him. He speaks with introverted feeling and extroverted intuition and is great at making presentations or training people. The ENFJ man puts greater feeling and emotion behind his public speaking to raise up and audience to action and is a great propagandist. The ENFP male is a more subdued speaker, showing you what he knows about people, the insight he has of the big picture, and the ENTP male can use his presentations to reveal his free thinking, inventive and adventurous attitude toward making the complex visual and vivid with technological or natural history.

This man is so full of energy, enthusiasm, empowerment, and excitement, radio talk show hosts may yell at him to calm down and talk slower. He can motivate and inspire you and the crowd to do anything ending in a big hug.

He needs to be told you love him. He'll get restless if you're not his ideal and stray or else have a lot of female friends. He can really work a room networking and flirting. He's not for the jealous, introverted woman.

## The ENFP Man Under Stress: The Darkest Side In Marriage

ENFP is so optimistic that he's aware of your feelings and makes a passionate lover or marriage counselor. He'll face today's problems with reluctance and will rather whisk you away to a more romantic place.

If you disagree with him, he'll take you on vacation to someplace exotic. The ENFP male wants to escape quickly into his imagination and into the future. He won't solve present problems, but makes the best companion for a woman seeking new age therapy or a good psychologist to dump on who'll end up in bed with her every time and give her a darn good massage.

After your ENFP lover dumps you for a younger woman, you'll end up with the INFP psychologist who proposes marriage if you're an introvert.

If you're also extraverted, stick with the ENFP and make wonderful parties together or give successful seminars on making marriage work. The ENFP male will wring out everything there is life through an old fashioned washing machine vise and then wonder why it's all coming out flat.

If you're an intuitive feeling perceiver who can inspire him by looking to future trends in order to plump up when he's steamrolled, you'll make science fiction together as world-famous trend spotters and journalists who reveal the future.

The ENFP man is likely to give up a career as a stockbroker for a career as a psychologist or career counselor. He would be the type most likely to major in psychodrama in graduate school or become an art teacher. He'd volunteer as a swimming coach and flirt, but as a travel companion to the INFP woman, he would be an excellent buddy or mate to travel with until his desire to meet new people, including new women surfaced. Your biggest problem with your ENFP could be that he may think the pastures are greener in the neighbor's yard. His desire to rescue damsels in distress is only equaled by the ISFJ male. Only the extroverted ENFP really must work a room at a party, meet new women, train them or rescue them, counsel or treat them all in the meantime looking for adventure.

He would give up a secure job to get into broadcasting or screenwriting, but would soon get ants in his pants at having to sit and write alone. The need to be with people working as a team with him as the center of attention would satisfy his need for rapport. This great guy flirts with women in your presence.

If you're an introvert and want a man all your own, beware of ENFP who is energized by people around him, usually pretty women. What he wants in relationships is rapport, the more the better, and would soon grow adventurous, like a roaming tomcat, with only one woman. He thinks there's a better relationships out there waiting in the wings for him, in case you don't tell him you love him every day.

He has to here you say it, but with his introverted feelings, the way he might say he loves you is to take you on a faraway trip. The ENFP man would match the INFP woman in the same introverted feeling tones and extroverted intuition textures, but his real perfect match could only be another ENFP woman. Another good match is the ENFP man and the ENTP woman. With this couple, she'd have to go out of her way to tell him she loves him and misses him when away, and say it daily. This twelve hugs a day man won't tolerate cold logic of ENTP's business-based home in a counseling-based marriage.

## The ENFP Woman

### Enneagram Type 7 or 9, Usually For ENFPs Of Average Scores On Extraverted Intuition And Introverted Feeling With High Score On Perceiving:
### ENFP: Extroverted, Intuitive, Feeling, Perceiving
### Dominant Extroverted Intuition With Introverted Feeling

ENFP, a quintessential Lois Lane reporter seeking Superman in Clark Kent's job. Driven by her dominant extroverted intuition to seek out, observe, and discuss any resource, she is a catalyst who rescues anyone anywhere through her suggestions of alternate pathways. Her intuition seeks patterns in everything. Like the ESFP, she uses the patterns in novel ideas with which to perform before an audience. She's focused on the future, however.

ENFP woman will find a thousand ways of avoiding dealing with details she finds boring. She hates housework with a passion, and won't maintain machinery from cars and appliances to computers. Her house looks like a rat's nest most of the time, and she couldn't care less because she lives in the fantasy that she has a wide range of interests, accomplishments, and memberships and need not follow anyone's rules.

ENFP makes flurries and often believes everyone should think for himself and question all authority, like the ENTP, INFP, and INTP. Her health problems are frequent, for she doesn't pay attention to bodily needs until symptoms finally bring her to the emergency room with dizzy spells, tachycardia, exhaustion, seizures, or other signs of physical collapse.

ENFP so overwhelms herself with projects and possibilities that she develops a variety of health-related symptoms-unaware that the sensations her body has been giving her for the past year went unheeded, unfelt, and unheard.

Poor ENFP's inferior sensing function. She hasn't stopped to listen to the signals her body has been giving her all along that it needs her to take responsibility for her health for the long term. ENFP needs to listen to her body.

She has inferior sensing. So bodily sensations are often ignored until they strike her down with nervous exhaustion.

Then the ENFP woman may take up exercising later in life, or belly dancing, if it provides the novelty she seeks from exercise. She's also interested in Tai Chi Chuan, and different forms of ethnic exercise combined with meditation.

ENFP won't obey time, and throws out watches and clocks or wish she could. She misses a lot of trains, planes, and busses and is frequently late without apology.

Thinking logically is the ENFP's third function, and she uses it when she needs to learn subjects to get her degree, but she says that she prefers to use intuition rather than thinking in her decision-making.

The ENFP woman can offer the world versatility. She can quickly learn to speak many languages, She relates to all people seeking novelty, variety, and accomplishment. ENFP woman wants to meet a mate she can impress as much as she wants to be impressed. She has had many accomplishments and seeks the same in a mate.

Her inferior function is introverted sensing, taking in and organizing details as in secretarial work. She usually hires an ISFJ to take care of her paperwork, while she remains the counselor, the people person, the publisher who talks about books her writers write for her.

The life purpose of the ENFP in marriage and in work is to see alternative routes, possibilities, and take on one project after another, so that life and work has as much variety as possible, as much change as can be handled to keep life from becoming routine.

The ESFP will put variety into an ENFP woman's life. If the ideal soul mate doesn't turn up, the ENFP will find a life in her many friends and activities, interests, hobbies, and projects. Her work is her play.

No matter how good her mate is, the ENFP will think to herself that somewhere over the rainbow her ideal mate stands waiting with open arms. She reads and writes a lot of romance novels and will search forever for the ideal mate who will improve upon the romance novel hero of pure fantasy. She'll never believe romance is unreal. She wants rapport and to be the center of attention at the parties she gives or the way she entertains in her living room artistic salon. Her right-hemisphere brain is dominant so she can take a piece of fabric and sew it into a perfect circular skirt without looking twice at her pattern. She's a natural linguist for foreign languages and an artist, excelling in drama, broadcasting, publishing, and psychology.

Meanwhile back home, her real mate can never live up to her ideal romantic. It's dominant extroverted intuition she's using to keep her introverted feeling behind the scenes. This woman is a rescuer of helpless men. Those she rescues may never live up to her ideal. She brags about her teenage years to her mate.

In romance, the ENFP woman will follow her own ideas and possibility resources to the ends of the earth searching for her soul mate. She will fly from job to job, project to project, and lover to lover seeking a new possibility at every turn.

She loves travel and meeting new people. Her extroverted intuition is dominant—perfect for looking for new sites, surprises, and events. At a party she works over a room. Through historical romance novels or suspense adventures, she will flirt and sashay before one restless ESFP swashbuckling male after another.

In her married life, once settled, she will be consistent and stable, dependable, and a dutiful wife, as long as her mate doesn't complain about her many friends and activities. The ENFP is the ultimate people person.

Only when matched with an ESFP, another ENFP, or a traveling salesman ESFJ soul mate and host with the most, can she follow her intuition to brainstorming sessions around the world. The life purpose of the ENFP woman is to bring out the best in any people around her, including her mate.

Values clarification is the game of the ENFP woman in marriage and in the workplace. She will try her best to swim through life without handling the details.

## ENFP: Under Stress: The Darkest Side Of Marriage

ENFP is the most stable of all the types under stress and the type most likely to emotionally cope under stress. However, with enough pressure, everyone has a snapping point, even if the ENFP is the last to go south under stress. Stress will hit the ENFP physically first, with nervous exhaustion.

Like the ENTP, the ENFP must be emotionally one step higher than you, and keep you down one rung below her. She will use guilt as a weapon to flay the ISTJ or ISFJ man.

His introverted sensing will rebel against her guilt-wielding one up-man-ship. It's a favorite ENFP and ENTP ploy, a manipulation technique used exclusively on SJ males.

The ISFJ or ISTJ male will respond with anger or physical violence, if pushed enough by her use of guilt to keep her man one step down, below her people-saving intelligence and verbal speaking and writing abilities.

The introverted sensing man falls silent and withdraws in anger under her guilt-provoking demands that he do certain tasks for her that he really doesn't want to do. Her presence embarrasses him, and he worries what others will think if she gets loud and pushy when he won't let her play the one-upmanship game to make him feel guilty and depressed.

His anger gets turned inward during the tension-building phase. In an explosion of verbal and/or physical violence, he will lash out at her for pushing him over the edge.

The ENFP woman bounces from man to man and job to job, in search of prince charming and the career that offers the most ideas. Her men friends see only the bouncing around from one project and friend to the next. They never see the real consistency and loyalty she gives to the pursuit of ideas and alternative ways of accomplishing tasks.

She's good at public speaking, but under stress, will challenge her mate to a brainstorming session in which it appears she can't discriminate. He'll label her as rattle-brained and fickle in her choices of men and careers. She's under stress because her mate forced her into an ISTJ mold. What she needs is a good job in the media or in counseling and rescuing others.

Under stress the ENFP's enormous range of interests and abilities-more than any other type (except the INFP), increases dramatically. The enthusiasm comes out more so under stress, to the point of paranoia when she's about to fall apart from pressures.

The ENFP woman becomes vigilant-of anything that could possibly be a threat to her. In a restaurant she'll ask you whether you think someone put poison in the saltshaker, then shake off her paranoid thinking with a joke about how salt causes hypertension if one's sodium-potassium pump is down, so it must be a poison.

The next day, she'll write articles to newspapers with paranoid fears pouring through-how much she's afraid that the fruit has been injected in the supermarket. So she looks for needle holes in every apple and peach. She tests the bottle and jar caps in the grocer's to check for tampering.

The ENFP woman under stress takes on more possibilities than she could handle in two lifetimes. Nothing is completed. Projects are started and discarded or delegated to someone else to carry out. Work piles up. Her Enneagram 7 or 9 and her ENFP inferior sensing prevents her from realizing the sounds her own body is telling her, thereby risking collapse from nervous exhaustion when she doesn't take time out to meditate and relax, or take on less work and adventures getting all the news, seeing all the travel sites.

Unfinished relationships, like unfinished work projects lie fallow with no answer to proposals of marriage. She always has many answers to the possibilities of career change suggestions and may seek work as a career counselor and apply what she learns at work to husband-hunting projects in her love life.

She'll give her future mate personality questionnaires. She may choose or lose her mate based on the results without questioning the possibility of the results not being valid for that time, place, and person because her mate was trying to live up to her expectations and requirements to qualify as a future husband.

The ENFP woman may not realize what skills she really needs, so flings herself into the job without the right ones and pulls it off by her public speaking ability. Her greatest skills like in creating project teams, and she'll do this with her male friends-bring them together to compete for her love.

Under stress, the ENFP woman's need for approval increases so that she'll turn up her motor in a flurry of activity and do anything and everything to be the center of attention-or to get attention. She's not above putting on a dramatic and mercurial act to call attention to herself in order to distract herself from the real issue-a fear of failure.

The ENFP woman becomes a motor-mouth under stress. She'll talk endlessly about possibilities, out-talking even the ENFJ. She'll get all flurried up. It's as if her motor gets turned on and her engine roars to attract attention in order to distract people from seeing her flaws or her real self.

To get a seat in the bus, she's not above pretending to limp or twist her wrist in such a way that she looks helpless or crippled, so that people will feel sorry for her and give her a seat. ENFP will flap her symbolic wings, run her mouth on nonstop, and make a lot of loud noises in a public setting to gain the attention and approval she craves.

What she needs to be doing under stress is analyzing people and their skills, and bringing people together for one project-such as an annual convention of some subject about which she's enthusiastic. The more stressful life is, the more the ENFP needs to be liked.

She will do anything for a positive word. Approval will be dug out of people at any risk and cost. Enthusiasm will take over. In the most exciting and breathless manner, the flirtatious ENFP will approach (usually an ENFJ) and scream how intimate and friendly she is toward people, even teaching swimming to children in her back yard-when she knows she really isn't interested in children. ENFP is a winged griffin, a fountain of news longing to tell all the latest.

She really wants to travel to hot spots in Peru to look for UFO evidence with her ideal man. If only her prince would turn up, but all who turn up are bums waiting for her to rescue them.

Under stress, the ENFP woman needs to work more with people as part of a supportive team. She knows what makes you act as you do and loves work and relationships where she can talk about why people act as they talk. Her ideal job is a radio talk show psychologist. Her ideal man is an ESFP physical therapist or physician who also loves to help people become stronger.

The higher your emotional state of hysteria or rage, the more sensitive she will be to your feelings. At the same time, her feelings will be hidden (introverted feeling). She likes to hunt down her soul mate in flirtatious pursuit, then reject him or punish him for the attention he has shown which she calls inappropriate. The ENFP woman is the type most likely to scream "sexual harassment" and not be exaggerating.

# ENTP

## Enneagram Type 5 With A 6 Wing Or ENTP On The MBTI™

### ENTP: Extroverted, Intuition, Thinking, Perceiving
### Dominant Extroverted Intuition With Introverted Thinking

12. ENTP is a salesman, presentations speaker, photographer, inventor, and adventurer who loves giving speaking presentations about an intangible product and an intangible wife. He's a video producer, photographer, publisher, computer systems analyst, marketing researcher, or journalist who likes talking before large groups of people more than he likes being and working alone. He must invent things, but he likes to invent with people around to bounce ideas off.

He is attracted to the ENFJ woman who is old enough to be getting in touch with her inferior thinking (shadow) function. She attracted to his dominant extroverted intuition and the way he takes in information and solves problems using introverted thinking because the ENFJ woman who falls for him uses introverted intuition to take in her information and extroverted feeling to make value decisions. Think of Thomas Edison's inventions and demeanor and you have a stereotypical ENTP figure to observe.

He can make the ENFJ woman walk out on the statue of an monastic INFP or reclusive INTP man for an ENTP adventurer. They would travel to hot spots around the globe and give presentations and talks together on intangibles.

So the ENFJ woman introverting her intuition and ENTP man extroverting his intuition are a good match for working together as well as being married-as long as she doesn't expect him to extrovert feeling like she doesn't because he thinks to himself and questions all authority. In the case of the INFJ man with the INFP woman, her extroverted intuition would rub his introverted intuition the wrong way so that she appears selfish to him.

Her introverted feeling would crush his extroverted feeling in that case of an INFJ marriage to an INFP. However, it works differently and well with ENFJ woman and ENTP man.

He's a freethinker and she's a free speaker. Together, they can talk up a racket training people as professional speakers. If you marry or fall in love with an ENTP man, he'll notice your housework is lousy and design a system that will help you clean the house rather than suggest you hire a maid with your executive salary.

He'll confront you about your unfinished housework or other work projects. Don't even consult him. Just do it or hire someone if you don't have the time.

ENTP males are looking for exciting challenges in ways like the ESTP male. With the ENTP, he's spouting ideas and intuition, imagination, inventions, and a need for a series of projects to work on with constant change. He's so inventive that he'll design systems for you that will make others look up to you in awe. This man would rather be an entrepreneur out in the world than sitting in a classroom learning academic theories. He will use theories, but as the owner of a business or as the owner of sales presentations techniques, photographic secrets, or investigative work.

Marry him if you want him to invent ways to beat the system. Your romantic life will be such that he will only trust logical reason. His use of logic and intuition toughens him. If you're an NF woman, his free thinking comments might cut down your magical thinking or beliefs based on faith and the paranormal. ENTP males are interested in proving how far evolution has taken society or how much we all need to grow to reach a rational thinker's height.

This engineer of adventure and intangible talk won't trust his impulses, only his intuition. He won't trust authority. Logic is absolute, grades and licenses mean nothing. If you call him a solipsist, he'll agree without having to look it up in the dictionary. He'd get bored selling tangibles and being with a sensing, tangible or practical woman, such as his opposite type, the ISFJ routine worker, such as a clerical supervisor, nurse, or elementary teacher.

If you're an idealist, you'll be this realist's best mate. You'll be aware of his ingenuity. His excursions lead to wisdom. He's attracted to you only because you appreciate his mind. You're intriguing to him because he can't fathom your mysterious depths.   As an idealist, you'll be an ENFP or ENFJ yourself. Your parties with other extraverts who intuit, will be filled with talk about whether there really was a flood in Noah's time.

Your romance will be based on him designing you a dildo to enhance your self life when he's too busy at his engineering duties. He'll pursue science endlessly, and you'll pursue his rational nature. But don't travel without him. If you're gone alone on vacation overseas for three months, don't be surprised to come home and find he wants to marry his secretary and he's already started divorce proceedings without you.

## The ENTP Woman

**Enneagram Type For Females Is A 5 With A 6 Wing High Score, Lower Score ENTPs Are Fives With 4 Wings, Approaching The INTP. She Can Also Be A 3 With A 4 Wing, If She Scores Lower On Thinking. Those Scoring High On Thinking Are More Like The Enneagram 5 With A 6 Wing.**

**ENTP: Extroverted, Intuitive, Thinking, Perceiving
Dominant Extroverted Intution With Introverted Thinking**

ENTP, an adventurous and impatient woman who must feel she is a little bit better than you in her occupation, presentations, and as a free-thinker. She wants use her ingenuity to replace your relationship with a better one and still keep you.

The ENTP woman is out to destroy the traditions and old rules. If it isn't broken, she will break it, and like the INTJ, improve it, or eliminate any thought about it. Five out of every one hundred people in the United States are ENTPs.

She needs her own type, or an educated ESTP to promote her presentations and create visibility and publicity for her business, but frequently who she marries is an INFP or INFJ who is more concerned with his inner world. Of all the men she meets, she's most likely to wind up with an introvert.

It's her mate who always takes the phone off the hook on weekends so as not to be bothered by people's petty intrusions. She has just had a call-waiting device installed so as not to miss anyone trying to speak to her. All she wants to do is to inspire.

The ENTP woman enjoys bringing anything that's complex and theoretical to groups of people. She's hired most often to give presentations and seminars, to counsel people about their jobs, or to lead a brainstorming session of executives to come up with better ideas.

In marriage, she wants to put her finger in every pie, to express her ideas on every subject imaginable as an expert or to seek out experts. She attends or creates conventions and conferences, and brings people together.

Her soul mate must have an adventurous and intellectual appeal to her. This is a woman so caught up in being around people, that if she misses a phone call, she'll worry what exciting event will she not be informed of that she should be attending.

The talkative ENTP woman will often corner her opposite type, an ISFJ man at a barbeque and not let him open his mouth the entire evening. Her enthusiasm and bubbly personality matches that of the

ENFP woman, with the exception that she doesn't like to put in writing what she can say on videotape.

Often, she's a media producer or entrepreneur, or a publisher, hiring ENFPs to work for her on written communication and people-meeting while she does her one-up-womanship presentations from a podium or behind a camera. ENTP women frequently go into technical photography or commercial advertising, working closely with ESTP and ESFP publicity and ad agency men.

She's too interested in people to be a writer in the way that the INFP or ENFP writes the news. Instead, the electronic media or publishing as an executive, is her forte. In a relationship, the ENTP can be distinguished from the ENFP because it's the ENTP who chomps at her bit to break any rules or traditions. Her opposite personality is the ISFJ.

The visionary ENTP woman avoids tradition as much as the ISTJ enjoys it. Just because it has been done that way before doesn't mean she's going to do it that way. As a freethinker, she'll pick her own research, and use her analytical skills to do something her own way-all the way through the marriage.

Typically, she, like the INFP woman, belongs to two-religions, for example, Unitarianism and Reform Judaism or Religious Science and Humanism, and enjoys the best of both when she needs those experiences. The ENTP woman is always looking for bringing two unrelated subjects or people together to make a whole new and different third creation. She's always searching for a better way to have a marriage or relationship.

The ENTP woman may reason that the traditional family is falling apart and that a new way to relate must be tried. So to find the new way, her dominant extroverted intuition is always seeking new and better mousetraps, new ways of doing things, and new projects to get involved with all leading to a better relationship, and of course, a freethinking soul mate.

She will ignore all traditional males with traditional values who have rules women couldn't break in the past. When the ENTP woman searches for her soul mate, she is looking for a man who will directly aid her in reaching her intellectual and financial goals.

A marriage that works for ENTP woman is one in which her husband will be supportive of her freedom to open one business after another, to try many avenues of entrepreneurship or job hopping without blame or complaint. She doesn't want an SJ mate to tell her what is good for her.

In marriage, she wants a challenge from a man. She wants to prove to him that she can make a commitment in marriage and reach for the stars in her career. She wants to prove she can have it all, that having a marriage and a career can be done. She will not give up an inch. Heaven help the man who comes between her and her career.

She seeks an INTJ man to do the impossible for her. (As in "Which INTJ male will walk on water for me?" Ms. ENTP asked.) She only can improvise using her spontaneity. With the ENFP male, she will make a fool of him in his efforts to rescue the underdogs who waste her valuable introverted thinking time.

She will rise to any crisis, but to do so successfully, she needs an ESTP soul mate. He will put out fires for her, meet the crises she creates and solve her immediate relationship or presentation problems. The restless, swashbuckling, adventurous ESTP promoter, always on the go, will work well in marriage with the freedom-loving, adventurous ENTP woman, ready to improvise with him in any venture.

In marriage, all the ENTP woman wants from life is power. All she wants for herself is competency, like any proper NT. All the ESTP male wants in a marriage is the freedom of action that the ENTP woman allows him to have. Because of her power and competency, she is totally independent of any man or family life.

He likes the reality of this type of sweet freedom she feeds him. They will work well together-he searching for action, fun, travel, and freedom, and she-searching for power through achievement and public recognition.

## ENTP: Under Stress: The Darkest Side Of Marriage

Falling apart, the ENTP woman becomes phobic. It's not so much the agoraphobia of the INFP woman, but a fear of specific things, such as heights, elevators, snakes, flying, work, angry people, driving, men, etc. She's prone to panic as her speech becomes more rapid.

This exquisite conversationalist needs to contact an ENFJ to put the ENTP in touch with her newly developing feeling function.

If single, a relationship or romance with an ENFJ may be what she needs to put her back on track. She'll carefully follow the garrulous ENFJ's talkability as one of the best mood elevators. Love between ENFJ and ENTP is more than a gambol or gamble as it would be with the ESTP wheeler-dealer-promoter.

It could be real romance between ages 21 and 35 when the ENTP woman is busy getting in touch with her third function, extroverted feeling and the ENFJ is getting in touch with his third function, extroverted sensing.

Or if both parties are over the age of 50, the ENTP woman is busy getting in touch with her inferior function, introverted sensing, and the ENFJ man is busy getting in touch with his fourth function, introverted thinking.

With the ESTP male, between the ages of 21 and 35, he's getting in touch with his third function, extroverted feeling, and she's doing the same. They have a goal in common. Between the ages of 21 and 35, the ENTP woman's getting in touch with her third function, extroverted feeling. So we have two soul mates here, both getting in touch with the same preference at the same time-extroverted feeling.

By the time the ENTP woman is 50 years old or more, she is getting in touch, at last, with her inferior (or shadow), her fourth function, which is introverted sensing. The ESTP man of age 50 or above, is now getting in touch with his inferior function, introverted intuition.

Her introverted sensing is opposite to the ESTP male's introverted intuition. They have nothing in common now and are like two ships passing in the night. They could find their differences overwhelming and split.

So what the ENTP or any other woman needs in a soul mate, depends on what era of life she's in. The first years until 21, everyone's getting in touch with the first two preference styles or functions, the dominant and the auxiliary, that is the best and the second best. Later in life you get in touch with your third best and finally, in mature years, your least best.

After the age of 50, the ENTP woman into introverted sensing with a rage (and probably into computers by now), needs a man also into introverted sensing. That soul mate is, of course, the ENTP man, someone so much more like her at each stage of life.

Therefore, under stress, the ENTP woman needs someone in sync with her own needs at that particular time of her life. As stress increases, the ENTP woman will argue more for the sake of argument. Her emphasis will not be on personal values, but on how intellectual things work.

Life as an intellectual game and one-upmanship can be so frustrating to the ESTP man, who's game must be exciting, that he will leave her for an ESFP performer. She will, under stress, and in the end, find kind solace with an ENTP man, so much like herself, yet so individually different, that she will enjoy his authority of competence.

Under stress, the ENTP woman's work style falls apart. Nothing can be done according to someone else's methods or schedules. People and values or feelings seem to be an intellectual game they use to gain authority over others. The ENTP woman, under stress, worries whether her life means anything.

To verify, she will seek out an ISTJ male to show her with just the facts, that her life has some meaning after all. Stress will push the ENTP woman to avoid taking needed rest. Like the ENFP, she is not aware of bodily sensations and warnings. She pushes herself to exhaustion.

The range of the interests and talents of the ENTP woman is challenged by the ENFP man. He could be her soul mate, if she accepts his challenge, and they could have a happy married life together, with him soothing her at the times she's most stressed. He would be constantly asking her to say she loved him, and she would be constantly telling him she'll show it by piling more filling in his sandwich.

To be centered and balanced under stress, the ENFP needs to take time to be alone and focus on her great need for rest (that was building up for years, unheeded).

Under stress, it's the ENFP who teaches the ENTP woman how many hundred paths she has to power. ENTP forgets to look critically at the alternatives. Stress to the ENTP means having to sort out the gifts from the trash.

A lonely marriage is an ENTP woman married to an ISFJ man under fifty trying to get in touch with his inferior function, extroverted intuition, which is the ENTP woman's dominant style. Between age 21 and 35, the ISFJ man is getting in touch with his third style, introverted thinking, and the ENTP woman of 21 to 35 is getting in touch with her third function, extroverted feeling-which is the ISFJ man's naturally auxiliary or second function.

The two (ENTP-ISFJ) attract like electric magnets, especially him to her and her talking him into a trance. Yet in the end, such a relationship could lead to abuse and violence. With the ISTJ man, there is less physical excitement between the two. It is the same outcome at different times.

He tries to get in touch with his third function, introverted feeling, or after 50, his inferior function, extroverted intuition. The ISTJ man is more likely to go for the ENFJ or ENFP mate than the ENTP. She falls through the cracks around the ISTJ.

Under stress, ENTP woman needs the rest and kind solace the ENTP soul mate gives her in the long run. It's a marriage made with energy and brainstorming.

# The ESTJ Man

## Enneagram Type 8 With A 9 Wing Or ESTJ On The MBTI™:
## The Business Leader And Organizer
## ESTJ: Extroverted, Sensing, Thinking, Judging

### Dominant Extroverted Thinking With Introverted Sensing

13. ESTJ is the epitome of the hard-driving executive who must manage everything, including you. He's like the ISTJ who monitors and critiques you all the time. However, the ESTJ is extraverted and prefers to boss groups of people around.

He's the organizer, the chief executive officer who focuses on productivity, not feelings. He's hard-charging, macho, who shows affection in a macho way by slapping you on the back instead giving you a hot oil back rub. He'll never come up to you in the kitchen and kiss you on the neck.

He'll goose you instead as you bend over the garbage can and say something abrasive like "you're all right for a girl." ESTJ gives affection with one hand and takes it back with the other. He won't say "I love you." He might say, "It's great the way you make lists and stick to them." Don't worry. He won't live that long, and he'll leave you plenty of money for that face lift, cruise, and young lover.

### Under Stress: The Darkest Side Of ESTJ In Marriage

ESTJ males are best suited to ESTJ females who challenge their macho sarcasm and wit. If you're a partner in a law firm and he runs a company that sells franchises on organizational management, the two of you can team up to create a Yuppie homestead in Silicon Valley.

Have your first child after forty when your career has long reached its peak and his macho sarcastic wit can't pull you down. Both of you are life's administrators who make decisions so quick that you get ulcers unless you both give in to Yoga lessons from an ENFP therapist.

The ESTJ male is a concrete expressionist. Anything impractical will be tossed out. Sex is done by standard operating procedures. Romance is acted out by a table of particulars.

The ESTJ male is tough on women who deviate from productive and ceremonial conduct in bed. Play is out and so is imagination.

If you're an INFP novelist, don't touch the ESTJ male with a ten-foot bus. If you want to daydream with an ESTJ or play, do it on your own time, not his. In bed you might be reprimanded for wasting time while he's "on duty" with insistence on extended foreplay.

The primary drive of the ESTJ male is economic. He runs a tight ship, the tightest ship in the head-of-the-household business called marriage. He needs to control the INFP woman as much as the husband in the play, "A Doll's House" needed to control his wife.

He's an excellent provider, but rarely will the kids know he's there. The economic problem is never solved no matter how much money he makes and is of primary importance in life.

If you love this man, be prepared to let art and imagination take a back seat. He'll order you to write his autobiography and tell you to get the facts from other people and not waste his time.  Marry him only for his security, expensive house, your allowance money for groceries, and get fun where you can. He'll never leave you poor in old age. It's best to romance with him after you're fifty and have already had loving rapport from someone else (unless you're a similar ESTJ woman).

The ESTJ male will give you financial security and a beautiful home and clothes. If it's a sugar daddy you want, seek him out. Don't waste his time demanding passion, romance, and fantasy. He will set you up in business, but don't expect his time or his deep conversation about reincarnation, UFOs, life after life, or theory and philosophy on the meaning of the life of a wife.

## The ESTJ Woman

## Enneagram Type 8 (High Score On Extraverted Thinking) Or 9 With An 8 Wing (Lower Score On Thinking And High On Sensing-Logistics) Or 8 With A 9 Wing (Higher Extraverted Thinking Score, Lower On Sensing)

## ESTJ: Extroverted, Sensing, Thinking, Judging
## Dominant Extroverted Thinking With Introverted Sensing

ESTJ, a woman in touch with her community, will seek a love match from her immediate environment. Most traditional, she will want to keep the faith, the ethnicity, and be the pillar of responsibility to her people. In childhood, she often sides for strength with her dominating father and rejects her mother as a weak and useless dreamer. Thirteen percent of the population of the United States are ESTJs.

If she wants something from a mate, it's responsibility. She marries a man she thinks would make a good father to her future children or good provider, worthy of someone as responsible as she is. With the ISTJ and ISFJ male, it's a good match, and equally good with the ESTJ like herself, and preferably an executive or physician with stability.

ENTJ men are too visionary for her. As mentioned, the ENTJ woman makes a good wife for the ESTJ man, but the ENTJ man is too argumentative about his empirical thinking for the down-to-earth ESTJ woman to accept because of her focus on his responsibility at home with the family when she needs him there.

The NT's search for power competes with the ESTJ woman's search for stability and security in the home, in short responsibility and exemption from burdens. She wants her man in the home working on down-to-earth details responsibly, loyally, and dutiful at all times. An ISTJ husband usually fills the bill until loneliness sinks in. In the end, she really wants an ESTJ exactly like herself, but all ESTJs differ as individuals.

Her married life is about organizing orderly procedures in home databases. Logistics is her game-detailing the rules of the marriage and family hierarchy according to the tradition she's been exposed to longest.

She's not rebellious and has much in common with the traditional, ISTJ male also respecting rules, laws, and household regulations as he does at work. Both could lead responsible lives spent judging and evaluating the lives of everyone around them.

Marriage is judged by its obedience to traditional operating methods. ESTJ woman demands a husband who follows her realistic and pragmatic rules without exception. She believes above all else, "If it's not broken don't fix it." Heaven help the INTJ or ISTP man who challenges her with his belief in, "If it's not broken, break it and then improve and change it."

The ESTJ woman is either loyal to her job security in a large corporation where she'll climb the ladder on track, or in her family's business. Once she has children, she will prefer working at home on flexitime until her children are grown.

Change is threatening to her. She is second least likely of all the types to ask for a divorce. (The first is the ISFJ male or female.) ESTJ woman is equally as reluctant to make changes or welcome unplanned surprises as ISTJ, ISFJ, or ESFJ types. She will find the perfect mate in an SJ temperament partner. Almost any SJ will accept the same duties of responsibility she demands.

ESTJ woman won't respond to her husband's or children's emotional needs like an ISFJ mate would do. She could be cruel to animals at times, horrifying the ISFJ partner or child. Yet, the ESTJ woman will sacrifice anything to "do her duty." She makes a good military wife. Many ESTJ women plan to have four children and stay married to a physician, happily organizing the home and friends. ESTJ women in careers enjoy public relations as account executives or go to pharmacy school.

Some of the subjects they enjoy most include chemistry courses, math, and business management. They excel in the logistics of running a home or business. ISTJ and ESTJ women may go to dental school. Most ESTJ women follow traditional religious beliefs, but this can vary with the individual. There is a focus on the family, but in a less emotional way than ESFJ's devotion to children and service. ESTJ is more about being the administrator than the service professional. In a marriage the logistics and organizational ability spills over into the home and may focus on buying and restoring old, traditional-type homes of historical value. Many ESTJ women become history instructors or work with archives. In the home this reaches to scrap booking an preserving old family traditional photos and portraits.

In a job, she will rise to the top of the glass ceiling, challenging an ENTJ woman who won't tell her how she broke through the glass ceiling barrier for women. She'll be hired for her ability to handle details and logistics. The ESTJ woman, daunted by duty, will turn to religion and civic clubs for recognition in the community if she is prevented from being all she can be at work or in the home.

Often she will marry to rise socially. ESTJ women without educations often target physicians as potential mates, hoping to rise in the eyes of the community by being a doctor's wife and fulltime stay-at-home mother. In this way, she's similar to the ESFJ woman. Both need anchorage in the community and in work with organized religious affiliations.

ESTJ woman demands punctuality, organization, and down-to-earthness in a man as well as a "real job" in the community, one that she can respect out of her inner need to make up for her lack and loss in her own educational achievements. She's daddy's girl in every sense of the word, often preferring the company of men to women.

If there's any established and traditional institution, it's the domain of the ESTJ woman's leadership and volunteerism for life. After retirement and in widowhood, she will be the ultimate full time volunteer at whatever is held in traditional esteem in her community, religion, or ethnic group. She is a walking ritual, a time-honored tradition. ESTJ and ESFJ are most likely on a Sunday afternoon to be pouring coffee in the cottage of her ethnic group in a park, dressed in an ethnic costume or purchasing her favorite ethnic food from specialty gourmet grocers.

## ESTJ: Under Stress: The Darkest Side Of Marriage

The ESTJ woman cuts off anyone who marries outside the ethnicity, faith, race or tradition. If her daughter marries a man of another race, religion, or ethnicity, she is more likely to be cut off than if a son takes a foreign or ethnically different wife.

This is due to the ESTJ's traditional stereotypes and prejudices learned from her parents. Frequently, the ESTJ woman treats her daughters differently than her sons. Old prejudices come welling up under stress. ESTJ women can often make their INFP female relatives sick by emphasis on family honor. The INFP emphasizes individual freedom of expression. The ESTJ curtails the INFP's enthusiasm to tell family secrets in published diaries.

Anything that smacks of the traditions of the "old world" being better is incorporated. Often, a son is sent to the old country to find a wife because the ESTJ parent thinks young girls in the old world are raised with less exposure to changes.

When an ESTJ woman divorces, she may take her children back to a country she considers better in which to raise children. The ESTP man takes his children back to the old country more to punish his wife by having them raised by his mother. The ESTJ woman takes her children out of the country because she honestly believes life is better where there is slower change in traditional customs and rituals.

ESTJ woman under stress, begins to have unrealistic fears about her mate or children abandoning the old institutions and ways. She's afraid of what's happening to the traditional family under radicals and liberals. She's naturally conservative, naturally right wing in every sense of the word.

Her life is anchored and stabilized by repetitive routine. If everything is no longer in it's place, she falls apart. Following family tradition is her whole life. Under stress, tradition falls apart with passing time and radical changes.

The more tradition breaks down, the more stressed ESTJ woman becomes. With an ESTJ soul mate, it's easier to live through the crises of seeing children rebel. An orderly home life is what she demands. When orderliness falls apart, she goes through motions to glue to family together by one ritual after the other.

Under frustration, she will create routines and rules. Every one of her laws must be obeyed. Every holiday must be celebrated in a traditional way according to the rules and at family functions prepared in a traditional way.

Meeting family and friends at traditional holiday dinners are the best things in life for the ESTJ, and they are never free. She spends her time planning these get-togethers. Everything is planned according to tradition-from weddings to wakes. To miss a holiday dinner and ritual would be an unforgivable rule violation.

ESTJ under the heaviest stress, is still dependable. She will develop physical symptoms, hypertension, stomach problems, but she will not break the rules. As stress increases, the ESTJ becomes a hypochondriac, using bad health as an excuse to seek exemption from responsibility and to break a rule or ritual.

If there's a break in the routine, ESTJ becomes unsteady, fearing loss and abandonment. ESTJ is consistent, even when falling apart and speaking constantly of her stomach problems and back aches from the heavy burdens. ESTJ is subject to depression, whereas her INFP opposite in personality is subject to chronic anxiety.

The more stress shoveled onto the ESTJ woman, the more she focuses her energies on the world around her. Her judgments that were impersonal, suddenly become personal as her inferior function, her flip side, her inferior introverted feeling bursts out.

She will make ritual trips to the old family photo album. For collecting family photos is more important in her life than her job. Under enough stress, the INFP, her opposite type comes out in her in its most inferior form. She becomes withdrawn and spends all her time alone. She focuses on judgments she makes about her lack of ability. Her self-worth and accomplishments are devalued.

If her husband tries to get her involved with people, she'll erupt with epithets and negative judgments, loud and clear about whoever bothers her. Her speech becomes destructive. She cuts off and disowns her children who won't obey her rules. She becomes overwhelmed by her ultra-conservative ties to her religion or ethnic group. She turns to fanaticism and begins to put down stereotypes of other peoples. She scapegoats. ESTJ will use her extroverted thinking to blast away at INFP's introverted feeling to the point where the INFP's mind will go blank when hearing criticism.

The ESTJ woman, normally has the qualities of what American culture values as masculine. Male ESTJs become more macho under stress. Female ESTJs lose their sense of femininity. On one hand, they act "inappropriate" for a "girl," in their traditional culture, and on the other hand, they are overwhelmed with the drive to be ultra traditional and conservative.

Under stress, the ESTJ woman is driven to think she should not aim as high as she wants to or should not be what she is naturally. Stereotyping is the biggest stressor for the ESTJ woman. Under stress, the ESTJ woman must express her practical judgment of people. Her soul mate, another ESTJ or any of the SJ males, or her platonic friend, business partner and visionary, the ENTJ man, needs to talk with her about how she can learn to run her self before she tries to run the world or her family.

In the film, "When Harry Met Sally," the enthusiastic ENFP man courts the orderly, organized ESTJ woman. Perhaps, an ENFP man needs to come out of the woodwork for the ESTJ woman (until she balks at the way he can't obey the rules of tradition), and help her to see that a lifetime spent on conserving her possessions isn't wasted at all.

Under stress, ESTJ woman needs to tone down her judgments about people. She's really a fun-loving, light-hearted lady in search of a teddy bear and security blanket. She finds both in traditional family togetherness. She must have material objects to conserve. Don't put her down for it.

Her role as a wife is a maintenance function. Life must run as efficiently as possible. She runs a tight ship, the tightest ship in the shipping business, like the ISTJ male and the ISTJ company.

To help her, keep her telling jokes and funny stories. ESTJ must balance her seriousness with playfulness. When she becomes playful, she knows she has found the right mate. She will not take herself seriously, except when she's under stress. By then, what she takes seriously is untrue.

Look at the ESTJ woman's car. Is it an old VW bug from the early seventies? Does she keep it repaired, driven regularly, and freshly painted after twenty years? Or is she buying/leasing a new car every year, the most flashy she can afford to show her possessions off to the community? The way she cares for a car will be the way she cares for a husband.

Under stress, the short-fused ESTJ woman loses her patience. She hates men who speculate. She rejects any mate who does not view everything the same way she does. Under stress, she wishes there were not so many choices.

Her soul mate will not demand she look over his emotions. This normally logical woman prefers to weigh the pros and cons on her list before picking her mate. She marries for prestige and economic security, not for emotional reasons. She marries a man who conforms to her view of how life's rules should be obeyed.

ESTJ woman needs to sort out what really matters in her life. The right man for her is really an ESTJ, ISTJ, or ESFJ. The ISFJ man is too miserly, withholding, and withdrawing financially for her. He's conserving his savings, and by Jiminy Cricket, she's not going to get into his wallet or 20-year old VW bug.

The STJ soul mates are the best ones to choose from who can naturally give her what really matters in her life-collecting memorabilia of family traditions, organizing administrative details, and fewer choices. If making too many choices is painful, then her true soul mate is another ESTJ. Two ESTJs will pay the bills on time.

He will give her the quick, logical, and reality-based decisions she asks for, not ENTJ futuristic leadership visions. He will not anger her with endless information like her opposite, the INFP would do. The ESTJ male would not make her feel guilty for not phoning to say "I love you" as ENFJ and ENFP males would. For the best match, an ESTJ woman would do well with either an ESTJ or an ENTJ man as both would use extroverted thinking to communicate. With introverted feeling types such as ISFP and INFP, the opposite type, ESTJ would unknowingly say words that could drive the INFP to illness and the ISFP to fleeing or gambling.

## The ESFJ Man and Woman

## ESFJ: Extrovert, Sensing, Feeling, Judging
## Dominant Extroverted Feeling With Introverted Sensing
## ENNEAGRAM TYPE 6 WITH A 5 WING

14. ESFJ is a dependable, harmonizing extravert desiring service-with-a smile in the quietude of the home or large institution. The ESFJ

male is a natural salesperson, traditional in values and looking to the past to imitate successful corporations and giant institutions. He wants to serve by setting up conferences or gathering people together in any place from a computer sales room for medical software to a traditional church. She is a homebody who likes to manage an office in one hand and entertain with her friends with the other.

In a divorce, it is the man, not the ESFJ woman who leaves the home, and it's never sold. It's given to her. She enjoys being of service, helping customers find what they want. Her goal is to organize details of her family's life or in an office-based file. She may love quilting and taking children to classes or teaching practical subjects or elementary school. The ESFJ male loves to bring people to one area and sell them something tangible.

ESFJ won't sell ideas if he can help it, but washing machines, computers, or software, office supplies or clothing is another story. Customer service is the badge of the ESFJ. These extroverted sensors enjoy detail and concrete thoughts about financial planning, good nutrition, and healthy living. At the same time, the ESFJ women may have heavy smoking habits they are afraid to stop. Time is filled greeting people. ESFJ makes good ambassadors to anywhere. They are the meters and greeters, hosts and event planners, and love to bring writers together at conventions. The ESFJ man and woman are similar.

Under great stress, her dependability will increase. In searching for a soul mate, her biggest error is not to recognize her attraction to irresponsible men who are often addicted to alcohol or drugs or other wayward vices.

Her soul mate search leads her to a rescue-rejection drama, an endless game that increases with the more overburdened with work she becomes. As her stress increases, she tries to do the right thing and gets beaten up for it.

## The ESFJ Woman

### Enneagram Type 6 With A 7 Wing Or ESFJ On The MBTI For The Female
### ESFJ: Extroverted, Sensing, Feeling, Judging
### Dominant Extroverted Feeling With Introverted Sensing

ESFJ, a woman who fits the American ideal of the 1950s passive, stay-at-home homemaker, elementary school teacher, nurse, secretary, and home economist-dietician dutifully married to her ENFJ school sweetheart. Her goal in life is to collect as much information about people as she can find sticking her nose into everybody else's business. Everybody really loves the ESFJ "typical" woman so much that they made her the standard female ideal type for all women. She's truly people-centered. The cheeful ESFJ hostess with the mostess frequently is named "Sunshine." Her most natural tendency is to mix among party guests and put them at ease by introducing the shy to the sly.

Two ideals count for ESFJ-responsibility toward people's feelings and respect for authority. She's every NT's ideal secretary, every NF's model mate. People walk away from the ESFJ woman feeling better about themselves. Her responsibility is to organize the way her mate and children act in public.

The ESFJ's dominant extroverted feeling exudes warmth to everyone equally. Details about people is what she collects and what makes her happiest in marriage and in work.

Her sense of responsibility causes her to seek a mate with a stable job, someone who's totally dependable and can offer her security. She don't want a man she'll have to support. The ESFJ is the woman who most likely had to work to put her first husband through professional school.

She made him feel guilty for doing it, that he owes her responsibility. So he left her to dump the guilt.

Now, in a second marriage, the ESFJ is not about to work and support another man or set him up in business. She's adamant about finding a responsible soul mate, someone as traditional as the ESTJ male, but who can fulfill her insatiable needs for emotional committment.

She wants a sensitive man with a secure job who will tell her how much he loves her every day. Yet she knows there is no such thing as a secure job. So she targets men most likely to have the next best-someone who can sell his skills in any town such as a doctor, dentist, or successful business owner of practical items.

She likes to read practical useful information such as how to make, build, repair, or restore, health material, and other useful information. She may read romance fiction or books on teaching children or nursing and office management. She reads material that will help her practice the skills she already knows. She'll study office management or open a boutique and sell fashions or import items to sell or distribute. However, she will escape on vacation with romance novels about women in practical careers, especially nurse stories (and books about women working in large, parental institutions like government, hospitals, and the military).

ESFJ woman wants concrete answers about anything. Questioning authority and thinking for herself are too painful if they don't give immediate concrete answers. The ENFJ or ESFJ soul mate will give her the concrete answers. ENFJ will calm her with endearments and "I love you" statements. ESFJ will give her quick, simple detailed answers that never touch on pondering the meaning of life.

The ESFJ woman is too involved with being warm to people to pursue an endless search for self-identity like the INFP or ENFP. Those mates would confuse, upset, and bore her. The SP temperament mate is too restless and adventurous in his freedom-seeking. The ESTP male, to impersonal, even though she worships his commitment and responsibility to his goals.

All the SJ wants, man or woman, is to be of service to people. The STJ is of service impersonally and logically, helping people by providing what they will buy to make a profit. The SFJ is of direct service to people, handling customer complaints, becoming emotionally involved, and collecting details about people or replacing what's wrong. ESFJ woman is a vendor, an excellent sales manager or salesperson.

ESFJ will sell directly tangible objects face to face, whether it be real estate, elementary education, clothing, cosmetics, medical diets, or appliances. She's a down-to-basics woman. She is not seeking power. She's giving service. Often the highest paid executive secretaries are ESFJs who are happy to work as secretaries after college. They frequently take degrees in business education or nursing.

The duty of the ESFJ woman is to stabilize relationships and to encourage commitment through attention to detail. They do not push for leadership and resent those who do, especially ENTJ men.

The ESFJ woman does not protest against the drive for leadership of the ENFJ man-because NF leadership is to motivate, inspire, train, propagandize, or help people get in touch with their feelings and preferences.

ESFJ woman sees ENTJ leadership as an impersonal, combative drive for power over nature. ESFJ woman sees ESTJ and ISTJ leadership as a greedy search for profit and real estate acquisition for the sake of collecting and separating the haves from the have nots.

What does the ESFJ woman really want in a marriage? Motherhood is important. Responsibility equally divided between each member of the family or couple. She is the third most modest of types (ISFP is most modest and ISFJ second most modest). ESFJ wants harmony among people, like INFP. Every task she does is done thoroughly, which is why she's rarely promoted up from secretarial ranks. She's such a good clerk-typist and limbic-brained bookkeeper.

If she insists on a promotion, she'll be given the concrete, detailed, down-to-earth details to work on using her introverted sensing auxiliary (or second style). She is frequently employed as a medical transcriptionist or medical transcription teacher for 30 years, all the while wishing the doctor would propose.

What she needs is a job allowing her to freely use her dominant extroverted feeling in a concrete way to be of service, such as a buyer of things that people want for emotional reasons. In marriage, it's the same story mate-searching. She needs a very personal search for a soul mate. She needs someone who like her is thorough, competent, and gets the work done before deadline.

Divorce or incompatibility in a relationship comes for the ESFJ woman when she is paired with a man who focuses on the future and on change. Dates from hell for her would be with ENFP, ENTP, ENTJ, INTJ, INFP, or INTP males, or with any of the SP temperaments.

The ESTP or ISTP males would leave her when they grow restless for adventure, excitement, new women, fun, and constant career and environmental changes. That narrows down the ESFJ woman's soul mate to ESFJ, ISFJ, or ENFJ.

Future and change is frightening because they bring up old fears of abandonment for the SJ woman. As much as ESTJ is masculine, ESFJ is feminine in the stereotyped traits associated with the old notion of masculine and feminine personality interests. She may enjoy sports as a sensing type or planning parties, events, conferences, or hosting writers' groups.

Home-oriented ESFJ women really need their own kind, ESFJ men, with all the similar blind spots to take the fear of change and to give the security blankets that ESFJs demand. It's a commitment to responsibly be of service to people while being warm and friendly.

ESFJ women insist on making concrete the golden rule because it's the only way to find the affirmation so deeply needed. All ESFJ wants is to be told that they have done a good job of raising their children, of sticking in the marriage, of giving their mate enough affection and attention. ESFJ needs constant approval that she has said the right words at the right time in the right place. She has done the right deed. She feels she will always be judged by people. Like ENFJ, she will try to say exactly the most appropriate words for the moment, or do exactly the right favor that's expected of her for instant approval. She appeals to people's feelings to get affirmation.

## ESFJ: Under Stress: The Darkest Side Of Marriage

As so much a people-person, she's usually hired as a customer relations clerk to take on every customer complaint and handle it tactfully. She believes the customer is always right, but she has to respect her boss and obey his rules.

Under pressure, the ESFJ becomes physically ill handling loads of customer complaints. She finds it difficult to step out of her feelings and look at the customer service job objectively as an ESTJ would do.

Dominant extroverted feeling rules her style, as it does the theoretical ENFJ. When she's falling apart most, she needs the love of her true soul mate, the ENFJ male. He uses his introverted intuition and his dominant extroverted feeling to meet her deepest needs in times of crises.

The ESFJ woman is full of "shoulds" and "should nots." She parents her husband, creating in his mind, the guilt of what he ought to do and why he shouldn't do this or that. She will force him to obey her authority figures.

He may fear authority figures as he feared his father, but she will push on until he feels confined. The ESFJ woman never really understands people who see things in a different way than she does. She may find under stress, only the ESTJ male or another ESFJ is really her soul mate.

This is especially true after the age of fifty when two ESFJs are getting in touch with their inferior (introverted thinking) style or fourth function at the same time. From childhood to age age 35, both

ESFJs will be getting in touch with their dominant function or style, extroverted feeling.

From age 21 to 35, ESFJ will be getting in touch with the auxiliary function, or second style, introverted sensing. During these years of education and internship on a job, or marriage and the establishment of a family, the ESFJ will be attracted to ISFJ (dominant introverted sensing with extroverted feeling) as well as ESFJ.

From age 35 to 50, both ESFJs will be getting in touch with their third style, extroverted intuition. And after age 50, ESFJ will be finally beginning to understand the inferior or fourth function or style, introverted thinking. At that time, in the more mature years, ESFJ finds happiness with another ESFJ of the same age, also reaching out to grab his undeveloped introverted thinking.

It's at this time that she'll also be attracted to INTP and ISTP men. Watch out! It's a phase you're going through, ESFJ. As a people person, stick with your own type.

Under stress, negative introverted thinking, the ESFJs inferior function is honed on family and friends. She will blurt out her shadow function consisting of harsh criticism. Her judgments will be harsher than those of an emotionally disturbed ISTP in a sadistic rage.

If her ENFJ soul mate says anything abstract or theoretical as NFs and NTs will always do, she'll dismiss it as "bullshine," or worse or fall asleep, or proceed to do aerobics. Everything must be made simple and concrete or she will toss it aside.

If it's not useful and practical, she will avoid it. At this time, the ISFP woman could prove a good pal to her in her time of need. Under normal circumstanced, the ESFJ woman who is not stressed will naturally avoid anything theoretical also. It's only that avoidance behavior becomes more exaggerated and extreme under pressure.

If she's stressed out, she won't listen to philosophy. She is not interested in asking about the meaning of life. Her faith and childhood teachings about the good book provides any answer that's concrete. The ENFJ man will naturally gravitate towards leaps of faith with her. All the ESFJ woman wants to know about life is whether she has done the right thing at the right time in the right place. Nothing more.

She is prone to cyclic depression. In a down mood, she's melancholic, and can suffer from emotionally-turned up hypertension and heart problems caused by worrying and depression centered around guilt about not doing the right thing.

ESFJ has been labeled the worry wart, much like anxietic ISFJ in a cycle of depression. The two can find solace in each other in times of stress. She's prone to start smoking when worried, just as the ISFJ is prone to take mind-improvement pills when the ISFJ feels inadequate, flawed or slow to learn. ISTJs eat and smoke when worried, and ESFJs eat, smoke, and volunteer under stress.

Under stress, the ESFJ judges herself impersonally and negatively using their inferior logic instead of their values clarification skills. If their mate pauses to think and reflect before answering a question, the ESFJ woman sees it negatively as a lie.

An ESFJ woman under stress needs a soul mate who will involve her with others. She needs an extroverted partner interested in the down-to-earth details of living within an established institution of political work, social volunteerism, or religious commitment.

Under stress, she becomes the critical parent telling everyone around what he should or should not do-what is right and what is inappropriate, what the neighbors should hear (only the good stuff), what card or gift should be sent for the appropriate occasion, how short a hair cut should be, what courses to study, and what "real job" is the most practical.

## The ENFJ Woman and Man (Together Because They Are So Alike)

15. ENFJ, a professional public speaker whose gift of gab comes so naturally, that she can act as a catalyst for anyone's personal growth. This

natural psychologist extroverts feeling as the dominant drive of her personality. She can express freely just the right feeling at the right time.

Marrying an INFP may be a disaster as his dominant introverted feeling withholds the expressed feelings ENFJ woman demands for a loving relationship, no matter how loving he feels inside and how much he worships her ability to express positive feelings to a mate and to the great masses of strangers lurking out there, waiting to disagree.

If her extroverted feeling clashes with his introverted feeling in a marriage, it can work well in a business partnership with the ENFJ doing the speaking and having face-to-face contact with the public, and the INFP working alone writing the speeches or publishing books on the topic spoken about by the ENFJ at seminars.

The ENFJ woman creates visibility for introverts who write by her natural gift for public speaking, including preaching religion, especially more liberal religion. (The ESFJ is more conservative in choice of speaking topics.)

ENFJ woman is a born public relations executive who will speak in public for those introverts who prefer the written word because public speaking drains their health and energy faster than it would an extroverted feeling or extroverted thinking type.

ENFJ woman in marriage becomes a natural teacher of adult education or personal growth courses. ENFJ wants to bring out all her husband's talents, push him toward his maximum personal growth potential. ENFJ woman often search for a husband who's an architect of whatever can be designed. The INTP man fascinates the ENFJ woman, especially if she can show off his logic-centered intellect. Thinking is her inferior function. Extroverted feeling is her dominant function.

She seeks a "mental" man as her soul mate, a thinker, then may call him a cold fish and accuse him of being unable to express how he feels with physical affection. He may stare at a point over her shoulder when hugging her or may be emotionally absent in an embrace. She may exude as much anger as warmth in her Jekyll-and-Hyde way, but with her INTP male, what you see is what you get, and what is hidden, you'll feel as a cold aloofness and dedication to work. She will say words that are touching to the emotions as much as he will look for flaws in words and theories to appear convincing, if ENFJ and INTP live together.

The INTP or ENTP she frequently marries or the ISTJ engineer she often picks usually comes at a time late in her life when she is just getting in touch with her inferior function, thinking. Late in life, the ENTP man is just getting in touch with his inferior function, sensing. They may pass like ships in the night without meeting each other's needs at the same time.

The ISTJ man, after fifty, is getting in touch with his inferior function, extroverted intuition, at the same time that the ENFJ woman is getting in touch with her inferior function (or shadow side), which is thinking. Between the ages of birth and 35, everyone is getting in touch with his or her dominant and second functions. For the ENFJ woman, that is dominant feeling and introverted intuition.

After the age of 35, all of us begin to get in touch with our third function. For the INFP man, that's introverted sensing. For the ENFJ woman, that's extroverted sensing. Introverted sensing rubs extroverted sensing the wrong way. Extroverted sensing exhausts introverted sensing.

From age 35 to 50, the ENFJ woman does well with a man who's getting in touch with the same function, that is, extroverted sensing. After the age of fifty, when all of us get in touch with our inferior function or shadow side, in a small way, at least and at last, the ENFJ woman is finally beginning to explore her introverted thinking.

She finds suddenly she's attracted to the intellectual style of the INTP man, the dominant introverted thinker. However, the INTP man after the age of 50, is getting in touch with his own inferior or fourth function, extroverted feeling-which is the ENFJ woman's dominant function throughout her lifetime.

So the INTP man and ENFJ woman attract and find they have a lot in common? Can this marriage be saved? Will it last? What the ENFJ woman needs later in life is a man who is in the same shoes as she is-another ENFJ who is getting in touch with the same function-be it third function or fourth, for the same age category (35 to 50) or (50 and beyond) as the ENFJ woman.

She needs her own type, an ENFJ or an ESFJ to marry, for her soul mate to to find her. Between the ESFJ and the ENFJ, the best bet at any age is the ENFJ if she's in a helping profession and steadily employed, or the ESFJ if she's not employed or in business other than the helping professions, such as sales of tangible products or certain intangibles needing a mate to join with her in the practical economics of the kind of service with a smile stability that the ESFJ represents.

The ENFP man has too much of himself split off from the type of intense emotional experience that the ENFJ woman demands. His extroverted intuition is too fast for her. She can't come up with the number of ideas as fast as he can. His ability to be a spontaneous resource person throws her off balance. She feels off-center around the ENFP man who outdoes her in public in brainstorming. Her introverted intuition is constantly "slapped in the face" by his machine-gun extroverted intuition firing off idea after idea without preparation in public.

She needs a man of feeling who also is a good provider. She covets an ENFJ or ESFJ. She needs someone as close to herself as possible, even with the same blind spots, to lead groups with her. Her outstanding talent is naturally to lead groups, including her own family. She must be followed, and another ENFJ man or an ESFJ will follow her as she follows him in turn with equal and mutual respect.

The ENFJ represents only five percent of the population. People come first, and children come before parents to the ENFJ.

All the ENFJ woman wants, like the ENFJ man, is involvement in a marriage and to be a good manager at work, play, or as matriarch of the family. ENFJ is the ideal people-manager type, sought by corporations for their ability to nurture at the same time they train and support large numbers of people in an audience. The ENFJ woman is a master of public speaking, a woman of steel with a satin glove.

They are motivational speakers at conventions or teachers. ENFJ approaches people with more warmth than their ENTP public speaking competitors. ENFJ women idealize their relationships.

When relationships don't meet their high ideals, they complain their mate doesn't live up to their standards of being romantic and communicative, or sensitive and caring. However, tolerance is the ENFJs specialty. They are usually totally honest and trustworthy, and sometimes ripped off by bad relationships with ESTPs or ENTPs who steal from them when they are most vulnerable and trusting of human feelings.

In marriage, the ENFJ woman needs most to be accepted for who she is and understood, since her specialty is clear speaking and oral communication. She has exactly the right words to say it, and says better in speech than in writing. When she talks, it's about people and their habits. She makes an excellent psychologist, working with people's feelings and understandly deeply how people share feelings with others.

It's important that she marry a feeling man, a man who can extrovert his feelings to her and welcome face-to-face conversation. Unfortunately, she frequently ends up married to an ISTJ who chases her back to her room if she tries to talk to her mate while he's at his computer using his dominant introverted sensing and wishing to be alone after work daily for the rest of the evening.

Like the INFJ, the ENFJ is equally as empathetic to other people's pain or joy. ENFJ woman identifies with her friends, clients, or patients and becomes wrapped up in their lives as she does with the life of her husband and children. She needs communication so much, she will quickly walk out of a relationship in which she feels emotionally neglected.

In contrast, the INFP woman will stick in an emotionally neglected marriage for years, asking nothing but enough money to survive so she can practice an unpaid art or writing hobby. The ENFJ, seeing she deserves so much more from love, will extrovert her feels, leave, and discuss before a live audience the kind of relationship she wants. She'll get it, even if she has to become an ordained minister, rabbi, or religious-organization counselor, psychologist, MFCC, or marriage broker to find her soul mate.

The ENFJ woman frequently starts up singles clubs in order to find herself a mate. She is one of the foremost corporate trainers on issues dealing with people's behavior and feelings. In her own married life, the ENFJ woman will speak out and reach out, extending herself emotionally to find her soul mate-even to the point of going to past-life hypnotherapists and regressionists to find out what in a past life is affecting her mate-seeking for Mr. Right Personality in this one.

## ENFJ: Under Stress: The Darkest Side Of Marriage

His or her hunches are right when their marriage sours. Under stress, the ENFJ woman makes decisions based on what it's worth to her happiness in a relationship. She must bond. She must mimic. She cares so much about other people's problems in her family, that it brings her down.

Her logic decisions could be coming from her shadow side. There is the tendency to explode in volcanic feelings, like the ENFJ male, and develop a Jekyll-and-Hyde, two-faced personality, one at home, and one charming, outspoken side with which to face the outside world. She cares too much what the neighbors will think, much like the ISFJ man.

The more stressed she is, the more she will read into people. Her highest talent is reading other people's personalities and feelings. She knows every game people play to survive. As a leader, the ENFJ woman doesn't dominate. Under stress, she leads by complaining how victimized she was by her mate.

The ENFJ woman wants a perfect relationship. Instead, what she finds usually is a perfectionist INFP mate. Soon she can't live with the

INFP when her need for affection is not fulfilled. The INFP nurtures and pleases himself first.

She wants to be first in her mate's feelings, but that's not what the INFP introverted feeling type does. So she may leap into the arms of the ESTP or ENTP promoter of her seminars or public speaking tours. The ESTP may steal her blind.

The ENTP may bill himself first in the seminars she set up for herself. She'll try to get in touch with his thinking function to have some common ground on which to meet. The ENTP practices his one up-manship with the ENFJ woman while she is still seeking to get in touch with her sensing or later, thinking function.

He's trying to get in touch with his extroverted feeling function (35 to 50) or finally, after 50, his introverted sensing, and he's running after his opposite, an ISFJ woman, possibly his "Gal Friday" who organizes the mundane details of his office life. The ENFJ woman hates dealing with day-to-day details.

Under stress, the ENFJ woman becomes meticulously organized. Not having her love life settled drives her up a wall. She'll open up a dating service before she'll see herself alone, without a soul mate. Loving human relations is the core of her life and spirit. She's broken when she isn't bonding to one significant other. She loves children, or a career that involves dealing with people's attitudes toward human relations and family life.

She needs to say the right words at the right time in public. At parties, she's looking around for a soul mate. The ENFJ, under stress, makes many critical judgments about people behind their backs.

To her, the back-biting words are merely given as information she wants the whole world to know about the people who bug her. ENFJ under extreme stress, knows how profound an impact she has on people. Under stress, she becomes determined to market her words, hopefully on tape.

The ENFJ is adept at capturing an audience and at holding attention. In the throes of marital stress, she will use this gift to create catchy slogans and go on talk shows to discuss the most intimate details of their lives and their mate's.

ENFJ becomes even more interested in people and "nosey" the more she's stressed out. She will lose herself in somebody else.

If she would work with people more and make less judgments about them before all the information flows in, she'd stop putting her foot in her mouth so many times when she feels stressed.

Her life becomes absorbed in making oral judgments about people and broadcasting it publicly. In short, ENFJ has a big mouth and loves it. Under stress, she needs more time alone to reflect before her mouth opens publicly before asking herself whether it will be worth it after the words are said on the air or in front of a group.

Logic goes quickly, when pressures mount. When ENFJ has been hurt by a particular type (frequently a restless and roving ESTP former lover who has taken a loan of money and never paid it back), the ENFJ loudly voices criticism of that entire ESTP type of man rather than focus on the individual kleptomaniac as the exception for his type under stress.

The ENFJ woman may extend her hurt feelings to ENTP men also, stating, "The ENTP male is a lot like the ESTP in his adventurer style and in the way he treats women." What the ENFJ woman is trying to express is her shadow side, her inferior introverted thinking. In her shadow side under stress, she turns introverted thinking into a sword to at slash herself. Her judgments are never impersonal.

Under added stress, the darkest side of her marriage consists in taking mundane details and using an inferior logic on them. Instead, the ENFJ woman needs to focus on alternative routes and possibilities, the "what ifs" of life. ENFJ woman will often forget her own needs under stress. As pressure increases, she looks outside herself to give to others in order to be the center of attention.

When her mate does not allow her to be the center of attention, she will stop her usual emphasis on positive alternatives and start twitching, ticking, blinking spasmodically, even having epileptoid-like seizures, when no organic illness can be found. What she needs under marital stress is to be recognized for the warmth she gives, rather than for her two-faced personality. It's people who put stress on the ENFJ-people who take emotional swipes at her without even knowing their impact on her feelings.

The two-facedness under stress consists in making critical and "bitingly illogical" judgments about her mate (or anyone else stressing her) behind her mate's or the stressor's back. In front of her stressor, she appears to be her usual fun-loving self. Under stress, if one man of a certain type does something bad to her, she rationalizes (using her shadow logic) that every man of that man's psychological type or background will hurt women in the same way the one example had hurt or stolen from her.

What she needs in her hour of need is to find a religious career or involvement, or a reasonable facsimile of one, and to reach out and touch another ENFJ or ESFJ soul mate for a "deep and meaningful relationship" that only the NF and SF can together experience both concretely and abstractedly in parallel realities.

The ENFJ woman thinks of herself and her soul mate as lop-eared stuffed toy rabbits dressed in cute, fluffy clothing. Under stress, she needs to restore this seductively cute image. Like a big, stuffed toy, she has to restore her total faith in other people, her sense of joy, and her enthusiasm for propaganda that motivates, inspires, and persuades a soul mate to "adopt" this cute "bunny wabbit."

## The ENTJ Woman

## Enneagram 8 With A 9 Wing Or ENTJ On The MBTI™
**ENTJ: Extroverted, Intuitive, Thinking, Judging**

## Dominant Extroverted Thinking With Introverted Intuition

16. ENTJ, an impersonal leader who thrives on making judgments-impersonal decisions about the men in her life. She lives her personal life by analysis. Lovers are meant to be organized in categories-the takeaway man, the tell me you love me man, and the clone me again man. ENTJs make up five percent of the population of the United States.

Marriage is challenge for the ENTJ woman. She demands that her man be led only by her, and she wears the skills and boots to make it happen. Her definition of love is to control and influence her man. She could be the most dominating of all dominatrices. She may not carry a literal whip as a dominatrix, but her figurative one is her leadership gifts, decisive ability, and executive action in the corporate world or in leadership positions at the helm of a company or career. Marriage consists of her blueprint for entrepreneurial success in the home. She is a take-charge woman who runs her household like a Fortune 500 corporation. She can't relax.

People are there for her to organize, not to live their own dreams. The drive for leadership in her marriage makes it essential that she marry an ESFJ, ESTJ, or INFP man who can offer her a chance to go off in another direction. All she wants out of life is to be in charge of the marriage.

For this, her ESTJ soul mate is the better bet, although she will choose the feeling man and lead him until his feelings rebel against her taking charge of his need for autonomy. With the ESFJ or INFP man, there is the change the NP autonomy will rebel and turn passive aggressive. He'll do little things behind her back to get even, to nurture his hurt or neglected feelings.

The ESFJ will get lost in being her host.

The INFP will welcome being the househusband, if she leaves him alone to his art work, cartooning, or writing at home as long as she brings in the larger income and leaves him alone to create in peace. The ENTJ woman's life purpose is to reshape her marriage so she can call all the shots. Unchallenged leadership is her goal inside the home.

## ENTJ: Under Stress: The Darkest Side Of Marriage

Her drive for quick closure increases as the pressure increases in her home life or at work. In her marriage, she wants things settled right now. She'll talk it out, but not for long. As stress increases, she demands her husband stop giving her information when she wants an immediate decision from him. Her INFP husband would only give her more information. That would infuriate her. She demands closure now.

She's prone to outbursts when she can't get an immediate decision from her spouse, child, or employee. What she needs is to take time to reflect and analyze in her mind. Of all the types, the ENTJ woman, like the ENTJ man, needs decisions immediately. There is lacking an inability to wait for more information to come in, to hold the temper from exploding, and to reflect. Introverts reflect before deciding. Extroverts explode first and decide later.

As a lover, the ENTJ woman under stress can be intimidating and humiliating to her mate. In bed, she's decision-oriented. So quickly will she form a judgment about her mate, that she runs the risk of categorizing him without taking the time for enough information to reach her. Don't make this woman your judge in the home, say introverted men who must take time to think, feel, and reflect before speaking.

If she's forced into having to reflect, she will take even less time. She needs time alone, much like the ENTP woman. When alone, she will reflect to herself. The more she reflects alone, the more she will increase the time she needs to make a decision.

Under stress, ENTJ woman can't look at love from all sides now. She needs to listen to the lyrics of that song. She has great difficulty turning matters over in her mind. It's painful.

She needs a mate who can show her how he looks at their marital problems from many different perspectives. This job usually falls into the lap of the INFP man to whom the ENTJ woman gravitates toward in her hour of despair. Soon she will be reprimanding him for only giving her information when she seeks decisions.

ENTJ woman under stress loses her private sector. She needs a man who will challenge her on her own terms only. ENTJ woman are not all alike. Some are hard, cold, impersonal, and shrill. Others appear strikingly beautiful and soft, but are tough in their jobs, which usually are television news show producers and commentators or interviewers. These take-charge women reach the top quickly as news television anchorwomen with high leadership roles.

The softer types appear frequently in the real estate business as realtors or business owners, training fleets of salespersons and putting people in "their place." Under stress, however, the balance goes quickly. From being aware of people, the ENTJ woman becomes less collaborative when making an executive decision. In the home, under stress, she will focus on telling her husband to focus on the details for her.

An ESTJ husband could be her soul mate, because he doesn't mind focusing on the details when she throws up her hands in impatience. She has the big picture on her mind and quickly dumps the facts in his hands. Usually only a sensing thinking type man will put up with her and actually take care of the facts and details or the more mundane side of running a marriage. He'll do her taxes.

Her best choice in a husband is the ESTJ, ISTJ, or, most naturally, her own type, ENTJ, provided they hire someone else to do the detail work. If she sticks by the ESTJ as her soul mate, she will find a detail man also as interested in leading people as she is, with him handling the logistics and details. For example, the ENTJ entrepreneur marries the ESTJ tax lawyer who handles her business and household mundane details.

Her inferior function, introverted feeling may be hidden by using her dominant function, extroverted thinking to make decisions based on weighing pros against cons rather than asking her personal feelings what's something worth in value. So she needs a husband whose personal style is not primarily making value judgments based on his own feelings. The ENFJ man could be a disaster with the ENTJ woman. He would have that case of wounded feelings all the time. The ESTJ man would be a soul mate, handling ordinary life for her while she's leading in the home, in political office, or in her career.

She is most likely to run for political office the more the stress increases in her marriage. The ENTJ woman under enough pressure develops a disorder of self esteem, an all-consuming self. She marry carry marital woes into political office and project them onto the people around her at work. If ENTJ has little genuine self esteem, she could create a huge self in order to keep on functioning normally on the outside, like the INTJ megalomaniac, and behave in her mind as if she were the most important person.

She would need that her husband and co-workers should recognize her leadership and importance. She would also need for everyone around her to put himself in his special place beneath her in order to maintain her aura of self-confidence.

Under stress, she needs to get in touch with her dominant extroverted thinking, but what comes out is her inferior feeling style. She has unending faith in herself. She must use this faith to fuel her willingness to lead.

The closer ENTJ comes to fall apart, the more likely she is to run to the INFP or ENFJ man to soothe her failing self-confidence. She could exploit others to get ahead in her search for NT power over all people and over all of nature. Under stress, the ENTJ woman will battle arrogantly for special treatment.

Under stress, she loses her ability to size up the situation. The INFP man helps her to perceive larger complexities, but she can't stand his giving her information when she wants closure-a decision-each time. Under stress, ENTJ believes she alone can take on her opponents. She really believes her competitors think she's better than they are.

The ENTJ errors in a marriage are political errors. ENTJ will manipulate others to get what she wants only until her impatience kicks in. The ENTJ under stress is prone to obsessive-compulsive behavior such as washing her hands all day until they bleed-to relieve anxiety. The obsessive-compulsive behavior is supposed to distract her from the real issue-a fear of impending failure and incompetence at leadership or a fear of loss of power in her marriage or career. She fears her drive to destroy her attacker.

Extroverted thinking when under stress becomes rigid, cold, and objective, according to Jung. She can find the visionary, changeable, and creative ENFP man a help under stress.

It is the realistic ESTJ man, who will become her long-term soul mate. He will bring her drive for leadership and power back into the sociability and activity of the real world.

The ENTJ man, like her, will be too changeable in a marriage, too much of a visionary to see that facts and mundane details make the marriage work. It's always the little things that make or break a relationship, the sensing details driven home by the ESTJ, at least between the ages of 21 and 35.

The ESTJ man focuses on the energies around him. The ENTJ woman focuses on the commandant style, taking over groups. Only after the age of fifty, can the relationship work well between two ENTJ partners. Both want to give structure to love.

# Chapter Eighteen

## Will You Marry A Bully?

Bullies are mean people who hurt others for a laugh. At one time others hurt them. These kinds of mates share many behaviors with anti-social people, paranoids, narcissists, and drug and alcohol abusers. Their lives are full of marital discord, work problems or constant unemployment, and legal hassles.

In childhood, these people were bullied. Many suffered physical, sexual, or emotional abuse, or grew up in a home where they saw their dad constantly hitting their mom. The rage builds up until the person finally wants you to feel what's inside the sadist or antisocial-the pain.

What's the biological basis of this violent behavior in the home? Low levels of serotonin in the brain have been associated with violent and impulsive actions. Serotonin serves in one way to slow down the central nervous system. With less serotonin, a person may not be able to slow down, cool off, and think before reacting to the impulse to beat a family member.

Violence-prone individuals have low levels of serotonin. In contrast, strong industrial leaders were shown to have high levels of serotonin. Researchers found that leaders in all walks of life, from fraternity leaders to leaders of nations had higher levels of serotonin in their brains.

Research currently in progress in neuropsychiatric laboratories will reveal future findings about the relationship of serotonin levels to violence or leadership. If your future marriage partner displays any sadistic, aggressive, or antisocial tendencies to cruelty or misogyny, you're in a no-win situation if you continue the relationship.

If you give in, you win only a temporary honey-moon phase of the relationship, before the cycle of violence comes around again. Abusers in a relationship people inflict pain without a reason. Wives have been beaten for serving soup too hot or too cold or for having soggy croutons in a salad.

The man who throws food or water in your face will escalate to hitting or punching you or holding a gun to your head. You've shown him that you'll tolerate "x" amount of violence now. So next cycling period he'll escalate the violence a leap further.

If you're boss is sadistic, quit your job. If you're the victim of a sadistic boyfriend or girlfriend, move out and don't renew the relationship no matter how sweet the honey-moon phase of the cycle becomes, for it will surely end.

If you are not yet married, but fearful of your safety, you can still go to a battered women's shelter. To find one in your area call toll-free: 1-800-333 SAFE.

If you can't leave a man who batters you now before marriage, ask yourself whether you have an unconscious need to suffer, defeat yourself, or sacrifice. If the answer is yes, read the book, *Personality Self-Portrait, Why You Think, Work, Love, And Act The Way You Do*, by John M. Oldham, M.D. and Lois B. Morris, Bantam Books, NY, 1991. Read the chapter on the self-defeating personality.

## Does Your Partner Have A Conscience?

Before you say yes to a relationship, move in together, or get married, find out whether your lover or friend is missing a conscience, compassion, empathy, and sympathy from his or her personality. It's like there was Swiss cheese holes in his or her brain where a conscience should be. Check the background of your partner, particularly if you met through online chat rooms, Web sites, or newspaper advertisements. What do other women have to say about him? If you're checking on a woman, find out what others who have dated her or are close friends have to say about how slow she is to anger.

## Does Your Friend Harass Others? Does He Have Trouble Holding A Job For Very Long?

Does he lie? Has he ever stolen without confronting anyone or forged a check? Has he ever forced you into sexual activity against your will? Did he ever start a physical fight with anyone? Was he truant? Did he ever run away from home overnight at least twice while living with his family? Has he robbed (in childhood or adulthood) anyone or committed burglary? Extortion? Purse-snatching?

Get a copy of the DSM-III-R and check your lover's behavior against some of the disorders listed to see whether any of his problems match those on that classifier of disorders. After all these disorders are extensions and exaggerations of normal behavior, but there's a point when the behavior is no longer considered normal, and you could get hurt. So look for warning signals and red flags that alert you to possible trouble ahead if your future is with this person. Although the masculine pronoun "he" is used here, the situations apply to man or woman.

Find out whether your partner has any of the problems listed there. Ask yourself the following questions about your future mate: Did he ever use a weapon in a fight (military duty excepted)? Is he cruel to animals? Did he bully children smaller than himself as a child? Have his physician test him for low levels of serotonin in his brain by taking a simple medical office blood test.

Is he cruel to children-does he pinch babies to make them cry and try to hide the act? Did he destroy or vandalize property? Does he paint hate graffiti on houses of worship? Does he destroy your property, such as rip your clothing if he doesn't like it?

Did he ever set fires? Is there trouble with his work behavior? For example, does he have unemployment for six months or more within five years when jobs are readily available? Does he show the same kind of problem with school if he's a younger person?

Is he continually absent from work and not ill? Does he abandon work and not make plans for other employment or study?

Does he break the law or pursue illegal employment that's grounds for arrest? Is he aggressive, irritable, and violent? Does he get into a lot of fights or beat his other girlfriends or family members? Violence to defend oneself, or required on the job, such as in military combat, is exempted.

Was he bullied and beaten as a child in an unstable family or in abusive foster care or grew up abused on the street? (This is NOT to imply that children from homeless families or kids who ran away and grew up on the street become antisocial or sadistic. Poverty does not cause personality disorders.)

Is he a policeman, prize fighter, or military officer often accused of or sued for and convicted of using excessive force and violence on the job? Does your boyfriend dishonor financial obligations? Does he default on loans or debts?

Is he accused of being a dead beat father by his ex-wife for never paying child support after ordered by the court to pay-and he is physically capable of earning income? Is he a runaway father? Does he travel from city to city marrying or romancing different women or maintaining many polygamous families with the intent to take money from different women?

Does your boyfriend or partner fail to plan ahead. Is he impulsive. Does he travel between cities or countries without a pre-arranged job, business, study/research, or goal? Does he know when the traveling will stop? Is he a drifter? Does he have no fixed address for more than a month?

Does he use different names or identities, aliases, and have no interest in telling the truth? Does he lie to close relatives or to romantic partners, conning them for profit?

Is his safety record reckless? Does he speed or drive drunk or drugged? Is he an irresponsible person or parent? Has he (or she, as the same qualities apply to females) neglected a child? Most of all, is he quick to anger and explosive, throwing things to the floor when frustrated by not getting his way?

Does his anger jump from one to ten in an instant? Is he addicted to carbohydrates, alcohol, or other fixes that he uses to increase the serotonin in his brain, although he may not know why he craves comfort food, sweets, or bread, wheat and other quick-sugar carbohydrates? Does he ask for a quick pill to fix an illness? Is he impatient?

Did your partner ever cause the malnutrition of a child, or failure to obtain medical help for a sick child? Was his or her child dependent on neighbors or nonresident relatives for food or shelter frequently?

Did your partner ever leave the house or car even for a short time so that a small child or children under 5 were left alone in the house or car? This includes running to the grocery on impulse for fifteen minutes, leaving a child alone and in harm's way.

Did your partner ever squander household money on personal items? Has your companion ever had a monogomous relationship for more than a year? (People too young for previous romantic relationships, excepted.)

So, does your friend have a conscience after all? Most important, does your friend lack remorse? Does it feel justified and all right in having hurt or stolen from someone else? Does your friend totally lack any compassion or conscience, empathy or sympathy toward other people?

People without consciences, guilt, or remorse are not the soul mates for you in your quest for Mr. or Ms. Right. These people physically, genetically, and biologically, are not able to care about the feelings of others.

They impulsively disobey the rules of society, committing vandalism and destruction of property, neglect of children and family members, and committing fraud and forgery to get what money they need. They are highly intelligent con artists who appear charming on the outside.

They live by lying and manipulating other people for their personal gain and profit. They marry the kind of spouse who is bent on changing and rescuing them, and they choose their mate according to the mate's weaknesses and vulnerabilities.

If you haven't read Dr. Forward's book on **Men Who Hate Women, And The Women Who Love Them**, it's highly suggested reading before you look for the person with whom you'll spend the rest of your married life. Also highly recommended is the book, **Verbal Abuse: Healing the Hidden Wound**, Grace H. Ketterman, Vine Books, 1993.

Ask yourself, why do you feel you must depend on such a mate for your future? By dating this person, in what ways are you sabotaging your success at finding a mate who truly loves you? Why do you think you deserve to have someone who loves you and a great career? Why don't you think you deserve love and success?

The deserve list should outweigh the "don't deserve" list. Three percent of American males and one percent of females are said to suffer from "antisocial personality disorder." In males it's five times more likely to occur among first-degree biologic relatives, and in females 10 times more likely to occur. A family background of alcoholism is common. Evidence strongly supports a biological factor that could prove to be genetic or inherited.

It has been said that poverty breeds more people with fewer consciences. Poverty also breeds Nobel prize winners. So regardless of your friend's background, check the person out before a charming façade seduces you into a relationship that may put you in unsafe situations.

Before you commit to a relationship, find out how your man treats his mother or how a female relates to her father. What relatives might display this problem in your partner's family? Is your soul mate's nervous system under aroused and excitement seeking in a dangerous and brutal way, or over aroused, panicky, anxietic, and avoidant? Does your partner have a history of being cruel, stern, or mean to animals or relatives?

It's the under aroused nervous systems of some antisocial people that get them into trouble trying to arouse their nervous systems by dangerous or cruel acts. The low levels of serotonin, and other biochemical and genetic factors, are only part of the problem. Such people get depressed often and turn anger inwards as well as outwards to you.

Biological factors aren't entirely responsible. If your friend is born to an antisocial parent, his or her risk is increased. Often antisocial parents were themselves abused or grew up away from their parents in unstable homes, and the problem often appears to be inherited or at least shows up in relatives.

Researchers also believe that children who never had adequate bonding to a parent within the first year of life have a good chance of becoming abusers of their partners who may also be loners who isolate their spouses from family and friends and treat them cruelly by breaking down their self-esteem. These people learn early in life that the world is hostile and frustrating. They have no responsible adult to show them how to channel impulses. They learn to trust and care for only themselves and to vent their emotions by violence. They don't want to change. They outsmart you by humiliation. All you can do is improve their mood or treat them for substance abuse. Because a person is a substance abuser, doesn't mean he or she has a personality disorder that drives the person to abuse a partner or relatives. One problem has little to do with the other.

Mr. Or Ms. Wrong is wrong for you when that person begins to manipulate you at the same time he or she breaks the rules that keep people safe. Mr. or Ms. Wrong wants you to feel his or her rage as your pain.

Protect your financial assets from manipulators and pull away. You deserve a mate who really loves you, whom you can trust with your life, and a safe haven at home. If you don't feel safe riding with your partner or in the same room over a long period of time, it's Mr. or Ms. Wrong.

Do you test your boyfriend's anger limits? If provoked, will he strike you or shove you? Any one of the 16 personality types on the Myers-Briggs Type Indicator (MBTI ™) can fall victim to spouse battering.

However, some types are more vulnerable in extricating themselves from such a relationship. What type are you, and are you more likely to be battered and stay in a relationship, falling victim to the learned helplessness of the battered partner's syndrome?

## Does Your Friend Mistrust You And Show Jealousy?

What happens, when he's so stressed out that he becomes mentally disturbed? When an ENFP male (or female) goes mad, he tends to act as if he were paranoid, even without such a diagnosis. It's a form of panicking into a great fear of being harmed, hurt, or swindled. He's capable of threatening to kill you and maybe even acting it out if the loss of self and love object he's obsessed with is that great. He's a charmer, a daydreamer living in his extraverted intuition, but when his flip side emerges, watch for vigilance, jealousy, possessiveness and symptoms of paranoia.

When and if your ENFP partner ever acts as if he is paranoid under pressure (and you know he's not), here's what to expect. Your ENFP friend expects to be harmed. He questions your loyalty and says you can't be trusted. He accuses you of lying, even though you've never given him reason. He reads hidden meanings or threats into your words and deeds. He holds grudges and won't forgive insults. He never confides in others because he concludes what he says will be used against him.

He reacts with anger to words he says slights him. He may counterattack. He is jealous and questions your fidelity without provocation. This man mistrusts relationships, both personal and business.

He is sure others mean harm and eventually you'll let him down just like everyone else does. He has learned to mistrust intimate relationships and close relatives as well as external business deals. He mistrusts anyone from his doctor and lawyer to the grocery cashier.

He acts this way to keep people from getting close. His guard is always up.

# Chapter Nineteen

## *Regardless of Personality Preference, Check Out Your Partner's Compassion*

What will you use as the litmus measure of human compassion, empathy, and devotion to you in your journey to growing to your maximum potential? Does your friend feel others take advantage of his weakness so that he will never trust anyone or become intimate emotionally? Is he wearing a false identity because he thinks you won't love the real him?

Is he very intelligent, alert, forceful, vigilant, ambitious and cautious? Is he successful at work because he trusts no one? Is there a corner of his life he's hiding from you for protection? Does he have trouble with supervisors and co-workers? Does he envy all in authority over them, even showing jealousy of their successes? Is he very uncomfortable with people of higher rank?

Has he picked you as his fiancée solely because you're non-threatening? Are you the only person he can let down his guard with because you're not powerful enough to be a threat?

Does he keep his innermost thoughts to himself out of fear you'll betray him? Is he too careful how he appears? Does he speak softly and gently in order to cover a seething innermost rage?

Is he overly suspicious of other's motives? Does he keep searching to confirm his doubts about everyone? Is he always testing the jar lids in supermarkets or in restaurants to see whether a jar or lid has been tampered with and perhaps poisoned? Does he act afraid to eat in restaurants because he thinks the help spit in the food?

Does he find what he's looking for because he provokes it in himself? Does he question your loyalty until you break off the relationship out of harassment? Then, does he accuse you of betrayal or his feelings of being unloved, or a confirmation of his lack of trust in you?

Is he always right and never says he's sorry? Is it always your fault when things go wrong, and does he blame and criticize you?

This man starts off as a verbal abuser blaming and criticizing you until it escalates to physical violence, or it may remain at the verbal stage with him blaming you or calling you names when things go other than his way. Does he accuse or blame you for ruining his life or not closing a deal?

Does he blame luck or destiny for bad things that happen to him when he can't blame a person or you? Does he magnify every slight? Does he constantly sue people for exaggerated misdeeds?

This man is never wrong, you are. He's the ultimate verbal abuser, expressing his usually introverted feelings in a negative way. What gives away the clue to his inner life is the fact that he's blameless and never admits to weaknesses.

The truth is people of any personality preference under great stress and frustration, feel so helpless, weak, blameworthy, and full of angry impulses that they project all their negative feelings about themselves onto you, the closest one to them, or onto other people who influence their lives.

They're protecting their brittle self-esteem by throwing accusations and blame at you.

The man you should steer clear of will blame you for making it hard to get close because he can never trust you with his life. Therefore, you can't trust him with yours. He'll find the smallest weakness in you and blame or criticize you constantly for that weakness with words like, "Why can't you tell me you love me?"

He fights off close relationships even though he's dying for a close, romantic, and intimate marriage. Inside he's craving dependency. When he realizes how much dependent he really is, it makes him hostile. He fears his inner dependency, which if realized, would ruin him.

He maintains his autonomy at all costs to function-by blaming you.

Filled with fear of his own dependency, he doubts others instead of himself. He sees you as doubting him. He can see in your facial expressions of your feeling that you betrayed him. However, he never really trusted you in the first place.

This kind of takeaway man is a lot like the narcissistic lover who is absorbed with his own ability to be loved. He's very seductive, charismatic, and flirtatious going from person to person in a group or party, spouting his intuition, touting the possibilities of life.

He's the romantic, but when and if this man ever does feel you are there to harm him under that extreme stress that leads anyone to severe mental disturbance, he'll see in your expression the projection of his own fears. He's of intuitive feeling temperament, and communicates through reading the emotion on your face. He makes his decisions by what really matters to him, his values, not his cold logic.

## Does Your Friend Show Low Self-Esteem?

*(The masculine "he" is used for the sake of brevity. The same problems in all cases can apply to females.)*

He's concerned with himself first and above all when he's paranoid, like the narcissist. He's punishing, self-righteous, and metes out harsh discipline to you when he's certain you disagree with him and of course, you're wrong.

He'll want his own way because his strength of purpose never yields. He's attractive to needy women. He's a natural rescuer in his normal state. When paranoid, this man finds needy women who are co-dependent on his charisma and extraverted intuition.

You'll find the takeaway man working as a cult leader or hatemonger. The normal, average, caring, mentally stable person might work as a counselor, psychologist, teacher, or group leader.

If you're boyfriend has a character disorder, he'll project his self-hatred and self-fear onto outside groups and scapegoats and head the attack on those selected. He sees the world in his own imagined reality, whether he thinks he's a famous person or whether he's a rabble-rouser. He's capable of threatening the life of the people who counsel him when he's in a paranoid state. Or he's capable of seduction using his charisma, when stable and lovable.

This man is never to blame in his own eyes. He'll not seek help from or trust a counselor. He'll live in isolation, mistrusting intimacy, and be well able to take care of himself. Surely, you can find a new relationships with someone else.

The 16 personality types worldwide act disturbed in 16 different ways when they go under enough frustration and stress. Mr. or Ms. Right has high coping skills under stress, and that's what you should look for in a date and mate—high coping skills in a person who is slow to anger.

## Is Your Friend Suspicious Of Others, Including You Because He's Concealing His Own Inner Weakness?

Is your friend extremely suspicious? Does your partner think people are talking behind his back about him? Does he have a paranoid personality style, but not severe enough to have the psychosis? Is he or she overly sensitive to criticism? Does he mistrust everyone and everything? Does this habit run in his or her family? Was the person abused as a child or witness battering at home as a child? Is this person's family or parents rigid, not spontaneous, or uncommunicative?

Does he get so hurt by criticism that he hits you? Are you on his list of people who hurt him? If you're building this man up to batter you, if he gets up by putting you down, back away. If you try to talk him out of his mistrustfulness, he'll see you as plotting with his betrayers against him. He sees everyone conspiring against him rather than a world conspiring for his success.

If you confront a man so mistrustful and fearful of his dependency on you (and hostility toward you) for betraying him with an argument (or insist on getting your way), he may resort to verbal abuse, emotional abuse, and threaten violence, or finally become violent.

He's trying to conceal his fear of his own inner weakness and dependence on people he can never trust. This man has been betrayed in childhood and fears intimacy. He has learned intimacy leads to fear and abuse. The reason behind his mistrust is that this man learned early in life that intimacy brings pain.

Mr. or Ms. Wrong says the following when you two talk privately:

"*I hate you, but don't leave me.*"

"*I don't trust you because you're not loyal.*"

"*I have so little self-esteem left after a life of abuse, that I must create a huge self that's always right in order to compete. If you don't recognize my special place in the reality I create myself, I'll punish you.*"

Any of these types can be male or female, victim or abuser. Mr. or Mrs. Wrong Mate shows little ability outside a fantasy life. Mr. or Mrs. Wrong is the most important person in his/her own world. His body can't take one more punch from you. Therefore, before you start punching, he'll punch you first.

Is your friend after success at the cost of anything, including health? Is he out to get attention by any means and however destructive to the self? Is he bitter about being unrecognized as great and out to punish those who won't recognize him?   For example, a rejected writer who thinks he's an unrecognized genius may use a false identity to date the editor, producer, or publisher who rejected all his creative work with the aim of hurting her like she hurt him. Does he take rejection personally?

## Does Your Friend Get Angry When Criticized And Hit You?

This man or woman can talk his or her way into getting hired by convincing employers of special abilities they fantasize they have. When it's time to produce their product, they may realize they've overestimated the talent it takes to compete in a glamour business or in politics. Others are talented, but hard to work with. These men readily exploit anyone to compete. They demand special treatment, such as getting to the head of the line without waiting their turn. When stopped, they will say, "Do you know who I am?"

A "who cares?" answer will elicit revenge for bruising what little self-esteem they have left. These men who feel inadequate strike out at women, beating them down to size.

Does your friend undermine his own effectiveness and ambition? Is he helpless, but arrogant? Does he make up stories about royalty in his family? Does he believe that alone he can take on the competition and win-but when loses, gets revenge on the judge or the winners? Does he hit you for criticizing him?

Is he jealous of your salary? Does he get angry when you don't recognize that he's better than them all because he says so? If you argue that he's not a celebrity and he imagines he is or will be shortly, does he hit you to make the pain of reality disappear?

Psychoanalyst C.G. Jung theorized that the extraverted man has an introverted 'anima' or image of the ideal woman, inside himself, whereas the introverted woman has an extraverted animus, or image of the ideal man, inside her. These inner images get projected onto persons of the opposite sex.

The result is that your attracted to your opposite and may wind up married to someone of the opposite type, according to Jung. (He wrote the famous work, *Psychological Types* published in 1923 on which the *Myers-Briggs Type Indicator* ™ was based.) After much testing, Jung's theories finally had credible statistics. The indicator was accepted by professional psychological testing associations and standardized as an instrument of research. The indicator reflects a collection of research, statistics, and other findings based on theory about personality type. It's one of the world's most popular personality indicators that classify personality types and has been translated into many of the world's languages.

## Opposite Types Attract Until the Novelty Wears Thin

What do you really have in common with your spouse after many years of marriage? Do you share any of the same interests in similar subjects? When opposite types attract and marry, it's because each type unconsciously complements the other. However, there's a catch that is of deep concern to researchers in domestic violence. When opposite types marry, they have the time to interact with one another.

As the years pass and the couple stands face to face each seeks understanding from the other. (See Dr. Keirsey's book, *Please Understand Me.*) The problem is that the more each partner seeks understanding, the more they find out that they have never understood one another. Opposite types speak opposite psychological languages of miscommunication. The conflict between the two opposite types grows with familiarity during long years of living together in close quarters. It's different than working together where you go home at night. When a husband wants to watch footage of World War Two and the wife wants to watch a documentary on secrets of ancient Egypt, is having nothing to speak about in common good or bad in a marriage after many years? What will you say to each other when there is no longer any sex in the marriage, when you sleep in separate rooms because you can't stand the snoring and gassing, and when his coughing keeps you up? What do you say other than criticize how you are treated by the other—controlled, that you can't turn on the heat in the winter or the air conditioner because he pinches the pennies and you feel controlled? What do you say to remain full of joy, cheer, and fun? Do you or your partner escalate little sentences into mountains of fear or evaluation?

Do opposite types married to one another also batter one another or engage in verbal abuse and violence? No one knows. All we can rationally say about opposite types is that they have different preferences.

According to statistics in various police surveys, more than half the women in the U.S. are routinely battered by their husbands, and a smaller number of men are routinely pummeled by their overbearing wives. Spouse battering is defined as either verbal, psychological, and/or physical abuse ranging from a push or shove or pinch to actual punching with a closed fist or being threatened with weapons. Beyond battering, there's emotional neglect, psychological abuse, and financial abuse—when a partner or child takes a mature parent's or spouse's personal money or property. Are you old, overheated, and your spouse won't let you turn on the air conditioner because of fear of the electricity bill?

Beware of contempt and being disvalued in a relationship. Increasingly, men are using unloaded guns in their wives' heads to get their attention during an argument. The wife has no way of knowing whether or not it's loaded. Fewer women use this tactic, as women are more likely to weld what they find in the kitchen or bedroom where they are cornered more often.

For example, a husband puts an unloaded gun in his wife's face to get her to do some household chore his way, not hers. That's wife battering. When a spouse is disvalued, or negation of value occurs, the frustration and stress level rises. Anger and rage is banked inwardly until it explodes. Battered wives feel crushed by the values held most precious by the spouse.

The reason why opposite types may end up disvaluing one another is because the struggle to communicate between two types often results in mutual depreciation. The value of one means the negation of value for the other, according to Daryl Sharp's book *Personality Types: Jung's Model of Typology*, Inner City Books, 1987, p. 31.

See also the book, *Jung's Typology In Perspective*, Angelo Spoto, Sigo Press, 1989, if you want to learn more about the famous psycholoanalyst C.G. Jung (1875-1961). For information on the MBTI,

Highly recommended is *Gifts Differing*, by Isabel Briggs Myers, Consulting Psychologists Press, Inc., Palo Alto, CA., 1990. (Myers designed and researched the MBTI based on her interest in Jung's work on personality types).

Opposite types attract, but relate in a socially inferior way after familiarity sets in. The natural attitude of one complements the natural attitude of the other.

The introvert is curious, but once married, the introvert becomes fascinated by objects other than the spouse, objects inside his or her mind or inside the house-such as a computer or specialized documents. Sometimes the introvert often cannot be induced to go out and dance on New Years' Eve in a crowded place because of an inherit fear that some accident or disaster will happen on the way to and from or in the center of social activity.

The extraverted wife feels empty and bored, suffering a loss of self when the introverted mate won't take her out once in a while. She's disappointed in her expectations. There's no romantic adventure has she imagined.

She doesn't care about her husband's excitement with the new computer software, she wants to join groups and meet people, but she can't get out without a car. He may withhold the money to learn.

Each partner's undeveloped attitude or shadow springs forth and doesn't care about the other person's values. It won't sacrifice it's own dreams, hopes, and interests that create excitement or preoccupation.

A spouse beater in a heterosexual or same-sex marriage hits because as much as he wants to command, he feels an equal fear of failure, dependence, hostility, and inadequacy. The worse in a marriage is a combination of an aggressive man or woman with an underlying feeling of inadequacy acquired in early childhood.

The victim is attracted to those who hurt him or her. The person is full of self-sacrifice, such as staying in an extremely abusive marriage for 50 years for the sake of the children who then both abuse and blame her for being an overbearing and self-sacrificing mother.

Are you one of those men or women who can't stand pleasure for long before you have an accident or out of the blue, fall ill with a life-threatening disease? Do you miss opportunities to have some joy or pleasure from life? Does happiness escape you?

When everything is going great, do you spoil it all by sabotaging your happiness? Are you a giant with feet of clay that crumble when you're at your career or relationship peak? Do you ruin chances for employment or success by an unconscious effort to throw a monkey wrench in the works?

Are you ruined by success? Does happiness make you feel that something terrible is about to happen and it's just around the corner so you hurry it up to get relief?

Don't let your partner frighten you into becoming self-defeating. An abusive man often won't let his wife leave the house to go shopping alone or visit friends.

Spouse and children are frequently abused both physically and emotionally by the one who uses dominance by force. Violence in marriage is biochemical. Violence-prone people have low levels of serotonin in their brains. Strong leaders have high levels of serotonin. This is what may distinguish between a normal aggressive type leader and a sufferer of a personality disorder.

If you are worried about whether your fiancé will beat you after marriage, if he's not doing so now, look for signposts. Marrying a man with the potential to beat you is a no-win situation. Chances for counseling are there, but will he come to counseling? Can you change him? Violence escalates with familiarity.

A big problem is that many abused women say they never saw the abuse coming before they married. Others left an abusive family to go with a less abusive boyfriend, who later became more abusive than the family left behind.

Giving in completely gets only short reprieve from the next violent episode. There are groups for wife batterers, and men have been helped and families saved. The chances are slim that he will come for help. Do you have an unconscious need to suffer in this relationship that will surely escalate into more violence.

**Are You Likely To End Up A Battered Spouse?**

Welcome to the future battered spouses club. Do you feel anxiety about people and problems all the time? Do you worry about what will happen to you in the future or about small things instead of the large relationship questions? Do you worry about trivia? Do you talk about other people all the time?

Do you stay up all night worrying over someone else's behavior or actions? Do you worry, but never find answers? Do you check on people constantly and in a suspicious way without reason? Do you try to catch people doing wrong constantly? Do you feel unable to stop talking about other people's problems-and your not in the helping professions and at work? Do you stop your routine because you're too upset to continue?

Do you focus your energy on other people's problems all the time and you're not a paid (or volunteer) helping professional? Do you wonder why you have no energy even though you follow a maximum healthy diet? Do you worry that you can never get anything done that you feel should be done?

Are you controlling, in denial, have low self-esteem, push your feelings down, are afraid to be your real self, are rigid and controlled? Are you dependent or dependent and arrogant at the same time, blame, threaten, or coerce or beg. Does this poor communication increase lack of trust and anger?

Do you let others hurt you, complain, blame, but remain in the relationship? Do you think you can rescue or change someone who's hurt you, but won't get help? Do you insist on your partner taking responsibility when he feels he's too inadequate to take responsibility?

These are all questions to ask yourself to see whether your potential for becoming a battered spouse is equal to your partner's potential for becoming your batterer in a relationship bond that both of you will find it impossible to get out of when the violence starts. Before family violence, wife battering, child abuse, elderly abuse, and fear happens, extricate yourself now.

To find out your type and relate it to domestic violence potential before it occurs, much research needs to be reported publicly. What's out there are a few new books each season, but the majority of research remains largely in doctoral dissertations on university library shelves and in personality type trade journals and away from the places the public frequents-popular bookstores, supermarket magazine and paperback book racks.

In case your own family is abusive, you may never know what normal, loving family life is supposed to be like. It's suppose to make you feel good about yourself and give you respect and encouragement or inspiration to be all that you can be, to reach for a wonderful life. Here's a checklist. Ask yourself whether your date or mate shows you abusive behavior. If the individual does, then leave the relationship immediately. You survived before you met that person, and you will get along fine without a toxic person in your life at any age.

Say to yourself, I deserve real love when the right time comes. Ask yourself the following questions:

**Abusive Behavior Checklist**

1. Does your partner's temper scare the hell out of you?
2. If you disagree, does your date explode in anger or frighten you?
3. Do you apologize when your partner treats you like a doormat?
4. Do you make excuses to others when your date or mate shows a short or explosive temper or is quick to anger?
5. Does your partner push you around, hit you, or throw objects at you-such as a glass of water in your face when your mate can't get his or her own way?
6. Is your date jealous? Jealousy isn't a way of showing how much a significant other cares about you or loves you. Jealousy is a way to control and punish you out of anger and fear-filled rage.
7. Does he or she force you to have sex?
8. Are you afraid to tell your friend, no?
9. How would he or she react to your telling your friend to go take a flying leap?
10. Do you have to explain and defend everything you do to sugar coat your mate's temper? Do you have to be perfect or walk on eggshells to keep his or her temper quiet?
11. Does your mate or date angrily accuse you of flirting with others when you're not? Does he or she check on you or spy on you? Does he

call constantly to monitor your every move or decisions about your own independence?

Are you a dependent person who shucks responsibility? Why do you feel you're nothing without a mate?

12. Are you afraid to do anything you like without his or her permission?

13. Why have you given power over yourself to this friend when all you have in this world is your power to choose for yourself the direction of your life now and in the future?

14. Does he or she drink or take drugs and then become violent as an excuse to let go his feelings of rage at you? Does your partner say, "look what you made me do?" when getting drunk or taking drugs-in order to punish you or manipulate you?

15. Does your friend believe you hurt the one closest to you when you're down on yourself? Does he or she get up by putting you down?

16. Does your partner threaten to kill himself if you leave? (After marriage he or she will threaten to kill you and your family if you leave.)

17. Is your mate possessive and controlling or patrolling?

18. Does your date/mate have a hair-trigger temper that the ones closest to him can set off the easiest?

19. Does your friend criticize or ridicule you or tell you without him you're nothing or a loser? Do you get the feeling your mate is not your best friend and never was?

20. Does your mate call you all the names in the book without realizing that it's exactly the way he feels about himself? (For example, he thinks he's a loser or stupid, so he'll call you a loser.

Then you'll think he's calling you a loser because you secretly blamed yourself for some failure at winning a success and silently or unconsciously called yourself a loser. This is all called self-sabotage. It's used to keep you from getting what you want in life.

21. Does your friend make you tell him what you did every moment when you were away from him? Does he accuse you of seeing other friends?

22. Does your friend think he owns you? After marriage the violent or verbally abusive relationship turns into possessiveness and total ownership of the victim who's willing to allow her body to be hit.

23. Is he or she verbally or sexually abusive? Maybe your friend doesn't hit you at this time because he doesn't own you yet through marriage, but does he verbally abuse you? Does he emotionally or psychologically abuse you? Is there sexual abuse? Does he think after marriage, you're his. Is a marriage license viewed as a hitting license? Would you have him put in jail if he hit you?

24. Have you been put down verbally or abused verbally so much by your parents and siblings that you don't recognize verbal abuse in a date, friend, or mate?

Does it seem normal to you when he tells you words that make you feel bad about yourself, hurt, and angry at him? Do you think you deserve it? No one deserves to be hit or put down verbally. You will become his doormat. Is this the normal pattern in your home, or do you really believe you deserve better?

25. When you try to break it off, does he refuse to let you go?

26. Do you go to your violent or temperamental friend just because you want to defy your parents who don't like him? Do you keep quiet about the abuse or make excuses or apologies for him so your parents won't hate him even more?

Are you hurting yourself to spite your abusive parents or to rebel against normal or abusive parents because you are supposed to rebel and assert independence?

27. Instead of asserting your independence and becoming self-supported and educated, are you asserting your declaration of dependence on a male you expect to take care of you like a daddy? Do you understand total financial dependence on this man or total emotional dependence

with you financially supporting him in part, is often chosen by women who don't have enough security or confidence in their own ability to take care of themselves?

**What Kind Of Mate Denies The Warning Signals?**

To get a closer look at what kind of woman makes a battered wife, in contrast to what kind of man becomes a batter, see Terry Davidson's book, *Conjugal Crime: Understanding and Changing the Wife-Beating Pattern*. In Davidson's book, therapist Carol Victor surveyed eighty clients, all victims of wife beating, all socio-economic classes.

In Victor's survey of 80 clients, four of the battered wives completed graduate school, six completed college, and seventeen had attended college. Nine of the wife beaters completed graduate school. Several were PhDs and MDs, and nine had completed college.

The stereotypical myth that wife beaters come from lower socioeconomic classes is false. Domestic violence from child abuse to wife abuse to elderly abuse cuts across all economic classes from dropouts to those with many graduate degrees, from the most poverty-stricken to the rich and famous celebrities.

In therapist Carol Victor's study, the type of women who were beaten listed their occupations as one or more of the following: "social worker, psychologist, librarian, teacher, artist, nurse, designer, manager, medical technician, computer programmer, law enforcement officer, banker, secretary, and accountant. One woman was a waitress."

The wife-battering men listed their occupations as: "physician, self-employed businessman, draftsman, engineer, teacher, pharmacist, medical technician, librarian, police, career military, and computer programmer. There was one sanitation worker."

Battered women are found in all walks of life, from members of the high IQ societies to physicians and lawyers. It's a myth and stereotype that women who hold independent jobs or who own and run businesses can't possibly come home and change like Jekyll and Hyde into a battered wife. Battered wives aren't only the stereotypical submissive, shy personalities.

They're also the outspoken, independent thinking women who refuse to defer to their husbands controlling, patrolling, manipulative behavior. By refusing to defer and standing their own grounds, asking assertively for respect, the hostile/dependent man is provoked. When he loses the control over a woman who seeks control over her own life, he batters her.

The other type of battered wife is truly the shy, demure woman who suffers from the "battered woman syndrome." She has seen so much domestic violence in her parent's home as a child, or escaping violence in childhood, feels unable to take responsibility for her own financial and emotional independence.

What kind of a woman becomes a battered wife? According to the book **Conjugal Crime**, on page 53, Terry Davidson describes the battered wife as *"a woman who looks down on all women, including herself, as inferior,"* according to Minneapolis therapist Mary Pat Brygger, who runs a rap group for battered wives.

## What Kind Of Man Becomes A Wife Beater? Does Your Boyfriend Feel Inadequate And Frustrated?

Therapist Mary Pat Brygger of Minneapolis wrote that the man who beats his spouse has "an overwhelming sense of frustration, inadequacy, consumes energy living up to the old-fashioned masculine stereotype, and then finds it too hard."

This man cannot care for his wife, Davidson writes, in the book, **Conjugal Crime**, and she can't care for herself either-emotionally and economically.

Unless a mate becomes violent due to an accidental head injury on the right temporal lobe that controls violent outbursts, there are family origins of wife-battering. There were no controlled studies of battered wives, according to Barbara Parker, instructor in Nursing, University of Maryland, when she and Dr. Dale N. Schumacher, M.D., M Ed. decided to study the variables that distinguish battered wives from the general population. Barbara Parker wanted to find out what might be done to reduce further abuse.

Parker wanted to research what else there was besides psychiatrists ascribing psychiatric labels to the victim and offender. Parker noted in the August, 1977 issue of the American Journal of Public Health, that reports which ascribe psychiatric labels to the victim and offender don't necessarily document mental illness such as masochism and sadism.

In the book *The Intimate Enemy*, by G. Bach and P. Weyden, Avon Books, NY, 1968, domestic violence was also defined by 'catharsis' or 'ventilation theory.' In concrete words this means "letting it all explode."

The letting it all explode theory viewed violence in the family as stemming from verbal battling. Verbal aggression was seen as actually increasing the use of violence.

Another theory appeared in the *Journal of Marriage and the Family. 1974; 36: 13-39.* "Leveling, Civility, and Violence in the Famil," by M. Straus, in which wife abuse was related to the cultural norms of society. Straus explained that some European and American norms license family violence. This violence may be encouraged implicitly.

In *Forward To The Violent Home*, Sage Publicatons, (Beverly Hills, 1972), author R. Gelles suggested that some people believe that battering a wife is a legal act. Researcher M. Straus in his article, "*Leveling, Civility, and Violence in the Family,*" *Journal of Marriage and Family*, in the seventies, suggested that the wife-battering husband is executing a role model learned from his own father. Other researchers during the next two decades suggested that the wife is carrying out a role model learned from her mother.

# Chapter Twenty

## *Is Wife Battering Related To Violence In The Victim's Childhood?*

Parker tested this theory in her study. She studied for five consecutive days all women who applied for legal assistance to the Domestic Relations Division of the Central Office of the Baltimore Legal Aid Bureau. Fifty women were given a confidential survey consisting of an open-ended, multi-purpose questionnaire.

What Parker defined was the Battered Wife Syndrome. A model for the study was the Michigan Wife Assault Task Force Study, directed at gathering dates on violence in the family with the aim of improving legal services.

### What Is The Battered Wife Syndrome?

Ask your boyfriend how he would define the battered wife syndrome (BWF). Note his answers and study them carefully before you marry. Parker defines the Battered Wife Syndrome (BWF) also known as the battered women's syndrome as-a symptom complex of violence in which "a woman has, at a time, received deliberate, severe, and repeated (more than three times) demonstrable injury from her husband, with the minimal injury of severe bruising."

Violence to such a woman in a nuclear family, is defined by Parker as "a positive response to the question, 'Did your father ever mistreat, hit, or beat your mother?'"

The researchers looked for more positive answers to questions asked to include the number of incidents, injuries received, and the amount of medical care necessary.

## Does Your Boyfriend Have Less Education Than You, And Was Your Own Mother A Battered Wife?

A high number of wife batterers are less educated or hold jobs which they perceive as having less status and income than their wives. They key point is whether these men actually view having less education, job status, or income than their wives as making them feel bad about themselves, in short, inadequate/incompetent.

Women who feel there's a shortage of 'princes' out there on the marriage market may marry men with far less education than themselves. The important point to find out before marriage is how does them man really feel inside about you having more education?

Even if you never worked outside the home for pay or earned any significant income, the fact that you have your degree and he doesn't-that you stuck it out and he didn't could set him off to become a batter-if he allows your degree to make him feel inadequate.

One of Parker's significant findings was that the husbands of battered women in the study had less education than those of non-battered women. The other finding was that if the mother in the battered wife's family was a battered wife herself, there was a statistically significant probability that the wife would be battered by her husband.

There was no "significant relationship to her abuse as a child," according to Parker's study.

## Would You Definitely Leave Your Mate After One Episode Of Violence? Or Would He Continue To Come After You To Get You Back Into The Relationship By Showering You With Love And Gifts?

Parker's data revealed a small number of "non-battered women" who were victims of violence on only one occasion and either divorced or threatened that "further violence would not be tolerated." These women, if further abused, sought outside aid. Parker designated these women as a sub-group of "Violence Syndrome Averters." Here, there was significantly less violence in the family when the women were children than in the family of battered women.

Where do you stand? Did you witness your mother being a battered wife? Violence is banked in one generation and spent on the next. It's passed down. Women who have not witnessed violence in their own families as children find wife battering inconsistent with their role. What you don't see as familiar, you avoid.

Violence is passed vertically in families. It's not that a woman who witnesses family violence will be more likely to beat her children. Instead, she'll most likely marry a man who will beat her and live in fear and submission, falling victim to the battered women's syndrome, afraid to speak out publicly that she's being hit or verbally abused to the point she unconsciously or consciously believes she is what he tells her-incompetent to take care of herself financially and emotionally without him. She will easily hand her children over to her husband when he demands custody and threatens her life.

Until Parker's study, primary prevention of wife beating was largely ignored by the media reports on domestic violence. Only in medical journals and public health reports was the problem starting to emerge to health-care workers. Preventing wife battering throughout all socioeconomic classes wasn't discussed with the battered wife. No one sat her down and told her here's how to spot a wife beater before you marry him-next time around. Parker and Schumacher suggested that heath-care workers must develop methods to break the circle of domestic violence from wife beating and child abuse to elderly abuse.

# Chapter Twenty-One

## Do We Really Fall Apart According To Our Personality Preferences?

When the persons who proudly announce their sixteen MBTI (Registered Trademark) types, thirteen styles, four temperaments, or nine Enneagram preferences-or any other number from the variety of personality classifiers-have a breakdown due to stress and other pressures, do they fall apart in sixteen, thirteen, four, or nine different ways?

Psychopathology shows the different ways in which the different personality types and styles fall apart when having a stress breakdown or other mental illness. Some types mimic real physical illnesses, but upon examination, are found to have no disease, degeneration, or sickness in the body.

Do we really fall apart sixteen different ways for sixteen different types? Are there thirteen mental illnesses for the thirteen personality styles? What about four ways to go "tactical" as Keirsey puts it for the four temperaments contained in the sixteen types-the NF, NT, SJ and SP temperaments?

Is it true that SJs have cycles of depression throughout their lives, SPs explode into sadists or implode into head-banging, razor-wielding, self-abusing masochists, NFs, dissociate and develop multiple personalities or go anorexic, amnesiac? Do ENFJs with no underlying organic disorder act as if they are epileptoid? Do INFJs under extreme stress spasm, convulse, or assume the stationery stance as if they were catatonic? Do we know these studies hold weight? Who is doing the research and why?

There's so much to investigate before you say "I do." How much can you really check out your partner's background before you commit to marriage or even a relationship? How much should you investigate? Would you want to know what happens when your partner cracks under the weight of unbearable stress? How much can he or she bear?

When NTs break down and fall apart under extreme stress, do they tend to become obsessive-compulsive or ritualistic, washing their hands all day or compulsively cleaning the house over and over? If they have been observed performing such rituals, how accurate are the studies and how many NTs were observed acting obsessively, washing their hands repeatedly or doing other similar acts? Is it important that you know all this about your prospective partner or mate?

How many ways do the different types cope with stress, falling apart, or mental illness? What do they do under pressure when they can't take it anymore? What is the tactical behavior they use to manipulate others? How do they appear paradoxical? They are not aware of being able to stop it when it occurs. Do they behave in tactical and paradoxical ways to unconsciously call attention to their cries for help when they are in great need to change?

Now that you have looked at some of the warning signals that could predict impending gender violence, go forth and pick you mate consider your personality preferences as well as many other criteria. Match your own behavior and preferences to your mate's character.

# Chapter Twenty-Two

## *Once You Know Your Preferences And Type*

When you find out your four-letter type, what do you do with it? Use it as a guide to achieve dating, marriage, and job comfort levels.

Your four-letter type can give you clues to what is measurable about your preferences as to a right-fit niche that's a natural. How you've applied your preferences to skills and skills to production and profit is only part of the picture.

Use your understanding of your own preferences and characteristics to find what's measurable in the company to which you're applying. Then try to match your characteristics to the character of the organization.

To understand how your preferences relate to job satisfaction, you need to know the meaning of the four letters of your type. A list of suggested jobs follows the discussion of each letter.

To have job satisfaction in the computer industry, you need to be both creative and disciplined. Do your job-related skills match your current preferences?

Did you learn the skills you have because they were easy to do? Or were you trying to please someone else? Did you learn what you do well only because you were told those skills were in demand or paid well? Do you deeply enjoy using your particular skills and competencies?

Would you use those skills as your hobby even if you weren't paid? Do your skills increase your energy, growth, or general health on and off the job? If not, what preferences can you include in your resume and use on a job that make a better match?

Use your understanding of how preferences relate to type in order to understand yourself better. Your preferences show up when you write your resume, go for an interview, or choose a job. Do people energize or drain you? Does working alone exhaust you? Why take a job that drains your energy when you can find one which energizes you with enthusiasm? Let's first discuss the difference between extraverts and introverts. Your first letter was either E or I.

## If Your First Letter Was E.

### E Is For Extravert

About seventy percent of the people in the U.S. are extraverts. They get their energy from being around people and people-oriented activities.

If your first letter was E, you see yourself at this time as an extravert. (It's also possible to be a closet extravert, and list yourself as an introvert, or to be an introvert at your core and list yourself as an extravert because that's what you'd rather be to fit in.)

You use your extraversion to talk about each part of your resume with people you meet at professional associations, job fairs, computer industry employees in your field, and job search committees. You're oriented toward working with a steady flow of people around and high people-processing activity.

Look for jobs requiring you to be outgoing, sociable, interactive, and enterprising. Look for breadth of skills or job activities rather than depth of expertise and concentration.

You're an external-oriented person. You also find it hard to maintain concentration on a solo activity if there's any interruption or distraction by people passing by. Extraverts make excellent receptionists, customer relations persons, vendors, and teachers or trainers. About fifty percent of computer programmers are extraverts.

You need extensive contacts with clients because people contact energizes you, and being alone drains you. Attend external events such as conventions, conferences, and meetings.

Involve yourself in planning events for the computer industry such as trade shows and exhibits. Marketing is an excellent way to get a foot in the door as is public relations. You are energized by talking, so volunteer to do public speaking on panels at conventions and meetings of professional associations. The ideal job in the computer industry would be where you can manage people, technology, or events.

If you're an extravert, look for a job in the computer industry which allows you to do the following tasks:

* Run national associations of computer professionals.
* Do public speaking and presentation graphics work.
* Sell and market computer tangibles (products) or intangibles (ideas, such as advertising).
* Produce software videos.
* Train employees how to use software or hardware, or teach in a school.
* Open a computer matching service for business partners.
* Organize computer camps for kids.
* Do many things at once.
* Work in an environment where there are many distractions.
* Work in the computer press arena as a journalist.
* Sell wireless telecommunications equipment and car phones.
* Do demonstrations for stores.
* Plan computer fairs on campuses.
* Direct marketing research and consumer tracking.
* Manage a large staff.
* Telemarket computers or software.
* Attend meetings and volunteer on committees.

* Plan office parties.
* Put your opinion in the company newsletter and ask to be columnist so you can interview many supervisors and employees.
* Work in the public relations and marketing communications department of a computer firm.
* Create visibility for all your ideas, working with a partner who can help you make your ideas realities.
* Make audio or videotapes.
* Don't spend too much time alone at work. Keep the door open.
* Practice listening skills when you feel you talk too much.
* Bounce your thoughts off 100 people a month.
- Get feedback from co-workers and employers on how you're doing daily. Don't wait until job evaluation week.

## If Your First Letter Was I.

### I IS FOR INTROVERT

Approximately thirty percent of the U.S. population are introverts. Introverts are energized from introspection, concentration, and working alone more often. They prefer depth to breadth.

What are your best skills as an introvert? Precision, vision, understanding, insight, analysis, objectivity, and reflection. The more quiet time you have, the more creative you become. Market your precision by creating visibility in written communication.

Introverts need more time to think and reflect on questions before they speak. Many jobs in the computer industry fit the needs of introverts desiring solitary activities where they can think, analyze, or express their creativity for long hours at a time.

If you're an introvert, you're territorial. The job you can thrive in must allow you to concentrate on one long project at a time with the office door closed for privacy. You're an internal-oriented individual.

Your skills focus in depth on one or two subjects. If the focus is too wide, energy scatters. Target a niche. Become expert in what gives you energy. Your worse mistake would be to become a dilettante, generalist, or jack-of-all-trades.

A second skill can be used as a backup when the first subject becomes obsolete or no longer needed by employers. An example would be to gain expertise in computer-aided design or corporate animation as your primary subject and in an unrelated second subject, such as a degree in entertainment law, computer law, computer security, or computer repair technology.

You're drained by people. Limit your relationships by finding a job that will conserve your energy levels. Your work is going to be guided by your internal reactions and reflections on your subject of expertise. Therefore, look for a job where you can work alone or with one or two other people on long projects requiring depth of concentration, such as writing computer books. Introverts are complex people who usually don't show everything they are feeling at the moment to the world without thinking about it first. When in a live interview, you will keep your best points to yourself. Your best points are put in writing on your resume or cover letter.

Since it's so hard to show your best, keep records of what's really driving your personality. Use those records to select a job that uses your best skills in depth. Otherwise, supervisors could undervalue your skills.

Interviewers need to allow for different response times and not confuse introversion with degree of enthusiasm for the job. Resumes and cover letters of introverts often use direct mail marketing techniques to illustrate enthusiasm.

Create visibility by publicizing the skills on your resume, brochure, or cover letter. Show samples of your work and a list of your achievements.

If you're an introvert, look for a job in the computer industry which allows you to do the following tasks:

* Work alone and enjoy the solitude as much as you need for recharging.
* Look for writing or illustration jobs.
* Choose long projects, like books to concentrate on with the office door closed for privacy.
* Deal with people through mail order or computer bulletin board.
* Limit your public speaking commitments.
* Choose distance teaching and correspondence courses if you are a teacher.
* Conserve your energy.
* Travel less than an extravert if you're in sales.
* Stop working when you're exhausted and take a break.
* Write down what you have to say and reflect on it.
* Concentrate on creative or analytical work.
* Interview people one at a time with as many breaks from foot traffic as you can get.
* Choose outdoor work where you spend more time alone that directing people face-to-face.
* Consider telecommuting or work in a home-based consulting business.
* Review software and books or tapes.
* Sell your listening skills.
* Keep your friendships down to a few close ones.
* Push out your ideas and give them visibility or hire a publicist.
* Do radio and TV interviews by telephone hook-up to your home.
* Don't allow colleagues to interrupt you in mid-sentence without a financial penalty.
* Develop your artistic talents with computer graphics software.
* Color desktop publishing is a new field to consider.

* Don't take telemarketing or telephone jobs where you have to make many calls a day. You'll wear out.
* Talking seems to waste your time. Put your communication in writing and sell it.
* Courseware design and instructional technology are excellent ways of using your teaching and training skills.
* Computer technology and robotics repair is one job where you don't have to talk to customers while your fixing their machinery.
- Some introverts prefer to work nights so they can work alone as computer operators.

## How We Take In Information
**Your second letter was either S or N.**

There are two ways we take in information—by intuition or sensing. Sensors (S types) gather information literally. They like information presented to them factually, chronologically, and sequentially by offering specifics.

Intuitives (N types) gather information figuratively rather than literally. Intuitives take in information holistically under a theoretical umbrella.

Misunderstanding or "lack of communication" at work or in the home often is due to the differences between those giving out information as sensors and those taking in the information as intuitives. Let's look at the differences between sensors and intuitives.

**If Your Second Letter Was N.**
**N IS FOR INTUITIVE**

The greatest job-related skill for you as an intuitive to develop is a technique for bringing your best ideas into reality and selling them. Look for the big picture behind the facts.

Intuitives are in the minority. Only about 30 percent of the world's population take in information using intuition. Therefore, it's going to be harder to do it your supervisor's way, unless you match your type with the organization's character.

If you're an intuitive, your resume needs to show how much you inspire and motivate people with your theories about the future. You deal in randomness rather than logistics.

Intuitives Need Change And Diversity

You wouldn't be happy for long handling routine details day after day, such as keeping records of accounts payable and accounts receivable or typing the same title insurance policy forms in the word processing department. You need diversity on a job. There needs to be change and variety—many projects, ideas, and possibilities.

You'd be happier working as a computer press newspaper or magazine reporter writing a different article each week on a variety of subjects than teaching word processing each semester using an upgraded version of the same software.

Look for a job where your main skills would be to persuade, motivate, and inspire alternatives. Introverted intuitives are happier writing, programming, analyzing, illustrating, or designing courseware than speaking professionally. Extraverted intuitives are energized by training managers, speaking in front of audiences, managing people at all levels, creating visibility, and marketing ideas.

Intuitives Offer Ingenuity

Intuitives are catalysts who bring people together from different walks of life and make great event planners of computer conventions. As an intuitive, you'd enjoy designing or writing a corporate video or managing a nonprofit organization which recycles used computers to schools.

Scientific programming appeals to intuitives. Many combine their background in healthcare or environmental sciences with computer programming for research, design, or training.

Intuitives who are introverts would feel more comfortable selling by direct mail order catalogues or electronically, where constant face-to-face contact wouldn't drain them. Extraverted intuitives can look to selling intangibles such as ideas to advertising agencies.

Intuitives thrive on theory. Regardless of whether you're an introverted or extraverted intuitive, if your second letter was 'N,' your best skill is your ingenuity.

Intuitives Need To Use Their Imaginations

Intuitives prefer to use fantasy and escape to sell the sizzle rather than use only the literal facts to sell the steak. Intuitives would bloom in the field of instructional technology. Look for a job which allows you to discuss patterns and possibilities. Your job-tasks should allow you to look at the big picture, or the "forest rather than the trees."

You'll be happier in a job where there's an audience for your speculations, ideas, or imagination, daydreams, or fantasies.

Therefore, use your resume as one technique for bringing your ideas into reality, by supporting your ideas with facts. Any job you seek must emphasize the use of your ingenuity, imagination, creativity, and ideas in a general way.

Any type can be creative or imaginative, but intuitive 'N' types are creative (more frequently) in general and future-oriented ways, and 'S' or sensing types are imaginative (more frequently) in specific, present-oriented ways. Intuitives need to sell fantasy.

The best computer-related jobs lie in designing computer video games, selling your interactive fiction, teaching and training others in your specialty, and working with theory. Your head is in the clouds more often than sensing types, so market "head in the clouds" products and services.

Sell escape. Use computers to teach at a fun-filled computer camp resort. Or involve yourself in the theories of neural networks and fuzzy logic and artificial intelligence.

If you're not an analytical-type intuitive, try corporate animation, desktop video, desktop publishing, technical writing, computer press journalism, computer graphics, and the more creative aspects of computing. You're also excellent motivating and inspiring others to enter the computer industry.

Intuitives are at home using persuasive communication, experimental art, and writing. Literally, many intuitive prefer to work at home as telecommuters with their computers hooked up to headquarters via phones, modems, VCRs, and fax machines.

Intuitives Look For The Alternatives

Use your intuition to study the possibilities in your resume. The best skills you have as an intuitive is your interest in looking at alternatives and possibilities. Consider what else can be done, how you could the job differently.

Looking for alternate routes to complete a project energizes you. Your best skill in a job would be as a resource person. You can find a thousand ways to market a product or service, or a hundred businesses that utilize one skill.

If you're an intuitive, look for a job in the computer industry that allows you to do the following tasks:

* Think of many things while working on one project.
* Work out alternate routes or new possibilities.
* Leave the boring details to sensors.
* Work flexible hours—as late as you want.
* Analyze how computers work.
* Work with words and creative writing.
* Explore hidden meanings. Create "back doors" in software.
* Find out how different things really are connected.
* Question all authority.
* Accept your general answers to specific questions without anger.
* Don't have to follow directions unless you create the directions.

* Sell escape, entertainment, fantasy, and imagination.
* Explore your creativity, whether in math fractals, publishing, or art. Desktop publishing and design and desktop video are good bets.
* Keep out of the accounting department, unless you're managing an accounting firm's public relations or personnel department.
* Find out whether a company is receptive to your need for variety and constant change in your work routine.
* Analyze the complex for research departments and think tanks.
* Computer engineering—when the emphasis is on computer languageanalysis rather than on continuous sorting of sequential details.
* Look into new uses of computers, and virtual reality used in new ways. Look to international markets for new possibilities.
* Wireless communications offers possibilities for global linking.
* Enjoy forecasting trends of the future today.
* Use foreign language abilities to design translation software.
* Enjoy futuristic pursuits.
* Evaluate and analyze inventions or work with inventors and patent attorneys.
* Improve or develop new products combining old things in new ways.
- Use computer technology in psychotherapy or rehabilitation.

**If Your Second Letter Was S.**

**S Is For Sensing**

Sensing deals with the way you gather information, and sensors like to gather information quite literally. The resumes of sensors reflect the perspiration more than the inspiration which drives their practical skills. You're in the majority. About seventy percent of the world's population are sensors.

The job most likely to make a comfortable fit will be direct, realistic, down-to-earth, unchanging, specific, factual, and tied to the present. You'd prefer to sell tangible products rather than ideas. The steak appears more real than the sizzle.

You like to sell what you can touch, smell, hear, or see through your five senses.

Look For Applied Solutions

Ideas are a dime a dozen to sensors. You want to see the ideas applied to real solutions.

To sensors, intuition means playing hunches, and hunches aren't backed up by concrete facts. You'd rather use practical, factual experience to take in information. Seeing is believing.

Sensors Are Literal

You're literal about data. You enjoy the tactile experiences of textures, videos, sounds, sights, and smells. Virtual reality is your stage. You want a job that uses your hands-on skills or troubleshooting ability. You're a tools master or a facts master.

Your ideal job needs a here-an-now aspect to it, like analyzing the systems in financial databases. Financial programming deals with the here and now.

You'd leave the theoretical programming to the physical scientists and mathematicians. You'll take applied math or programming—applied to the real world's day to day problems that you can take in through your senses. Sensors are comfortable in the business world.

If you're a sensor, look for a job in the computer industry which allows you to do the following tasks:

* Deal with details and specifics.

* Work at jobs that use more common sense than book-learning.

* Explore computer security and computer law professions.
* Work with applied sciences. Theory puts you to sleep.
* Enjoy lots of physical activity at work. Move around. Walk.
* Troubleshoot and repair technology.
* Learn computer-aided drafting or engineering graphics.
* Deal with accounting or applied mathematics.
* Apply your financial knowledge to artificial intelligence.
* Create technical illustration, typography, or applied art.
* Robotics technology and computer-aided manufacturing require your literal, hands-on skills.
* Concentrate on one project at a time.
* Take only jobs that offer immediate, tangible results. You want to see where your craft ends up.
* Work at jobs that deal with the present reality. Thinking too much of the future wastes your time.
* Work with figures or facts. Routine is important.
* Choose programming specialties in financial database management or healthcare fields.
* Use your imagination to summarize the facts.
* Work sequentially and chronologically.
* Learn step-by-step and teach computer subjects the same way.
* Simplify the complex using facts and details.
* Don't make sweeping generalities when you can supply exactness.
* Give clear instructions and ask for them as facts in sequence.
* Ask for the details immediately.
* Question authority before taking anything literally.
* Look for the trees, not the forest.
* If you believe everything you see, appearances may be deceiving.
* Keep dated memos and records of how you're treated at work or anything odd or unusual.
* Deal with reality.

* Sell tangible products.
* Instead of trying to fix what's not broken, ask an intuitive toshow you all the ways a disposable copy of it can be improved.
* Look for low employee turnover in a company.
* Comparative shop.
- Use software for fashion design.

## Thinking And Feeling
**Your third letter was either 'T' or 'F.'**

There are both thinkers (T types) and feelers (F types) in the computer industry. Let's first look at thinkers, who are found in large numbers in programming, software engineering, scientific research, and systems analysis positions. Fifty percent of the world's population are thinkers. However, two thirds of the thinkers are male and one third of the thinkers are female.

**If Your Third Letter Was T.**

### T IS FOR THINKING
Thinking deals with how you make decisions. Here's where you focus your need to come to closure when you decide on anything—be it what to put on your resume or where to work. Thinking also deals with how you judge.

You're going to judge something by logic if you're a thinker. That means you wish to step back from getting emotionally involved in a decision.

According to Otto Kroeger, management consultant and author of Type Talk At Work,(How The 16 Personality Types Determine Your Success On The Job), Delacorte Press, Bantam, Doubleday, Dell Publishing Group, Inc., 1992, 96% of the corporate executives at the very top echelon are thinking judgers (TJ types). Only four percent of corporate executives who have risen to the top CEO level are not thinking judgers (TJs).

For example, suppose you're a thinking, judging person, a 'TJ.' According to Otto Kroeger, "As long as our system is profits-and-productivity-driven, TJs will rise to the top."

Profit is a key factor in determining how those who run the computer industry make their decisions. On a resume, how much money you made for a company last year really does influence your desirability.

So if you're a 'T' or 'TJ,' connect with organizations that have a similar character to your own. The same goes for any of the other preferences: connect what you are to where you work.

Hard Heads And Firm Words

You'll try to be as fair and objective as you can by distancing yourself from sentiment. You'll try to be calm and clear-headed. Sometimes your clear-headedness will be perceived as hard-headedness. You'll talk straight rather than make up little polite lies to avoid hurt feelings.

Thinkers value logic and downplay sentiment. They'll chose being truthful over being kind. Thinkers prefer executive action over socializing. They will question authority if the authority's conclusions aren't backed up by factual, scientific evidence.

Question Employer's Authority

Being natural skeptics, it's comfortable for a thinker to critique and evaluate. You may insist that the boss is wrong until the person proves he or she is right. This is not the same as being guilty until proven innocent, however.

Thinkers like to organize either facts (if you're also a sensor) or ideas (if you're also an intuitive) into logical order. Thinkers hate redundancy. In the computer industry, you'll find many thinkers who are business-like, brief, and curt on conversation. Thinkers are impressed with logical statements.

Thinkers feel most comfortable performing intellectual criticism if they're also intuitives and common sense criticism if they're also sensors. Thinkers enjoy solving the problems of machines, software, business, or technology more than solving the problems of people—unless they can administrate or manage the people at a distance from an employee's raw emotional issues.

Thinkers love to expose and blow the whistle on any wrongs in a company. These problem-solvers often "take over" situations where a feeling (F type) employee needs to think logically and impersonally about some job-related task. Thinkers in such a work environment become the guardians of the feeling type co-worker's thinking.

It's more important for you to be right, and you couldn't care less who likes you. You don't need harmony at work. You need a calm environment.

If you're a thinker (T type), look for a date, mate, or job that allows you to do the following tasks:

* Settle disputes objectively.
* Analyze securities, facts, or computer systems.
* Troubleshoot and repair computers or peripherals.
* Sell technical instruments.
* Write technical software or hardware user manuals.
* Design software or hardware.
* Design and program computer games.
* Handle accounting problems.
* Manage financial databases.
* Invent more efficient computers.
* Sell cable television to telephone companies.
* Use your cool-headedness to investigate computer security problems or crime.
* Practice computer, tax, or entertainment (computer animation) law.
* Design computers for military robotics.

* Write technical textbooks for professors.
* Open an electronic university to teach computer sciences.
* Teach critical thinking to employees or in community college.
* Volunteer to make your company's most difficult decisions.
* Become a computer consultant, solving problems.
* Work as a systems analyst.
* Be an expert witness or professional skeptic for TV talk shows.
- Use computers for scientific, economic, or financial research.

## Feeling Types

F stands for feeling types. About two thirds of all females in the United States are feeling types and about one third of males are feeling types. In the computer industry, feeling types feel more comfortable in jobs that use their drive for creative expression and to simplify the complex within communication with language, art, or music. Feelers seek rapport with people working closely with them, either through correspondence indirectly or in person. Feeling types have a deep need for harmony and lack of conflict in the workplace and in the work task itself.

Although thinking types are found in music, art, and literature, their verbal language and technical illustration tends to become complex and analytical, seeking to evaluate or critique. Feeling types, on the other hand, seek to praise rather than critique, evaluate or analyze. They ask what is the project worth and seek inner values leading to serenity in the project or work environment.

If you're a feeling type, a computer job or task may be highly technical or of a repair nature as well as creative and expressive. However, if the work can't be directly applied to helping people or enhancing people's lives, environment, imagination, or healing, the routine technical machinations wears thin pretty fast.

You're process-oriented rather than task-oriented. Your overview and career goal is always either self-growth, service with a smile, or geared toward creativity enhancement through caring about the inner value of the work in the long run. What does the work mean to your growth and the growth of those around you who use the product, service, information, or idea?

Feelers can be found in everything from artificial intelligence and neural networks to nanotechnology and biotechnology. The ultimate question, is whether the work will benefit people sooner rather than later. In the computer industry, feeling types are frequently found working as trainers, editors, public relations directors of software companies, writers, illustrators, and event planners.

**If Your Third Letter Was F**

You have a high need for affiliation and rapport with those around you at work, even if it's only through correspondence with those that work closely with you. You're loyal to your boss as long as the workplace need for harmony and rapport with the employees around you aren't overlooked.

When under stress, rather than list the pros and cons to make a decision objectively, you'll ask yourself whether the outcome is worth it. That's a feeling decision that you can trust.
Sell creative expression as a tool for healing.

In the computer world, software is viewed as a tool for healing or learning through entertainment, escape, play, or creative arts therapy. Sell software that you feel is "worth it" to your deepest values about work and life.

You'd rather work to do good in the world than work solely for a paycheck doing impersonal, high-tech work. If people's benefits aren't involved in the technology, the motivation to do the work routine wears thin pretty fast.

The feeler's niche is communication.

Your niche or best fit is communication with compact disk-interactive courseware design and creativity, CD-ROM, virtual reality, animation, desktop video, desktop publishing, the computer press and journalism, public relations, communicating about the people in the computer industry, people management or human resource management, people-oriented research, and personnel trend studies, electronic publishing, video production, psychology, multimedia, special effects, telecommunications, local and wide area networks, wireless communications, and graphics design or illustration.

Feeling types frequently design software for preschoolers.

You'd feel comfortable designing preschool software and games, making people feel better about computers, cable, or phones-linked-to-computers, and expressing yourself using computers as a tool for an aesthetic, communication, personal service, or visual experience. Educational technology, designing or selling software as entertainment or education is what you do best.

You're a natural communicator and teacher, either in writing or illustration, if you're also an introvert; or teaching, sales, event planning, and speaking if you're an extravert or at least like to work around them. As a feeling type, you would prefer to sell escape as entertainment and learning at the same time.

Feelers need feedback from the workplace as well as from customers. Feeling types like to give feedback, according to Otto Kroeger in his book, *Type Talk*. Feelers prefer to consider the feelings of everyone around them before making a decision.

You're either a service with a smile type repairing machines directly for people-helping, or an idealist, an ultimate optimist who would enjoy making computers simple to understand by a lot more people so they can be used as a tool for learning about life. Instructional technology and courseware design are your niches.

Use your drive for communication and rapport to create visibility or publicity.

You're empathetic, concerned about your own feelings as well as others, walk in other people's shoes and viewpoints, and try to please those around you. In the computer industry, feeling people need rapport with a mentor to start up services to help more people understand computers through linking with satellites and distance teaching that put computers into rural schools. You need harmony in your work life and flexible time. You desire security with the opportunity for frequent change of projects and learning new skills for self-growth or service.

Find new ways to use computers for music and the expressive arts.

You'd enjoy putting Javanese gamelan music on computer midi synthesizer disk to create a background for historical fiction on CD-ROM or write CD-I fiction so readers can be interactive with their novels and stories or poetry and cartoons. You may even write scripts for computer games.

If you're a feeling type, look for a job in the computer industry which allows you to do (and place value for growth) on the following career experiences:

* Write articles or books about careers in the computer field.
* Write stories, articles, books, or design computer software to teach through escape, entertainment, suspense, romance, idealism, service, or helping people achieve more harmony.
* Write fiction for CD-Interactive software to open up the imagination of children or adults of all ages.
* Travel to sell computer software to hospitals.
* Do public speaking to sales groups.
* Become a public relations director for a software company.
* Work as a journalist in the computer press.
* Express yourself in courseware design.
* Train employees or students in healthcare or education.

* Help people use computers to enhance the environment.
* Use computers in psychology and therapy.
* Animate corporate training films.
* Use computers and video in multimedia productions.
* Put books on software.
* Use desktop publishing or desktop video to create books or ads.
* Write software user manuals to help people learn a skill.
* Use computers to help people see others in ways they can't see without the computer use.
* Manage the marketing communications department of a software firm.
* Plan events and conventions for professional associations.
* Publish a newsletter on ergonomics and the healthy use of computers.
* Train healthcare personnel in computer use or write and produce training films for healthcare personnel.
* Work as a computer illustrator, graphic designer, or ad designer for an advertising agency.
* Animate cartoons and special effects for corporate training films or advertisements using multimedia hardware and software.
* Teach computer skills to the physically challenged.
* Place employees in jobs at an employment agency, temporary service, or in the human resources department of a corporation.
* Work in outplacement for retiring or career switching computer-personnel.
* Sell medical records technology software across the country to hospitals as a traveling salesperson.
* Plan computer trade shows and exhibits.
* Sell or design computer adventure games.
* Design preschool software.

* Work for or open a software talent management agency to sell the work of clients who design software for games, learning, or entertainment.
* Publish a newsletter on how to use software for creative expression.
* Teach creative writing using word processing software.
* Teach computer-aided design and illustration.
* Write books about computer careers or about people behind the scenes of the large computer corporations.
* Work as an investigative reporter specializing in computer industry trends.
* Compose music on a Midi synthesizer or use computer equipment to create music, work with sound and lights, or edit films.
* Teach new uses of computers for people.
* Use creative expression to communicate about software.
* Create national clearinghouses for new databases that package information about human resource management, psychology, technology, or education.
* Use computers therapeutically for healing.
* Engage deep enthusiasm and loyalties for technical writing projects.
* Work as a documentation analyst, technical editor, of software translator.
* Use or design computer software for church-related information or religious and historical studies.
* Do investigative reporting on computer issues that affect people.
* Improvise at sales meetings to train corporate managers.
* Use desktop publishing software to create pop-up books.
* Use your love of nature and sympathy with animals to create new kinds of portable computers or software.
* Design software and hardware or robotics devices to help the blind, deaf, or paralyzed worker to become more independent.

* Plan events and trade shows to bring in large audiences for computer conventions or exhibits.
* Work in telecommuting jobs at home so your time can be as flexible as possible to do creative work with computers or software.
* Design special effects for films and video using computers and software using music, lights, sounds, animation and textures.
* Build robotic devices for museums and exhibits using computers, special effects technology, and models of prehistoric animals or people. These could be moving models of dinosaurs, apes, insects, prehistoric people, or other exhibits.
* Combine 3-dimensional sculpture and animation for new computer software, simulations, or techniques in computer graphics.

## Judging And Perceiving

**Your fourth letter was either 'J' or 'P.'**

There are both judging types (J) and perceiving types (P) working in the computer industry or anyplace else.

Many times it's the Judging (J type) or Perceiving (P type) preference that is the reason why some employees are terminated for "not fitting into the group." They really are competent, but are matched with people of the opposite preference in a particular work situation.

In fact, the J or P preference may cause all types of conflict, tension, hostility, and arguments at work—from tardiness to disorder, from rigidity to waiting too long to make a decision.

Why would judging or perceiving cause so much conflict?

The J or P preference deals exclusively with the way you structure your environment. The judger (J type) wants order. The perceiver (P type) wants flexibility. The need for structure and order opposes the need for flexibility and spontaneity.

When you write your resume, you may be a P type who needs a flexible working environment, including flexible hours. You can adapt to many types of work situations on demand. As a spontaneous, creative person, you can meet unexpected surprises at work and meet needs as they arise. You'd make a good cop on a beat or computer video games artist.

When you send your P type resume to a J type employer. It may get tossed in the round file. The J type employer is looking for an applicant who can be controlled in a routine. The person in the employer's mind must be decisive, orderly, scheduled, deliberate, and work well under pressure only during certain hours. If you diverge from the J character of the organization (or the employer), you won't fit in. You'll feel there's a wrong fit. Your goal is comfort. After all, you want to work where you're type is welcomed.

As a P type, you want to keep your mind open for new information. The J type wants quick closure that makes sense. Judgers will make decisions instead of adapting themselves to the new information constantly streaming in. So while judgers judge and you adapt, there's conflict. You're feeling exploited and reactive.

**If Your Fourth Letter Was J**
**J IS FOR JUDGING**

About fifty five percent of the world's population are judgers. You seek structure in everything—"the planned life," as Isabel Briggs Myers writes in her book, Gifts Differing. Everything has a place in your system of order. Judging is what you do best—making quick decisions.

You're a natural controller, a fixed person who likes routine, stability, security, and working for the same company many years. You're a saver rather than a spender.

On your resume, you seek closure. You want everything at work decided as quickly as possible, and you want to make the decisions. You're methodical, scheduled, and organized. Your traditional in many ways and have a need have roots or to belong to the group of your choice. This structure-seeking behavior shows on your resume.

There is a definiteness about the way you organize your resume. It's frequently chronological, organized, and exact in precision. You work to deadlines, which is what every employer must have. You need a plan for everything from writing your cover letter to the last follow-up call entered in your computer.

You make use of day planners and clocks. You are all about counting, measuring, and controlling, and you make up 90 percent of top-level executives in the world. You hate constantly changing information. The biggest problem in writing your resume is that you have to keep revising it. J types have a harder time relaxing than P types.

In a job, you need to seek balance and moderation. Instead of becoming angry at P types for taking too long, look to them to provide many alternative routes to the same goal. Look to the spontaneity of the P to teach you how to play at work more. You're a master at records management and making lists to remind you to finish the work on time.

P types see you as an authoritarian father figure to be feared, regardless of your gender. Your perceived of by perceivers as the girdle into which the P type is squeezed whenever the P type grows another inch toward self-determination. You see yourself as the parent scolding a P type child, instead of equals at work.

If you're a judger (J type), look for a job in the computer industry which allows you to do the following tasks:

* Records management and filing. There's a place for everything.* Executive level or junior executive trainee work in computers.

* Programming

* Accounting

* Systems analysis

* Financial database management.

* Applied artificial intelligence.

* Software Engineering
* Clerical supervision or clerical work
* Word processing
* Desktop publishing
* Arbitration and mediation in labor disputes
* Computer security
* Drafting
* Robotics technology; computer-aided manufacturing
* numerical control
* Electronic mail processing
- Manager of multiple projects, objectives, and deadlines.

**If Your Fourth Letter Was P**

### P Is For Perceiving

About forty-five percent of the world's population are perceivers. Tight schedules cramp your style. You like to wait and see what happens. You're adaptable and flexible about careers and working hours. You go with the flow. Surprises are welcome.

You seek changes, the unexpected, and variety in your work projects, even in your jobs. Your plans are tentative.

You wish to create your own deadlines and work whenever you feel the inspiration or motivation to do your thing. You won't work to anyone else's deadline unless the recognition of your creativity or your entire financial security depends on it.

Your work must be fun and play or you won't do it. If you adapt yourself to a J type's rigid schedule or plan, your health could be affected. Your spontaneity makes you a good cop on the neighborhood foot patrol beat—or the equivalent in the computer security field. Your resume will change its slant many times as you work at temporary jobs in many different fields.

You're leisurely and laid-back. However, you often work near deadlines to cram everything in the short time you allowed yourself. You may thrive on the adrenaline, or go the opposite way. As a stress avoider, you also may avoid the work if it makes you tense—or get it out of the way early so you can play.

P types are free-spirited intrapreneurs, entrepreneurs, independent contractors, and freelancers who often work for someone else if there's autonomy and flexibility on the job. Above all, a job must offer you a chance to move freely. You need variety. Express your creativity or restless need for action, movement, and change on your resume by exploring the less familiar ends of the computer industry. Stay away from records management jobs where you have to organize and file facts all day. You'll be distracted.

If you're a perceiver (P type), look for a date, mate, or job that allows you to do the following tasks:

* Use your curiosity about new uses of computer technology.
* Adapt your resume to changing plans or frequent career switching.
* Look for a constant flow of new experience in a job.
* Don't take a decision-making job because you want to keep decisions open.
* Learn all you can about your employer's company or your job.
* Choose a job where you'll know what others are doing.
* Job tasks could focus on exploring how other people's work comes out—like an inspector or securities analyst.
* Start up many different new businesses for others or new projects at work. Then leave the project when the newness disappears.
* Work at tasks that are flexible and adaptable.
* Choose work situations where tolerance is a virtue.
* Choose a job where you won't be nailed down.
* Traveling computer or software sales was made for you.

* Get into research, working with think tanks where you can design your own models—especially if you're also a thinker/intuitive.
* Video game design will use your spontaneity and creativity.
* design and illustration/animation accommodates your need for a variety of projects.
* Technical writing of software manuals accommodates your need to keep options open as you work on changing projects.
* Explore the unknown about the relationship between computers and the needs of the physically challenged in robotics engineering.
* Work must be play, so why not write interactive fiction for CD-Interactive and CD-ROM laser disks?
* Courseware design and instructional technology give you time flexibility.
* Plan computer industry conventions, conferences, trade shows and exhibits, where you can work your own seasons or hours.
* Learn skills that are transferable from one career to the next. You don't want to be limited by only one career. An example would be desktop publishing skills or word processing and programming.
* You don't have to be definite about a career, only about a specific job.
* Instead of planning schedules, making outlines, or following plans, wait and see what changes will alter the requirements anyhow.
* Manage your files on computers software disks such as in databases, where you can change them as needed, instead of using paper file folders.
* Use spiral notebooks where you can add or remove paper.
* Your job search could be international.
* Take a job where you can depend on last-minute spurts of energy.

* Look for new ways to transfer past experience to many different careers.
* Don't look for a job where the primary requirements are control, order and neatness or sticking to the subject.

Now that you've learned your four personality type (or preference) letters, let's put them all together and come up with sixteen personality types, based on the principles of the Myers-Briggs Type Indicator (MBTI) (Trademark). These sixteen types are as follows: ISTJ, ISFJ, INFJ, INTJ, ISTP, ISFP, INFP, INTP, ESTP, ESFP, ENFP, ENTP, ESTJ, ESFJ, ENFJ, and ENTJ.

On your preference classifier you came out as one of these four-letter types. All you have to do is combine the characteristics of E or I, S or N, T or F, J or P. These preferences represent your four-letter type.

---

Recommended are books on type and temperament such as the following bibliography:

Discovering Your Personality Type (Enneagram), Don Richard Riso, Houghton Mifflin Co., NY, 1992. (The Enneagram Questionnaire).

Please Understand Me by Dr. David Keirsey & Marilyn Bates
Prometheus Nemesis Book Co., Del Mar, CA 1984

LifeTypes, by Sandra Hirsh & Jean Kummerow, Warner Books, 1989

TypeTalk, Otto Kroeger and Janet M. Thuesen, Dell Publishing,
NY 1988

Sixteen Ways To Love Your Lover, Otto Kroeger and Janet M. Thuesen, Delacorte Press, 1994.

Winning Resumes for Computer Personnel, Barron's Educational Series, NY 1998.

---

Below you'll find a fun dating preferences classifier, a self-scoring questionnaire. If you have a date, soul mate, best friend, partner or family member, have your significant other also answer all of the 74 questions about making choices. Compare your personality preferences or styles and see how unique or similar you are. Then take a scientifically-based personality classifier. For fun purposes of entertainment only, you can spend a rainy date evening or afternoon with your partner taking this classifier. Here's the questionnaire/classifier:

## For Entertainment Only: Your Date Night Fun Interests-In common-Preference Classifier

1. You get a phone call from a blind date. You plan to go out for fun on a Saturday night. You would rather:
a. actively go ethnic folk dancing, line dancing, or square dancing in a wholesome, crowded coffee house.
b. play video games alone while your date watches, or have you and your date order take-out food and sit in your living room playing games only two people can play. You take the phone off the hook and don't answer any doorbells from solicitors. You dislike when people disturb you and your date.

2. Computers are your hobby. At work you have time to show your hobby to your future mate during your two-hour lunch break in your flexible-time job. You choose to:
a. Play computer virtual reality martial arts video games as a sport purely for entertainment.

b. Design programs for forecasting the weather daily for 100 years into the future.

3. You would enjoy a soul mate who requires that you:
(a.) select from many details in planning your wedding and point out which details need improvement in shape, texture, mood, or color, and keep accurate records of facts.
b. You would enjoy planning an ancient-themed wedding that entails making farfetched decisions about Egyptian coronation wedding theories. You might enjoy discussing ideas and attitudes that people have about marriage in different times and geographic locations.

4. You have a date with two possible future mates. Which mate would you choose as your very own soul mate and possible marriage partner according to whether her interests more exactly matches yours?
a. The mate (male or female) whose job is to analyze stocks and stock market trends and apply artificial intelligence strategies to forecast upturn or downturn and who also analyzes computer systems using impersonal, objective logic all day.
(b.) The mate more interested in what makes people tick who works as a director of human resource development. That mate uses a gifted understanding of people to head the personnel department or research training and human relations in the corporation. That mate's main duty is to place the right people in the best jobs. In each case, both mates bring work home from the office a lot and each day discuss their jobs as part of the relationship.

5. You work with someone you'd like to date, someone who you'd hope to marry, if things worked out right. At work, you're told to fire your blind date for taking too long to come back after maternity/paternity leave.
a. You terminate the person as ordered, telling the employee that the company cannot afford the loss of productivity and profit directly attributed

to the individual's absence, but it's only fair that you two can go on dating and deepening your relationship as that person would make you a good future spouse.
(b.) You refuse to terminate the person as ordered. Out of empathy you advise the employee to sue the company for family leave discrimination and side with the person because of circumstances.
You ask that person out on a date and tell him or her of your romantic intentions and hopes that a meaningful and deep relationship leading to marriage could be a possibility.

6. When asked to shop on your lunch hour for your boss, you:
(a.) Visit many different stores all day looking for exactly the right product at the best price and quality.
b. Impulsively buy the first overpriced item you see that fills your boss's requirements so you can take the rest of the afternoon off to play and have fun. You tell your boss you had to spend the time hunting down exactly the right thing at the right price to save money.

7. You paid a nonrefundable $200 last month to reserve a ticket to attend a career-related convention five months from the present in Las Vegas. Today you found out there's a singles only (your preferred age group) mystery writer's convention on the same day in Rio de Janeiro that you'd rather attend because it's more exciting. You are:
a. comfortable sticking to your original plans to attend the Las Vegas career networking convention because it doesn't require change.
(b.) feel deprived of an open-ended exciting experience, and wish you could afford to lose the $200 and take off for Rio de Janeiro at a moment's notice instead.

8. To give yourself more visibility among singles you'd like to meet:

a. you'd take a paid weekend job hosting a two-hour radio talk show, answering questions on the air about computers or software in your specialty.
(b.) To give yourself more visibility among peers, you'd take a two-hour weekend job writing a singles column for newspaper about your own interests, reading, reflections, or research.

9. You would take an assignment in order to have:
a. job security and a high salary to spend any way you please.
(b.) the chance to have your work made into a film and plenty of worldwide recognition at conventions, but only a $1,500 pittance for your work.

10. You'd rather take a mate whose interests match your:
a. realistic attitude and practical skills in keeping records.
(b.) your imagination to create movies that sell escape.

11. You wished you would have majored in a subject at college that:
a. allowed you to decide logically, and objectively in order to analyze strategies, map out models, or keep records to solve problems about production and profit at work.
(b.) Gave you the warm fuzzies from understanding what people value most about their careers.

12. On which five specialties would you focus within a college major if you knew you would be offered a great job after graduation:
a. systems analysis, programming, logic, science, and math, or:
(b.) illustration, professional writing, creativity studies, psychology, and human resource management.

13. Your supervisor gives you an assignment to write an article for the company in-house employee newsletter on 10 home-based businesses you can operate with your personal computer. You would prefer to:

a. Create a plan and outline first, and then follow it exactly to organize the article. Then write the article.
(b.) Write the article first, from whatever springs into your head at the moment. Then weed out what doesn't belong when it's finished.

14. You're researching an international electronic database for a long list of articles and books on U.F.O. abductions in Russia for an Ivy League university professor of psychiatry. You get a call from a Nobel-prize winning astrophysicist asking you to stop your work immediately and tape record what he has to say before he leaves the country. You prefer to:
a. finish your research for your psychiatrist-employer and tell the astrophysicist you'll write to him later. It's annoying to have to stop in the middle of a project and switch to a new task.
(b.) You drop what you're doing and look forward to the surprise, change in routine, and excitement of taping the astrophysicist's startling statistics on a different subject.

15. You meet many possible mates at a series of parties who ask whether you're married, what you majored in, what's your hobby, what do you do for fun, and how old are you because they want to know you better. All of them could be Mr. or Ms. Right Personality Type, a possible future spouse for you. You tell the strangers:
(a.) everything you can think of about yourself. You reveal all that interests you. You ask all the strangers to lunch and want to know all the details of their lives.
b. you're a private person and don't want to reveal personal information, but you'll gladly ask the strangers questions about anything related to their interests.

16. You want a high-paying, prestigious job or business of your own that uses all you have to offer and that you'll be able to keep until:

a. you retire in 40 years with major benefits such as health insurance, a paid-off home mortgage, and a livable pension.
(b.) a better job offers you an opportunity to use your wild imagination yearning for adventure, change, intellectual achievement and/or creative expression, and the next future possibility.

17. On Thursdays, your workplace lets all employees out at four to attend personal enrichment classes. You have a choice of two workshops. Which one would you attend?
a. How to repair your home appliances or computer.
(b.) How to write novels about the future of employment.

18. You are asked to evaluate an employee. You would first consider
a. The employee's productivity and profit to the firm.
(b.) The employee's warmth, friendship, and personal service toward the customer.

19. You have a choice of working for two supervisors. Would you prefer
(a.) The boss who talks to you STRAIGHT about dating his adult child, but uses harsh words and sarcasm to make you improve your image but not your income while keeping you from getting personal or asking questions about his adult child or a raise.
b. The GENTLE boss who tells polite lies to protect you from knowing why your work was rejected, then asks the top honcho to reprimand you for errors. Finally, the boss approves of your dating interest in his grown child, but tells the honcho behind your back that you're a social climber trying to worm your way into the family.

20. Your job finishes at 5:00 p.m., but your departing manager says you can leave early if you want or hang around and start tomorrow's work. You won't be paid extra or less either way. No one's left in the office to see you working. You

(a.) start tomorrow's work and leave exactly at five, according to your usual daily schedule. You'll know exactly which place to start again in the morning with no confusion.
b. Drop everything in midstream, take off, and head for that new movie you're eager to see. Leave tomorrow's work for tomorrow, and have fun when you can grab it.

21. You work in a field you simply love with many singles in your age group around making life exciting. Your work is always
(a.) completed and well-organized long before the deadline.
b. finished exactly at deadline or just after. You enjoyed the exhilaration of rushing to complete it on time.

22. You're asked to train a group of visiting students in your field or specialty. There's someone in the group who you'd like to date and could possibly marry if all works out.
You're training employees that psychological type is used to open doors with people, not to close them off in labeled boxes. You're more comfortable:
(a.) giving an ORAL presentation and live hands-on demonstration on opening doors for people to a large group of eligible singles of all ages in your company conference auditorium. You want to make that special other notice you. You love talking face-to-face with large groups of people who share your interests and hope a romance works out of this meeting.
b. distributing the latest written book or newsletter you WROTE to that special person and the other students. You wish they could learn independently in school, at their own place of employment, or at home. You find giving an oral presentation to a group positively exhausting. You'd rather train students by letting them read what you WRITE (books, manuals, articles, or newsletters) as part of a correspondence course. Public speaking makes you sick.

23. In marriage, or within a family unit, you'd be happier as
a. one dependable business-focused logistics mate grounded in the present time and the real world who deals with troubleshooting and repair household appliances and remodeling; or in the sorting and selection of details in doing your spouse's taxes and financial planning.
(b.) future-looking absent-minded professor who uses neural networks technology from the biotech industry to create new possibilities classifying people as the most compatible mates to create the healthiest, happiest children.

24. You bought an old car or antique lamp at the best price you could find. Three years later you still (a.) use your car or lamp as is. If it "isn't broke," you don't need to fix it or change it.
b. continue to upgrade your car or lamp to keep up with technology, tastes, or styles. Everything has room for improvement and change.

25. When asked what you think of the concept of time, you're most likely to say that
(a.) Time is impersonal.
b. Time makes you feel guilty if you don't use it to help people.

26. There are two job openings—one for a spy and the other for a journalist. You have all the qualifications for both. You choose to
a. design software to track government legal cases on harassment in politics and to merge databases with a secretly-modified "back door" to allow intelligence agencies to access foreign computer systems for their own espionage purposes.
(b.) be a journalist who achieves visibility while investigating healthcare injustices, welfare scandals and law enforcement brutality.

27. You find it easier to
a. follow directions exactly as planned or told to you by others at work. You prefer looking at the other person's plans or schedules and following them as directed. You'd rather do the company's thing.
(b.) break regulations and do the work your own way.
You find it harder to follow someone else's plans to the letter because you can't get into the other guy's head to know what he wants, and there's no way you can please him. When you try to follow other's rules, the work comes out wrong. You'd rather do your own thing.

28. You're better at
a. time management of your home life after work.
(b.) adapting your workplace job to unexpected changes in your mate's or family's homelife schedule.

29. You're an unemployed and homeless typist down on your luck with a nickel in your jeans. An employment agency with a government grant pays for your training in word processing and sends you on two jobs. Both employers want to hire you with equal pay for similar firms near the same location.
Which job would be least stressful?
a. receptionist guiding heavy foot traffic all day in and out of a romance novel publisher's public relations or sales office, answering constantly ringing phones while typing reports and press releases and running errands.
(b.) back office word processing specialist in a quiet, but successful and long-standing one-person serious mainstream fiction publishing office where the boss usually is out and no one comes in or calls. You can have total solitude as you type one long mainstream novel after the other.

30. You'd be a mate whose conversations your spouse must listen to all day would more naturally be about topics or people focusing on a. common

sense, present, practical, useful, direct, realistic, actual, down-to earth, factual, specific, and traditional events.
b. futuristic, conceptual, inspirational, motivational, random, possible, intellectual, kooky, imaginative, fantastic, theoretical, ingenious, generalized, non-traditional, and creative events.

31. The toy manufacturing company where you're employed is adding a corporate animation department. You're offered a choice of two jobs. You decide to take the job as a
a. marketing and sales manager of toys.
b. designer and researcher of animated holiday-theme robot cartoon characters, and scriptwriter of commercials.

32. Your lover says you would prefer to do what's a. fair and truthful than do what will make your lover happy.
b. needed and valued to make your lover "like" you or to accommodate your lover's family and friends.

33. It's more important to you
a. to know you are right and not care whether you are liked.
b. to be liked, and know you are right, but everyone thinks you're wrong.

34. You want a marriage where you can
a. thrive on order and know pretty well what your home life relationships will be like.
b. explore the unknown without being pinned down. You want to keep all home life and relationship options open.

35. You prefer to spend blizzard weather weekends at home
a. completing projects and getting them out of the way by the end of each day.

b. turning your home-based projects into play. You believe if your work can't be play, you won't do that particular job.

36. Your lover offers you a choice of two jobs at the same pay and benefits handling a customer base of Fortune 500 clients. You ask to be placed in the
a. sales department to use your telephone skills talking to people all day with little paperwork to do.
(b.) publications department working ALONE reading about new information in your area of interest.

37. If you were promised the same salary and job security, you'd prefer to spend the next four decades
a. dealing with details and your common sense instead of your imagination to fix what's broken on the job or be of service to people who need your help. You'd enjoy customer service, or checking, locating, or troubleshooting details for accuracy.
(b.) as an investigative journalist and suspense novelist who writes about the connections and interrelatedness between competing entertainment corporations. You use imagination to absorb global impressions or create new ideas.

38. You pick your mate or date by
a. making judgments based on past experience.
(b.) making decisions based on gut-level guessing.

39. The type of people you wish you could be more like are
(a) able to stay calm and objective when others panic.
b. able to walk ten miles in your shoes.

40. If you could pick a mate most like yourself, that person would

(a.) welcome challenge, rebuttal, and confrontation, sacrificing harmony for clarity.
b. prefer harmony, even at the sake of sacrificing clarity to avoid conflict.

41. You would prefer a mate who
a. wants everything orderly and in its place—always.
(b.) Doesn't plan to have a place for everything, because the adaptive person with messy closets and desks you are planning to marry would rather wait and see what living with you demands at different times.

42. You're hired to interview blind dates in order to pick one to escort you on the world cruise for two you just won. Each applicant gets a half-hour interview. You now have only ten minutes to choose the winner. You'd prefer each applicant to
a. come only at the scheduled time of the interview.
(b.) walk in off the street when they felt like it and surprise you with their impressive credentials.

43. In a home-based business you'd prefer to
(a.) run your own public relations, advertising, sales, and marketing agency for authors, doctors or lawyers.
b. index the back of books and periodicals for doctors, lawyers, publishers, and library databases behind closed doors, where you'd work alone, with no close supervision and no phone calls or interruptions.

44. You find the future
a. best put off until it comes because it's too scary.
(b.) full of exciting possibilities for your imagination.

45. In your school classes you enjoyed best the courses that emphasized
a. hands-on practical skills leading to a comfortable job in the real world as quickly as possible.

(b) theory about the futuristic possibilities your mate might be capable of once microchips were enmeshed with human DNA molecules to form neural networks.

46. All appliances/machines/electric power/phones break down at the same time. Your first impulse would be to
a. keep things in perspective and push for precision and clarity when directing others to fix what's broken.
(b) try to understand how human error impacts the people affected by the power meltdown.

47. In a marriage, you'd rather
a. solve analytical problems and increase efficiency.
(b) express your creativity by sharing communication or service with a smile.

48. You must choose your mate from among three suitable friends you've been dating for more than two years. Each gave you a deadline day, and an ultimatum to make your decision. You'd rather
a. keep your decision goal-oriented and reach a closure as soon as possible for relief.
b. stay open-ended without goals because new information may come in before deadline.

49. As a newly hired writer with a B.A. in English, you're asked to manage the technical writing department. You never worked before and no nothing about technical writing. It's your first day at work. You would like to
a. hurry permanent decisions, turn solutions into action, and implement communications right into the word processing department.
b. keep the staff from going with the first decision, keep offering better solutions, and hold communications until you've cleared it with the tech-

nical illustration department—before turning the current iteration over to the word processing department.

50. You just graduated from college. Two employers are eager to hire you. Each offer equal benefits.
You'd rather
a. use your natural, terrific public speaking skills to train MANY PEOPLE—employees and students in how to act a certain way at work to win friends and influence people, or how to do a certain job.
You'd love to do lots of demonstrations and give great presentations for people. You think or communicate best on your feet.
b. organize records for a healthcare management firm monitoring production runs and performing backups of corporate data working ALONE. Or illustrate magazine articles and children's books, working ALONE for the communications and publications department.

51. You prefer to work side by side with your mate at home in a hobby you love that deals mainly with
a. using practical, real, tangible, specific, common sense, hands-on troubleshooting skills based on practice, usefulness, and experience.
b. using your imagination and forecasting trends to show others how to find hidden escape routes, back doors, advantages, alternatives, theories, and new ways of doing things.

52. If you were a salesperson, you'd rather sell
a. TANGIBLE PRODUCTS, like fashions, appliances, computers, modems, and peripherals, financial database software to accounting firms, or medical records technology and transcription software to hospitals.
b. IDEAS, like advertising, public relations, public speaking, logos, desktop video productions, technical writing, event planning, neural networks and fuzzy logic, artificial intelligence solutions, trend forecasting, interactive fiction, presentation graphics productions, and virtual reality games.

53. You're retired and contemplating marriage again to find happiness for the final third of your lifespan. Your dates are most likely to call you
a. a tough-skinned, hard-headed date who clawed your way to the top by your achievements, power. intelligence, persistence, and education.
b. an empathic, persuasive self-made date who always put first—above your own greed, your friend's need. You live by your personal values and your own gut-reactions about people and situations.

54. You're asked to give a presentation to people with the same hobby as yours at a fun-filled, leisurely convention not connected to your job. You'd prefer to
a. convince the audience by logical analysis to clarify definitions, facts, or trends.
b. persuade the people by communicating to their values, sentiment, and identity with a stirring videotape or film.

55. When searching for a mate, you
a. grab the first date you find so fast that you're disappointed later.
b. switch relationships or dates as frequently as you switched majors in college or tech school.

56. You want a good marriage partner who is
a. reliable, stable, serious, secure, unchanging, controllable, orderly, routine, familiar, scheduled,
methodical, organized, and dependable.
b. flexible, adaptable, leisurely, playful, fun, spontaneous, changeable, open-ended, and creative.

57. At your deepest level, lots of people contact activity after work or on vacation makes you feel
a. energized and eager to talk and share your life experiences. Your phone and door are kept open for the sounds of people networking.

b. sick, drained, exhausted, anxious, tense, pressured, and bored by a continuous, crushing crowd on whom you wish you could close your door when you want some recreation and peace of mind after work or on weekends and vacations. You disconnect your phone.

58. If you learned how to design your own parlor game to entertain your date, you would
a. produce a new product that will appreciate in value over the years, even when the board game becomes outdated. You'd patent the new product and save the profits in your retirement plan.
b. have some fun teaching kids how to use it and then donating the game to an imagination- stretching camp high in the mountains. Afterwards, you enjoy a vacation as a guest of the camp.

59. You have a choice of two conferences to attend during the holiday season. You're lonely and single. Neither conference is related to your present job. You'd rather attend
a. a conference on improving your practical skills that will allow you to pass a qualifying exam for a more secure job at a higher salary.
b. a conference on military abductions, advertising evidence presented by a distinguished military general, a Nobel-prize winning physicist, an Ivy-League university professor of psychiatry, and three security guards who witnessed autopsies on space aliens at a secret military testing site's underground base.

60. When you criticize your date, mate, or yourself, you're more apt to see
a. the errors of clarity and organization and how the person or his/her attitudes can be improved or made more efficient. You want to critique and analyze it, or see how and where the person's actions went wrong. You welcome challenge and rebuttal. You want a mate who makes objective and impersonal decisions.

b. the way he or she motivates, inspires, excites, and persuades you to understand his or her feelings, personal values, likes and dislikes, choices, and attitudes by his or her smooth- talking style. You praise your mate or date for using propaganda in the home for meeting your needs for simplicity and harmony.

61. You're hired to train the co-workers on your team and to mentor beginning students in your field of interest. You let the students know that
a. you're more interested in the subject than in the student's personal problems, learning needs, or motivation.
b. you're more interested in the student's personal needs and motivation, inspiration, growth than you are in the subject.

62. You'd rather enter a marriage
a. where every minute of your day is PLANNED and SCHEDULED, and you use a day planner or make a list of what you'll do each day, including weekends and vacations. You wouldn't mind if your mate assigned you specific chores to do around the house, and you'd give your children chores to do around the house. You believe idle hands get into trouble, and the day is wasted if you don't get some work done. You don't mind following someone else's rules to the letter.
b. where you have many hours of FREE TIME to see what leisurely and SPONTANEOUS activities can be fun-filled or full of your creative expressions. Heaven help the mate who crushes your autonomy at home or asks you to work at something that doesn't interest you. Work at home or outside should be playful.

63. On weekends you
a. make a list of every chore that needs to be finished and every item you have to buy. You'll visit stores only when you need to buy a specific product on your list.

b. let whatever happens spontaneously take over the day depending upon your energy level, who calls, or what movie is playing. You dread working on your free time, and prefer to see what fun happens as the weekend progresses. You'd rather browse.

64 On your resume you would be certain to emphasize
a. your interest in giving presentations, speeches, or talks on your area of interest or experience.
b. your preference for communicating via the written word in memos to co-workers and as little face-to-face talking as possible.

65. You'd rather take those thick, dry, dull books catching dust on university library shelves and
a. review them for a practical, how-to, hands-on magazine.
b. turn them into spectacular 60-minute multimedia instructional videos for beginners.

66. You'd rather repair
a. machines in buildings.
b. attitudes of people.

67. You want to duck out the door and take a break when
a. your date or mate cries openly.
b. you say something negative that you really mean.

68. You're a healthy, energetic age 57 and forced to retire against your wishes to continue having fun in your occupation. You wish you and your same-age mate could
a. analyze, challenge, and confront ageism with the truth.
b. deny that ageism exists in your specialty and convey optimism, energy, and enthusiasm by affirming your desire to offer service for pay.

69. To propose marriage, you need most
a. an agenda with handouts and flow charts.
b. room to move in all directions by self-pacing, a chance to change the agenda, and diverge from the original plan.

70. In a marriage, you'd rather have
a. ideas about theories of how life arose on Earth, faith, imagination, fantasy, and compassion as the best quality attitudes you can show for your mate and family. Imagination and intuition are more important than reason. Your senses could be deceived. Imagination offers comfort in greener pastures. You want to be proud of yourself, even though no one else ever notices. (You may secretly keep records in a log-book or keep a locked diary.) You'd rather be loved than right. And you know what you see isn't real. You feel there is a hidden reality beyond the senses that reason is not yet evolved enough to track and record.
b. self-determination, reason, rebellion, reality, and skepticism in the face of disagreement by the majority in your community or family. You'd rather be right in your own mind than win in the eyes of others. You believe others want to be deceived if the deception offers comfort and reward. You know what you see isn't always real. You prefer working or living at the front lines so you will know everything isn't always wonderful.

71. You're always willing to
a. share personal experiences by talking and expressing your opinions; volunteering to work on committees and attend meetings, functions, office parties or after-work cultural or sports events, and speak on panels at conferences.
b. write an inner personal journal. Research, reflect, meditate, and blow the whistle— especially when a co-worker or mate interrupts you in mid-paragraph. You'd not hesitate to write a published book about your mate.

72. On a date, the first things you would tell a new friend and possible prospective mate are
a. only those realistic, practical, useful, routine, hands-on skills or experience that specifically fulfill the requirements of the job description. You'd hand your date your resume.
b. express yourself by abilities or examples of creativity. Convince the date or partner to consider possibilities which don't yet exist in the present, to accommodate your ideas. You'd even propose on the first date.

73. Your employer is giving you an "employee of the month" award. You'd prefer the prize to be
a. a win/lose award for beating out the rival firms.
b. a psychology book on "why women see competition as loss of self."

74. You spend too much time
a. rigidly impatient with relationships and making lists and pre-nuptial contracts in order to arrive at a quicker decision about who will become your partner or mate—or about whether you chose the right person for an important relationship because changes are upsetting.
b. gathering endless information about other people, but not making any commitments or final decisions about a relationship, hoping new information (or a better prospect) comes your way. You believe that time changes pre-nuptial contracts anyway. So why be so final?

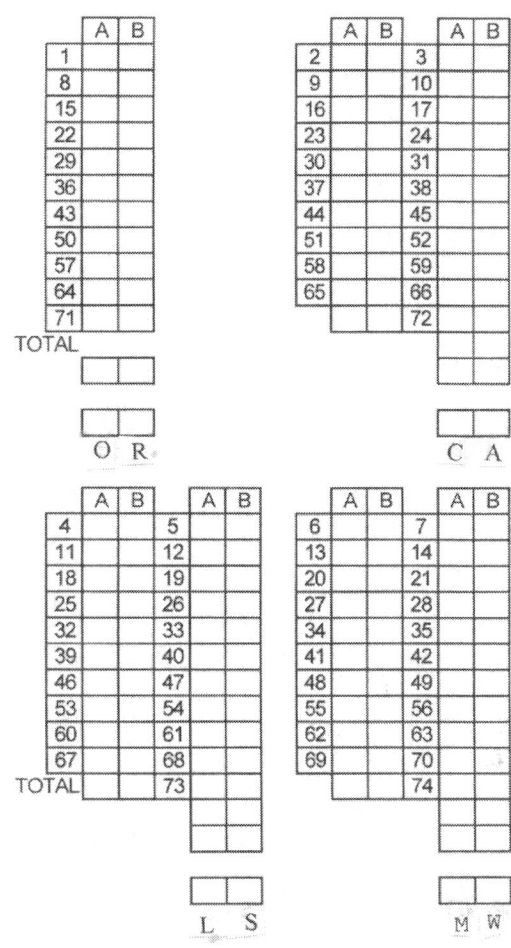

YOUR PREFERENCES

O= Outgoing      R= Reflective     C= Concrete
L= Logical       S= Sentimental    A= Abstract
A= Abstract      M= Methodical     W= Waiting

# 388 • Power Dating Games

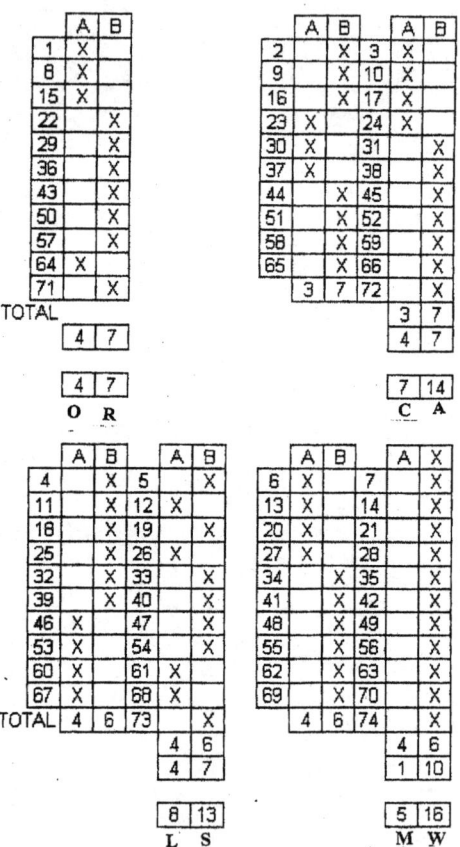

YOUR PREFENENCES

R  A  S  W

If you want to compare this fun preferences questionnaire that you can take with your partner or mate, to the four letters of your type out of 16 personality types of the scientific MBTI™ that I highly recommend that you take, this classifier key when compared to the MBTI™ is as follows below:

## My Fun Preferences Questionnaire

O= Outgoing

R= Reflective

L= Logical

S= Sentimental

A= Abstract

C= Concrete

M= Methodical

W= Waiting

## Letters of the MBTI™

E=Extrovert

I= Introvert

T= Thinking

F= Feeling

N= Intuition

S= Sensing

J= Judging

P=Perceiving

---

To score your answer sheet, follow the example of my scored sheet that contains my four preference letters, which are **RASW**. That corresponds to the letters INFP on the MBTI™ which is an entirely different personality classifier. However, I know, even thought the classifiers have nothing in common, that R shows I'm reflective. An introvert is reflective. My second letter is A for abstract, which means like other people who like abstract ideas and theories. I'm an intuitive person. So the letter A (abstract) corresponds to the letter N (intuition) on the MBTI ™.

My third letter is S for Sentimental. The art of sentimental journeys relates to feeling. So I can surmise I'm a sentimental feeling time, which corresponds to the letter F on the MBTI ™.

The fourth letter here is W for waiting. I wait for more information to come in before making a final decision and remain open for additional data. So W corresponds to the MBTI's "P" for perceiving, which means I'm enjoy exploring, probing, and waiting for new information to arrive before making a decision and I'm spontaneous. Put all the letters together and RASW spells a reflective, abstract, sentimental person who waits with an open mind for surprises or more information before choosing. Isn't that fun? Now take the real personality classifiers like the MBTI™ or any other organizer of personality styles, preferences, and attitudes. Now enjoy your fun classifier.

\* \* \*

# *Epilogue*

## How Personalities Fall Apart

Although There May Be No Organic Disease, Unconsciously, Each Personality May Mimic A Particular Problem. Only Your Mental Health Professional May Know For Sure. (So go see someone who is a mental and physical health professional to have yourself or your mate checked out before you make any decisions).

The four letters here are representative of those used on the MBTI™ and studied in many research investigations on the relationship of personality to symptoms when there is no underlying organic cause of the behavior, tactics, or display. Investigate personality stereotypes and compare your new insights to the latest research on the biological bases of personality. It's all part of understanding how people take in information and make decisions and choices based on preferences. What do you think of personality-based dating?

Problems (with no underlying physical/medical/biological causes) sometimes scene and being studied as related to different personalities:

| | |
|---|---|
| ENFJ | Tics, twitches, convulsions. |
| ENFP | Dreads he'll be harmed by you or others |
| ESTJ | Health worries fill the days |
| ESFJ | Sad feelings and exhaustion |
| ENTJ | Compulsive washing or obsessive rituals |
| ENTP | Fear-Centered Agoraphobia, Phobias, sociophobia |
| ESTP | Thievery Entitlement Shoplifts, or Steals |
| ESFP | Hooked On Highs of Substance Abuse |

INFJ  Inward Curled and Stays In One Position
INTJ  Immortal and Invincible Conqueror with obsessive rituals
INFP  Denies/Forgets, Anorexic, Multiple Personalities, Dissociation
INTP  Speechless in Public with Fear Of Incompetence
ISTJ  Tiredness, Impatience, Frustration, Volcanic Emotions, Exhaustion.
ISFJ  Anxiety, short temper, explosive feelings, ape-like gestures, depression.
ISFP  Self-mutilation, cutting the self, head banging, unkind to own body.
ISTP  Abusing others.

# How The Nine Enneagram Personalities May Fall Apart Under Extreme Stress

7,4 Convulsive (Non Organic) Seizures, Twitches, Tics

4,6 Feels Impending Injury from others, afraid others will hurt him

1, 2,4 Physical Symptomatic Health Worries

2,9,4 Sad, Resentful Depression,

5 Compuslive, Obsessive Washes Hands, Cleans, Goes Through Rituals

5,4 Fear-Driven Agoraphobia, Phobias

8,4 Theft For Pleasure Shoplifts, Steals

8,1,3,7 Hooked On Whatever Alleviates Low Self Esteem
Alcoholic & Drug Abuse

4,9 Curled Inward Stays In One Position

3,8,1 Immortal-Minded Thinks Nothing Can Hurt
Him Or Her, Immortality

4,9 Denial, Forgetful Amnesiac, Anorexic,
Times Agoraphobic, Anxietic
Multiple Personalities,
Dissociation

5,1 Fear Of Saying It Wrong
Unable To Speak Before Groups, Goes Blank In
Middle Of Talking

1,2,6 Exhausted Fatigue, Tiredness,
Exhaustion, Sadness,
Depression With Physical
Pain And Back Aches
Hypertension

8,1,5 Sadistic Hurts Physically Those
Around Him Or Her


4,2,9 Volcanic Anxiety To Wife Or Child
Directed Outward, Inward To Strangers
Depressed, Turns Anger

Inward, Abuses Wife
Verbally, Sometimes
Physically, Charms
Boss At Work, Cycles
Of Anxious Depression
Coupled With Anger Pool
Worries About Job Security

2,4,6 Self-Mutilating Self-Abuse To Punish
Others, Razor-Cutting
And Head-Banging

# *About the Author*

*Award-winning textbook author, behavioral science journalist, and novelist, Anne Hart holds lifetime community college Teaching credentials, a graduate degree, from San Diego State University, and a B.S. from New York University. She has written 55 books, booklets, plays, articles, stories, and learning materials and focuses on writing behavioral science books, learning materials on personality research, multi-cultural fiction, and books on career development as well as scripts, plays, and new media learning materials. Hart has been writing books full time since 1963 as her primary occupation. Her recent books include* **Winning Resumes for Computer Personnel** *(Barron's*

Educational Series, NY 1998. She may be reached by email at anthropojournalist@hotmail.com

Anne Hart was awarded a KFMBTV (Channel 8 News) Harold Keen graduate scholarship in professional writing in 1977. Winner of Mensa National Essay Writing Competition Scholarship, 1979. Scholar Incentive Award, NYU. Book editing. Book and software reviews writer. Columnist and frequent online teacher on the subject of "The Business of Writing."

Like multiethnic/multicultural suspense novels featuring female sleuths? Read author, Anne Hart's latest novel, A Private Eye Called Mama Africa, available in paperpack when ordered from http://www.iuniverse.com. It's an action suspense novel featuring a female sleuth, judge, and forensic psychologist from Egypt who makes house calls with video camera and niece in tow to solve problems visually when it comes to figuring out what makes people do what they do.

Or read the startling novel by Anne Hart, The Courage to be Jewish AND the Wife of an Arab Sheik. It also can be ordered from http://www.iuniverse.com. It's fiction with conviction that will make an impact—all about what a Jewish girl from Brooklyn is doing married to a Bedouin Sheik living in two kinds of deserts.

Read Anne Hart's resource, skills, and promotion/marketing book for writers: Writer's Bible, available at www.iuniverse.com or may be ordered from most bookstores.

Need how-to writing mentor books? Also at www.iuniverse.com in paperback is Anne Hart's nonfiction how-to book for freelance writers on opportunities in digital video and electronic print on demand publishing, on 25+ unique home-based online businesses for freelance writers, producers, and other creative people to start called The Freelance Writer's E-Publishing, Digital Media/Video Guidebook.

# *Appendix*

| | |
|---|---|
| APPENDIX A | Bibliography on Personality Type, Temperament, and Preferences |
| APPENDIX B | Publications and Research on Personality or Relationships |
| APPENDIX C | Associations for Personality Research or on Relationships |

---

APPENDIX A

## Helpful Books On Personality

## Bibliography

Gifts Differing, Isabel Briggs Myers, Consulting Psychologist's Press, Inc., Palo Alto, CA 1980.
Do What You Are (Discover the Perfect Career for You Through the Secrets of Personality Type) by Paul D. Tieger and Barbara Barron-Tieger, Little, Brown, Boston, MA 1992.
Personality Self-Portrait by John M. Oldham and Lis B. Morris, Bantam Books, New York, 1990.
Positioning (How to be seen and heard in the overcrowded marketplace) by Al Ries and Jack Trout, Warner Books, NY 1986.
Positioning: The Battle for Your Mind, McGraw-Hill, New York, 1986.
Power of Self Esteem (The) by Nathaniel Branden, Health Communications, Florida, 1992.

Type Talk, Otto Kroeger and Janet M. Thuesen, Dell Publishing, NY 1989.

Type Talk at Work (How the 16 Personality Types Determine Your Success on the Job) by Otto Kroeger with Janet M. Thuesen, Delacorte, NY 1992.

16 Ways To Love Your Lover, Otto Kroeger and Janet M. Thuesen, Delacorte, NY 1994.

When Smart People Fail by Carole Hyatt and Linda Gottlieb, Penguin Books, NY 1987.

Winning Tactics for Women Over Forty by Anne deSola Cardoza and Mavis B. Sutton, Mills & Sanderson, Bedford, MA 1988.

Working Together by Olaf Isachsen and Linda Berens, Neworld Management, Coronado, CA 1988.

Lifetypes by Sandra Hirsh & Jean Kummerow, Warner Books, NY 1989.

Manual, A Guide to the Development and Use of the Myers-Briggs Type Indicator (Registered Trademark), Isabel Briggs Myers and Mary H. McCaulley, Consulting Psychologists Press, Palo Alto, CA 1989

The Power of Optimism, Alan Loy McGinnis, Harper Paperbacks, Harper Collins, NY 1990.

Please Understand Me, David Keirsey and Marilyn Bates, Prometheus Nemesis Book Company, DelMar, CA 1984.

It Takes All Types, Alan W. Brownsword, Baytree Publication Co., San Anselmo, CA 1987.

When Smart People Fail, Carole Hyatt and Linda Gottlieb, Penguin Books, NY 1987.

Falling Apart, Dr. Michael Epstein & Sue Hosking, CRCS Publications, Sebastopol, CA 1992.

Survival Games Personalities Play, Eve Delunas, Ph.D., Sunflower Ink, Carmel, CA 1992.

True to Type, William C. Jeffries, Hampton Roads Publishing Co., Inc., Norfolk, VA 1991.

Personality Types, Jung's Model of Typology, Daryl Sharp, Inner City Books, Toronto, Ont., Canada, 1987.
People Types & Tiger Stripes, Gordon Lawrence, Center for Applications of Psychological Type, Inc., Gainesville, FL 1989.
The Neurology of Psychological Type and Language Style, A New Theoretical Model, Sheila Davis, Solar Systems, NY 1994
The New Science of Giambattista Vico, Cornell University Press, Ithaca, NY 1991.
Frames of Mind, Howard Gardner, Basic Books, NY 1983.
Metaphors We Live By, Lakeoff & Johnson, Univ. of Chicago Press, Chicago, IL 1980.
Left Brain, Right Brain, Springer & Deutsch, W.H. Freeman & Co., NY 1989.
Brain, Symbol & Experience, Charles D. Laughlin, Jr., et al, Shambala, Boston, MA 1990.
Cyberscribes.1 The New Journalists, Anne Hart, 1997 (reviewed at www.amazon.com).
Winning Resumes for Computer Personnel, Anne Hart, Barron's Educational Series, NY, 1998.
The Courage to Be Jewish and the Wife of an Arab Sheik, A. Hart, www.iuniverse.com, 2001
A Private Eye Called Mama Africa, A. Hart, www.iuniverse.com 2001.
The Freelance Writers' E-Publishing (and digital media/video) Guidebook, A. Hart, www.iuniverse.com, 2001.

# APPENDIX B

## Type-Related Publications

Bulletin of Psychological Type,
Association for Psychological Type,

9140 Ward Parkway,
Kansas City, MO 64114
(816) 44403500

Journal of Psychological Type,
Dept. of Psychology,
BOX 6161
Mississippi State University,
Mississippi State, MS 39762
(601) 325-7655

Follow Up
7781 E. Oxford Ave.
Denver, CO 80237
(a publication designed to keep
your knowledge of the MBTI alive and growing)

Type Reporter Inc.,
524 North Paxton St.
Alexandria VA 22304
(703) 823-3730
(newsletter)

The NF Journal, (newsletter for intuitive feelers)
PO Box 65214
Washington, DC 20035
(FAX 202/234-5210)
E-mail on the Internet: NF Journal @aol.com.
(newsletter)

(Also local APT chapters around the nation
have local newsletters going to APT members)

News Groups on the Internet

See the Usenet News Group: alt.psychology.personality.
Or search your MBTI ™ personality type on the Internet by the four letters. For example. Direct your search engine to INFP or your own type.

# APPENDIX C

## Type-Related Associations

Association for Psychological Type (APT)
9140 Ward Parkway,
Kansas City, MO 64114
(816) 44403500
(There are local chapters of this national association)

Center for Applications of Psychological Type, Inc. (CAPT)
2815 NW 13$^{th}$ St.
Suite 401
Gainesville, FL 32609
(904) 375-0160
(CAPT does MBTI training on applications for MBTI, and also publishes books on type and related issues)
toll free fax number 1-800-723-6284
Internet computer ID: mbti@nerix.nerdc.ufl.edu

MBTI TYPE TRAINING COURSES, WORKSHOPS, AND SEMINARS
Otto Kroeger and Associates
3605-C Chain Bridge Rd.

Fairfax, VA 22030
(703) 591-6284

Type Resources
101 Chestnut St.
#135
Gaithersburg, MD 20877
301) 963-1283
(Also publishes and distributes books and pamphlets on type)

Consulting Psychologists Press
(publishers of the MBTI)
3803 East Bayshore Road
Palo Alto, CA 94303
(415) 969-8901
Offers training, MBTI and other questionnaires, and books

Temperament Research Institute
16152 Beach Blvd.
Suite 117
Huntington Beach, CA 92647
(714) 841-0041
(Offers training, newsletter, and distributes books on type)

# *References*

1. *The Intimate Enemy*, by G. Bach and P. Weyden, Avon Books, NY, 1968
2. *Battered Wives,* Del Martin, New Gilde Publications, 1976.
3. *The Battered Woman*, Lenore Walker, Harper & Row, 1979.
4. *Conjugal Crime*: Understanding and Changing the Wifebeating Pattern,
Terry Davidson, Hawthorne Books, 1978.
5. *Straus, M. "Leveling, Civility and Violence in the Family."*
6. *Journal of Marriage and the Family. 1974; 36: 13-39.* "Leveling, Civility, and Violence in the Family," by M. Straus.
7. *Forward To The Violent Home*, Sage Publications, (Beverly Hills, 1972), R. Gelles.
8. *Gifts Differing, Isabel Briggs Myers,* Consulting Psychologist's Press, Inc., *Palo Alto, CA* 1980.
9. *Personality Self—Portrait,* John M. Oldham and L.B. Morris, Bantam Books, NY 1990.
10. *Type Talk,* Otto Kroeger and Janet M. Thuesen, Dell Publishing, NY 1989.
11. *The Neurology of Psychological Type and Language Style, A New Theoretical Model*, Sheila Davis, Solar Systems, NY 1994.
12. *The New Science of Giambattista Vico,* Cornell University Press, Ithaca, NY 1991.

# *Bibliography*

Gifts Differing, Isabel Briggs Myers, Consulting Psychologist's Press, Inc., Palo Alto, CA 1980.
Do What You Are (Discover the Perfect Career for You Through the Secrets of Personality Type) by Paul D. Tieger and Barbara Barron-Tieger, Little, Brown, Boston, MA 1992.
Personality Self-Portrait by John M. Oldham and Lis B. Morris, Bantam Books, New York, 1990.
Positioning (How to be seen and heard in the overcrowded marketplace) by Al Ries and Jack Trout, Warner Books, NY 1986.
Positioning: The Battle for Your Mind, McGraw-Hill, New York, 1986.
Power of Self Esteem (The) by Nathaniel Branden, Health Communications, Florida, 1992.
Type Talk, Otto Kroeger and Janet M. Thuesen, Dell Publishing, NY 1989.
Type Talk at Work (How the 16 Personality Types Determine Your Success on the Job) by Otto Kroeger with Janet M. Thuesen, Delacorte, NY 1992.
16 Ways To Love Your Lover, Otto Kroeger and Janet M. Thuesen, Delacorte, NY 1994.
When Smart People Fail by Carole Hyatt and Linda Gottlieb,
Penguin Books, NY 1987.
Winning Tactics for Women Over Forty by Anne deSola Cardoza and Mavis B. Sutton, Mills & Sanderson, Bedford, MA 1988.
Working Together by Olaf Isachsen and Linda Berens, Neworld Management, Coronado, CA 1988.
Lifetypes by Sandra Hirsh & Jean Kummerow, Warner Books, NY 1989.
Manual, A Guide to the Development and Use of the Myers-Briggs Type Indicator (Registered Trademark), Isabel Briggs Myers and Mary H. McCaulley, Consulting Psychologists Press, Palo Alto, CA 1989

The Power of Optimism, Alan Loy McGinnis, Harper Paperbacks, Harper Collins, NY 1990.

Please Understand Me, David Keirsey and Marilyn Bates, Prometheus Nemesis Book Company, DelMar, CA 1984.

It Takes All Types, Alan W. Brownsword, Baytree Publication Co., San Anselmo, CA 1987.

When Smart People Fail, Carole Hyatt and Linda Gottlieb, Penguin Books, NY 1987.

Falling Apart, Dr. Michael Epstein & Sue Hosking, CRCS Publications, Sebastopol, CA 1992.

Survival Games Personalities Play, Eve Delunas, Ph.D., Sunflower Ink, Carmel, CA 1992.

True to Type, William C. Jeffries, Hampton Roads Publishing Co., Inc., Norfolk, VA 1991.

Personality Types, Jung's Model of Typology, Daryl Sharp, Inner City Books, Toronto, Ont., Canada, 1987.

People Types & Tiger Stripes, Gordon Lawrence, Center for Applications of Psychological Type, Inc., Gainesville, FL 1989.

The Neurology of Psychological Type and Language Style, A New Theoretical Model, Sheila Davis, Solar Systems, NY 1994

The New Science of Giambattista Vico, Cornell University Press, Ithaca, NY 1991.

Frames of Mind, Howard Gardner, Basic Books, NY 1983.

Metaphors We Live By, Lakeoff & Johnson, Univ. of Chicago Press, Chicago, IL 1980.

Left Brain, Right Brain, Springer & Deutsch, W.H. Freeman & Co., NY 1989.

Brain, Symbol & Experience, Charles D. Laughlin, Jr., et al, Shambala, Boston, MA 1990.

Cyberscribes.1 The New Journalists, Anne Hart, Ellipsys International Publications, Inc., San Diego, CA. 1997 (reviewed at amazon.com).

(Match your personality preferences to the right writing job in the computer and new media industries.)
Winning Resumes for Computer Personnel, Anne Hart, Barron's Educational Series, NY, 1998.
The Courage to Be Jewish and the Wife of an Arab Sheik, A. Hart, www.iuniverse.com, 2001
A Private Eye Called Mama Africa, A. Hart, www.iuniverse.com 2001.
The Freelance Writers' E-Publishing (and digital media/video) Guidebook, A. Hart, www.iuniverse.com, 2001.

## Type-Related Publications

Bulletin of Psychological Type,
Association for Psychological Type,
9140 Ward Parkway,
Kansas City, MO 64114
(816) 44403500

Journal of Psychological Type,
Dept. of Psychology,
BOX 6161
Mississippi State University,
Mississippi State, MS 39762
(601) 325-7655

Follow Up
7781 E. Oxford Ave.
Denver, CO 80237
(a publication designed to keep
your knowledge of the MBTI alive and growing)
Type Reporter Inc.,

524 North Paxton St.
Alexandria VA 22304
(703) 823-3730
(newsletter)

The NF Journal, (newsletter for intuitive feelers)
PO Box 65214
Washington, DC 20035
(FAX 202/234-5210)
E-mail on the Internet: NF Journal @aol.com.
(newsletter)
(Also local APT chapters around the nation
 have local newsletters

Made in the USA
Lexington, KY
18 September 2015